Three Books of Polydore Vergil's English History

By

Camden Society

Published by Forgotten Books 2012

Originally Published 1844

PIBN 1000417540

THREE BOOKS

OF

POLYDORE VERGIL'S ENGLISH HISTORY,

COMPRISING THE REIGNS

OF

HENRY VI., EDWARD IV., AND RICHARD III.

FROM AN EARLY TRANSLATION,

PRESERVED AMONG THE MSS. OF THE OLD ROYAL LIBRARY IN THE BRITISH MUSEUM.

EDITED BY

SIR HENRY ELLIS, K.H.

" Ornatissime Polydore, Opera tua sunt eleganter et feliciter excusa."
Erasmi Epist. fol. Lugd. Bat. 1706, *Ep.* DCCLX. 5 *Sept.* 1525.

LONDON:

PRINTED FOR THE CAMDEN SOCIETY,

BY JOHN BOWYER NICHOLS AND SON, PARLIAMENT STRE. Γ.

M.DCCCXLIV.

C17

No. 29

PREFACE.

POLYDORE VERGIL, otherwise named de Castello, was a native of Urbino in Italy; born in the latter half of the fifteenth century, and educated in the University of Bologna. Of his family we know but little. Burton, who wrote the History of Leicestershire, says his father's name was George Vergil;* he himself tells us that Antony Vergil, his great-grandfather, taught philosophy at Paris; and he had a younger brother whom he mentions with affection, John Matthew Vergil, a professor of Philosophy at Pavia,† who died at a premature age. He had also a

---

* See Burton's MS. as quoted in Nichols's Hist. of Leicestershire, vol. iii. pt. i. p. 538.

† " Habes enim (prout probe scis) Antonium Vergilium proavum nostrum Archetypon, qui medicæ etiam rei ac astrologiæ peritissimus olim apud Gallos, in Lutetia Parisiorum, philosophiam docuit, quam tu Patavii in præsenti publicè profiteris.

" Non est infima utique laus, duos ex Vergiliana familia viros in duobus totius orbis præcipuis gymnasiis, haud longo temporis intervallo, professores bonarum disciplinarum non absque nominis gloria publicitus extitisse. Sed tu qui proavum jam longe relinquis, efficies (spero) ut aliquando posteritas

b

kinsman of the name of Adrian de Castello, of whom more will be said hereafter.

Polydore himself was first known to the literary world by the publication of a Collection of Proverbs, " Proverbiorum Libellus," printed at Venice in 1498, gathered chiefly from Latin writers, and dedicated to Guido Ubaldo then Duke of Urbino.* It was the first attempt of its kind, and the author was subsequently not a little mortified when Erasmus claimed that same priority for his " Adagia." Polydore Vergil gently reproached him in the preface to his next work: Erasmus protested his unacquaintance with Vergil's previous book ; and Polydore expunged the censure. Of this literary collision Polydore's biographers have said more than was sufficient. It created a friendship between these eminent scholars which lasted to the close of Erasmus's life, cemented by the congeniality of their pursuits, and evidenced no where more strongly on Erasmus's part than in his Correspondence.†

dicat, fuisse olim Polydorum quendam, qui illum Joannem Matthæum Vergilium a puero bonis moribus atque disciplinis nutrierat. Vale, Londini nonis Decembris, An. M. D. XVII."

* Other editions of the " Proverbiorum Libellus " were 4to, Ven. 1506 ; Argentor. 1510 ; 8 Basle, 1524, 1532 ; 12° 1536, and 8vo 1541 and 1550. To the edition of 1536 is subjoined a short commentary upon the Lord's Prayer, afterwards, about 1554, said to have been printed separately.

† See particularly the letters DCCLX. DCCCXV. DCCCLIV. MCLXXVI. in Erasmi Epist. fol. Lugd. Bat. 1706.

In 1499 Polydore Vergil published his second work, a Treatise " de Inventoribus Rerum." This also was the first publication of its kind, subsequent to the revival of Literature. It gained him great reputation; was afterwards much enlarged by its author; passed through numerous editions in different countries;* and was translated into several of the modern languages of Europe.†

* " Polydori Vergilii Vrbinatis de Inventoribus Rerum, Libri tres," 4to. Ven. 1499 ; reprinted there in 1503. This work was increased to eight books in the Basle edition of 1521, followed by other editions from the same place in 1524, 1545, 1550, 1554, and 1570, in 8ᵛᵒ and 12ᵐᵒ ; printed at Leyden in 1544, 8ᵛᵒ ; at Amsterdam, 8º, 1571, and by Dan. Elzevir, 12º 1651 and 1662; Rome, 1576, 8º ; Lyons, 1586, 12º ; Frankfort, 1599; Geneva, 1604 ; and Argentorat. 1606, 8º and 12º.

† Two editions of an Italian translation of this work, by Pietro Lauro of Modena, occur, 8º Ven. 1543 and 1545. A Spanish translation by Fr. Thamar Medina, appeared in 8ᵛᵒ 1551.

Wood in his Athenæ Oxonienses, edit. Bliss, vol. iii. col. 435, says, that Bale translated Polydore Vergil's work " de Rerum Inventoribus" in the time of Edward VI. but in rude and old English. He does not say whether this translation was published. Three if not four editions of an Abridgement, however, in English, appeared much about that time ; viz. One, " An Abridgemente of the Notable Woorke of Polidore Vergile. Conteining the deuisers and fyrste fynders oute as well of Artes, Ministeries, Feactes, and ciuill ordinaunces, as of the Rites and Ceremonies commonly vsed in the churche: and the original beginnyng of the same. Compendiouslye gathered by Thomas Langley." Dedicated to Sir Antonye Denny. " Imprynted at London by Richard Grafton, Printer to the Princes Grace, the xvi. daie of Aprill, the yere of our Lorde M.D.xlvi. Cum priuilegio ad imprimendum solum." Square 12ᵐᵒ. Printed also " xxv. Januarie," 1546, which stands as a second edition. A third, " Imprinted at London by Richard Grafton,

Soon after the production of this Treatise we find Polydore holding the office of chamberlain to Pope Alexander
the Sixth, by whom, in or soon after 1501, he was sent to
England as sub-collector of the tribute called Peter-
Pence, under the auspices of Adrian de Castello his kinsman, already mentioned, who had been raised to the
purple under the title of Cardinal S^{ti}. Chrysogoni, and
who was his superior in the office of treasurer and collector of the Papal tribute.*

What was Polydore's immediate reception at the English
Court is not recorded, but he is known to have been
recommended to Henry the Seventh by those who were
acquainted with the king, whilst Earl of Richmond, in his
exile.† Polydore's relation, the Cardinal S^{ti}. Chrysogoni,

Printer to the Kynges Majestie. Anno 1551. Cum priuilegio," as before. 12mo. The fourth edition, " Imprinted at London by Jhon Tisdale
dwellyng in Knight rider's streate neare to the Queenes Wardrop," $12°$.
without date. This is the latest edition of " The Abridgement," as we
know of no work from Tisdale's press earlier than 1550.

Bayle in his Historical and Critical Dictionary says, " The treatise de
Inventoribus Rerum contained several things which the Inquisition disliked,
wherefore it approved of no edition but that which Gregory XIII. caused
to be printed at Rome in 1576, which was purged of all those passages
which displeased the Inquisitors. See also the Index Librorum prohibitorum
et expurgatorum, p. 850, et seq. 1667, in folio. " Polidori Virgilii de inventoribus rerum Liber, nisi fuerit ex correctis et impressis ab anno 1576."

* Harl. MS. 6966. Excerpta ex Reg. Cath. Wellen.

† See what Burton's MS. says, Nichols's Hist. Leic. ut supr. respecting
Guido Duke of Urbino, Polydore Vergil's first patron.

speedily became Bishop of Hereford, and Polydore himself in 1503 was presented to the rectory of Church
Langton in Leicestershire.* In the following year, Oct.
20th 1504, when the Cardinal S^{ti}. Chrysogoni was translated from Hereford to the bishopric of Bath and Wells,
we find him enthroned, by commission from the archdeacon
of Canterbury, in the person of Polydore as his repre-
sentative.†

In 1507 Polydore Vergil was collated to the prebend of
Scamlesby in the Church of Lincoln ;‡ and early in 1508,
at the King's nomination, to the archdeaconry of Wells.
In the instrument of appointment he is named " Mr.
Polydor Vergill, otherwise Castellen."§

It was now, or a little before, that Henry the Seventh

---

* "1503. Nov. 16. Dominus Polydorus Castellen. jurium, reddituum,
et proventium Cameræ apostolicæ in regno Angliæ debitorum Vice Collector
generalis, admissus ad Ecclesiam de Langdon Ecclesia in Archidiaconatu
Leycestr." Reg. Smyth Linc. Episc.

† " 1504. 20 Oct. Hadrianus tit. Sancti Chrysogoni Presb. Cardinal,
translatus ab Episcopatu Heref. auctoritate papali inthronizatur (per com-
missionem ab Archid. Cantuar.) in persona Polidori Virgilii subcollectoris
in regno Angl." Excerpta ex Reg. Cath. Wellen. MS. Harl. 6968, p. 45.

‡ "1507. 13 Apr. Dominus Polidorus Castellen. clericus collat. ad
Preb. de Scamlesby in Ecclesia Linc. per mortem Magistri Willelmi Elyot."
Reg. Smyth ut supr.

§ The Harleian MS. 6966 contains an abridged copy of the instrument:
" Whereas Adrian Card. de Chrysogoni and bishop of Bath and Wells
hath, by his sufficient writing granted unto us the nomination . . . Wherefore

requested him to undertake the History, of which a translation of three of the later Books is here presented to
the reader. Polydore states the fact circumstantially in
the address to his brother, dated at London in 1517,
prefixed to the edition of the Treatise " de Inventoribus "
which issued from the press of Frobenius at Basle in
1521.

He says, " Veni post hæc, missu Alexandri sexti Romani
pontificis in Britanniam, quæ nunc Anglia est, ut quæsturam pontificiam apud Anglos gererem. Ubi ne bonum
ocium tererem, rogatu Henrici ejus appellationis Septimi
Regis præstantissimi, Res ejus populi gestas scripsi, in
historiæque stilum redegi. Quod hercle opus duodecim
annos sub literatoria incude laboratum, obstante fato,
nondum absolvere licuit."

Antony a Wood mentions Polydore as at this time in
great favour with Fox, Bishop of Winchester,* and
from several of Erasmus's letters we learn that he was on
terms of familiarity with the persons most eminent for

we woll that ye confer for this time only the Archdeaconry of Welles unto
Mr Polydor Vergill otherwise called Castellen. Geven 6 Jan. 23. regni."
The Cardinal de Chrysogoni resided away. Hence Polydore Vergil was as
frequently styled Collector as Sub-Collector of the Peter-Pence.

" 1507–8. 6 Feb. Polydorus Vergilius alias Castellen. per procur. install.
in Archid. Well. et prebend. de Brent annex. installatur personaliter 10
Sept. prox. sequent." Ibid.

* Fasti Oxon. edit. Bliss, 4° Lond. 1815. coll. 8, 9.

rank and learning who moved within the sphere of the court. Sir Thomas More, Pace, Linacre, Tunstal, and Latimer (the preceptor of Cardinal Pole), are especially enumerated as his friends.*

In the beginning of Oct. 1510 he was naturalised ;† and in 1513, upon being collated to the prebend of Oxgate in St. Paul's Cathedral, he resigned his prebend of Scamlesby.‡ In 1514 he was employed in assisting Wolsey

---

* Erasmi Epist. fol. 1706. Two Letters, one from Polydore to Erasmus, the other from Erasmus to Polydore, will be found in the Appendix, Numm. III. IV.

He had a short friendship too with Gawin Douglas, bishop of Dunkeld. In the third Book of his History, edit. Bas. 1556, pp. 52, 53, noticing the earliest accounts of the Scottish kings, he says, " Nuper enim Gauinus Douglas Doucheldensis episcopus, homo Scotus, virque summa nobilitate et virtute, nescio ob quam causam, in Angliam profectus, ubi audivit dedisse me jampridem ad historiam scribendam, nos convenit : *amicitiam fecimus :* postea summe rogavit, ut ne historiam paulo antè a quodam suo Scoto divulgatam sequerer, in rebus Scoticis explicandis, pollicitusque est se intra paucos dies missurum commentariolum de his neutiquam negligendum, id quod et fecit." He adds, soon after, " Verum non licuit diu uti frui amico, qui eo ipso anno, qui fuit salutis humanæ MDXXI, Londini pestilentia absumptus est."

† Pat. 2 Hen. VIII. p. 1. See the Letters of Naturalization, in Rymer's Fœdera, tom. xiii. pp. 290, 291. They were granted, without fine or fee, Oct. 2, 1510.

‡ " 1513. 11 Junii, Polider Vergil Castellen. coll. ad preb. de Oxgate in Eccl. S. Pauli Lond. per mortem magistri Johannis Pratt." Reg. Fitzjames Ep. Lond.

" 1513. 12 Jul. Magister Oliver Cosen collat. ad preb. de Scamblesby

to attain the Cardinal's hat,* though it seems doubtful whether either he or the Cardinal S^{ti}. Chrysogoni gave all the aid to Wolsey which that minister expected on the death of Julius II. Certain it is that in 1514 both fell out of favour.

The Cottonian Manuscript, Vitellius, B. II. contains various Letters and Papers, some burnt and injured, which it may not be improper to refer to here. The folio 101* of that volume preserves a Letter of the Cardinal S^{ti}. Chrysogoni, from Rome, to Wolsey, entreating the continuance of favour to himself and Polydore. He refers to long service on his own part : and says, " taceo meam antiquam fidem, et servitutem viginti quatuor annorum." He resided constantly at Rome, and was one of Wolsey's earliest tools. The same volume, a few leaves on, preserves another Letter, addressed by the whole College of Cardinals to Wolsey, dated Rome, 1st Dec. 1514, recommending the Cardinal S^{ti}. Chrysogoni, and his " succollector " Polydore, to Wolsey's kindness. At folio 123 we have a long letter from Polydore Vergil himself to the Cardinal S^{ti}. Chrysogoni dated from London in 1515, giving various intelligence from England ; burnt at the edges and im-

in Eccl. Linc. per resign. Magistri Polydori Vergilii." Reg. Smyth Linc. Ep.

* MS. Cotton. Brit. Mus. Vitell. B. ii. fol. 76, Letter from Polydore Vergil to Wolsey, dated 20 May 1514, but without the name of place.

perfect; possibly an intercepted letter, or it would hardly have been found in the Cottonian Manuscript; in which he says, " de Denariis Sancti Petri pauci sunt qui vellent solvere, dicentibus plurimis se velle videre finem litis; inter quos est etiam *noster bonus Abbas Sancti Albani* "* It was just at this time that Wolsey received the Abbey of St. Alban's in commendam, and he is probably the person meant. In folio 126ᵇ we have a fragment of a note to Wolsey, from whom does not appear, but it advises him to caution the King against both the Cardinal and Polydore, and recommends the interception of their letters.†

* Another copy of this Letter occurs in the same volume, fol. 127.

† Polydore Vergil, in his history of the reign of Henry the Seventh, gives the following account of the Cardinal.

" Legarat Innocentius Rom. pontifex Hadrianum Castellensem, hominem Hetruscum natum Corneti, quod veteres Castrum novum vocarant, qui in Scotiam proficisceretur, ad tollendas ipsius autoritate ex illorum principum animis discordias. Is quamvis magnis sit itineribus profectus, tamen cum pervenit in Angliam, cognovit ab Henrico rege, ad quem etiam a pontifice mandata habebat, se tardius venisse quam res requireret, quare ejus monitu, sibi jam pedem referendum, ac ex Anglia non excedendum ratus, vix bidui moram fecerat, cum nuntius cædis Jacobi venit. Mansit deinde Hadrianus in Anglia aliquot menses, in quem a primo Joannes Mortonus Cantuariensis archiepiscopus omnia humanitatis officia conferre studuit, hominis doctrina ac moribus ductus, quippe qui eum in summa etiam apud regem gratia posuit. Atqui Henricus cum hominem sibi a Mortono commendatum videret non minimi esse usus, jam tum mirifice diligere cœpit, ejusque opera cum apud Innocentium, tum apud Alexandrum sextum pontifices, ita deinde usus est, ut primum Herefordensem, et ex eo mox relicto, Batho-

c

The next we read, is of Polydore in prison, succeeded
in his sub-collectorship of the Papal dues by Andrew
Ammonius, the King's Latin secretary. The original of

mensem et Wellensem episcopatum ei detulerit. Cæterum Hadrianus brevi
post tempore Romam reversus, per omnes honorum gradus in Collegium
Cardinalium venit : nam Innocentius eum primo Collectorem, id est, Quæs-
torem pontificium in Anglia, et Protonotarium unum ex septem creavit, postea
Alexander pontifex eundem diu secretiorem familiarem habuit, Cardi-
nalemque fecit. Sed quotusquisque est, qui ista, quæ ignavis juxta atque
solertibus et dari et auferri possunt, miretur? Alia nempe Hadriani laus
est, et hæc quidem æterna : erant enim in eo plurimæ literæ non vulgares,
sed reconditæ, ac summum bonorum delectus judicium, qui memoria nostra
primus omnium post illud disertissimum Ciceronis seculum, suis scriptis
mortales excitavit, ad perfectas literas de doctissimorum autorum fontibus
hauriendas, docuitque modum pure, nitide, ac luculenter loquendi, sic, ut eo
doctore, in præsentia ubique gentium latinitas ab integro renascatur."
Polyd. Verg. Angl. Hist. lib. xxvi. edit. Bas. 1556, pp. 580, 581.

Some of the circumstances of Castello's subsequent life are incidentally
alluded to in a later page of Polydore Vergil's History. He was deprived
of the bishopric of Bath and Wells, in 1518, at the time of Cardinal Cam-
peggio's approach to England as legate, and while he remained at Calais :
undoubtedly to please, if not at the request of, Leo the Tenth.

" Venit in Angliam Laurentius Campegius homo Bononiensis inter
jurisconsultos jureconsultissimus, vir paratus meditatusque, cui datus fuit
collega Volsæus ; is etenim partem Henrici assiduitate petendi rogandique,
partim Francisci regis autoritate, a Leone pontifice Romano sub idem
tempus legatus Angliæ creatus erat. Atqui Campegium ubi Caletum pervenit, sive casu, sive dedita opera Volsæus monuit oportere eo loci dies
aliquot morari, ac interim multa promissa faciendo, hominem tentare cœpit,
ut vellet per Literas apud Leonem pontificem agere, quo HADRIANUS
CARDINALIS BATHONIENSIS privaretur episcopatu in quem jam ipse
paratus erat invadere. Fuit autem in promissis Episcopatus Sarisberien-

Ammonius's appointment to this office, from the Cardinal S[ti]. Chrysogoni under Leo the Tenth's direction, dated at Rome, 26 March 1515, follows at fol. 130.

The incarceration of Polydore caused a lively interest to be taken in his fate at Rome. The same volume from which so many documents have been already cited preserves two Letters, one from the Pope, the other from the Cardinal de Medicis to Henry the Eighth, referring to the fact, and soliciting for Polydore's release, and for the restoration of whatever had been seized at his residence.

sis, quem non multo post vacantem ipse Campegius assecutus est, eoque uti frui tandiu licuit, quoad non multo post lege sancitum est, ut absentes in Anglia sacerdotia non possiderent." lib. xxvii. p. 654.

In the next page of Polydore's History we read of the Conspiracy in which Adrian de Castello had previously joined against Leo, and of the vengeance which followed it, of which the deprivation of his English bishopric was no doubt a part.

" Interea Leo non immemor noxiæ, si qua fuerat, Hadrianum et Franciscum [Volaterranum] mulctavit, at non contentus ea præda, ejus satellitum præfectus deinde ad Hadriani ædes quæsitum ivit, si quid intus esset, quod rapi posset. Ejus injuriæ indignitate Hadrianus valde commotus Venetias se contulit, ubi, sicut ejus moris erat, in divinis atque aliis bonis literis, Leone non invito, jam acquiescebat, cùm ecce, inimicorum operatione deturbatur de sui episcopatus possessione, quem Volsæus repente voravit."

Castello now fled from Venice, and little more was afterwards heard of him. The editor of Chacon, who is followed by Godwin, says, " quo vero tempore Hadrianus hic noster obierit, incertum ; circa annum 1518 scribit Ciaconius : die 16 Januarii anni 1526 illum jam fato cessisse affirmat Contelorius : ferunt in Traciam, Constantinopolim usque, necis metu perterritum fugisse, ibique obscurum ac latentem clausisse diem extremum."

How long he remained in prison we know not, but his letter to his brother, dated at London, in 1517, is endited as from a man at liberty and ease, and we are certain that he forfeited none of his preferments but the sub-collectorship. And that was a loss which he was little likely to deplore.* The Pope's letter however states that he had been imprisoned for many months, before Henry the Eighth was written to.†

In 1522, when Charles the Fifth made his visit to England, in the List of lodgings set apart in London for the Emperor's train, we find, " Item, Poloderus in Paules Churche Yarde ; hall, parlour, iij. chambres, iiij. beddes, with all necessaries." Polydore's place occurs in two other lists ; in one, with the addition of " wyne i. hogg. bere ij. hogg." Polydore's place, as it is called, was, no doubt, his residence as prebendary of Oxgate.‡

Polydore had long taken the decision to pass the remainder of his life in England, and now devoted himself

* Chalmers, in his Biographical Dictionary, is wrong in representing Polydore Vergil as the last collector of this odious tax in England. He is never subsequently mentioned as returning to the appointment.

Noticing this tribute as established in the Saxon times, Vergil says, " numi illi argentei vocantur vulgo Denarii divi Petri, quos pontificius quæstor, quem non inscienter Collectorem nuncupant, exigit. *Nos hanc olim quæsturam aliquot per annos gessimus*, ejusque muneris obeundi causa primum in Angliam venimus." Hist. lib. iv. pp. 89, 90.

† See these two Letters in the Appendix of Documents, Numm. I. II.

‡ Rutland Papers, published by the Camden Society, pp. 91, 94.

more than ever to his studies, and to the completion of his English History: leaving no inquiry unpursued among our older chroniclers.

It is not generally known to his biographers that in 1525 he published the first genuine edition of Gildas, from a manuscript he himself possessed, collated with another which had been furnished to him by Tunstal, Bishop of London.* This and the just remarks he makes in his own history upon that of Geoffrey of Monmouth, fully evidence the discrimination as well as the care with which he compiled.

In 1526 he published a Treatise " de Prodigiis," 8vo. Lond. consisting of Dialogues and Attacks upon Divination.† This work was reprinted at Basle by Bebelius in

---

* " Opus novum. Gildas Britannus Monachus cui Sapientis cognomentum est inditum de Calamitate, Excidio, et conquestu Britanniæ, quem Angliam nunc vocant, author vetustus a multis diu desyderatus, et nuper in gratiam D. Cutheberti Tonstalli, Londinen. Episcopi formulis excusus.

" In hoc authore preter multiplicem hic illic Historiarum interpositionem, videre licet gravissimus illius temporis Regum, Principum, Ducum, Eporum, Sacerdotum, Clericorum, &c. correptiones, vehementı undique spiritus impetu, densis sacrarum literarum testimoniis fortiter armatas." 12º.

The Preface addressed to Tunstall is dated 8 id. April 1525.

This work was reprinted in the " Opus Historiarum, nostro seculo convenientissimum," 8º Bas. 1541 : and again, by Josceline, in 1568, dedicated to Archbishop Parker, with the restoration of some passages which had been intentionally omitted by Polydore.

† The preface, addressed to Francis Maria Duke of Urbino, is dated London, 13 cal. August, 1526.

1531, and again by Isingrim in 1545. To it were prefixed three other Tracts by Polydore, " De Patientia et ejus fructu, Libri duo ;" " De Vita perfecta ;" and " De Veritate et Mendacio."

In 1528 we find him dedicating the translation of a short piece by St. Chrysostom to his friend Erasmus.*

In 1534 his English History appeared in twenty-six Books ; printed in folio, at Basle : the dedication of it to King Henry the Eighth, dated at London, " mense Augusto, 1533." A second edition came out at Basle in 1546. These bring the History down to the year 1509. Immediately upon his death a third edition appeared, in twenty-seven Books, fol. Bas. 1555 ; bringing the History as low as 1538 :† this was followed by another edition, fol.

---

* Whether this Translation appeared in print earlier than 1550 the editor is not certain. It was then appended to an improved edition of the " Adagia." " Polydori Vergilii Urbinatis Adagiorum æque humanorum ut sacrorum opus, per autorem anno isto M.D.L. rursus novissime jam, ac diligentius recognitum, et magnifice locupletatum. Item Divi Joannis Chrysostomi de perfecto Monacho maloque Principe Libellus, eodem Polydoro interprete." 8° Bas. 1550.

Herbert's Ames, i. 342, 388, mentions " A Book conteyning the Commendations of Matrimony, by William Harrington, LL.D." as " Imprinted at the instance of Polydor Virgil, archdeacon of Wells," 1528, 4to. with a preface by him in Latin. Herbert quotes as his authority " Mr. Baker's interleaved Maunsell's Catal."

† " Polydori Vergilii Vrbinatis Anglicæ Historiæ Libri viginti septem, ab ipso autore postremum jam recogniti, adque amussim, salva tamen historiæ

Basle, 1556 : by a fifth, in 2 volumes in small octavo, Ghent, 1556-7 : by a sixth, fol. Basle, 1570 : and a seventh, an octavo, edited by Thysius, who forgot the reign of Henry the Eighth, and then prefixed it to the whole with an apology, 8°, Leyden, 1651.

Burnet acquaints us that, as a member of the Convocation of the Clergy, Polydore Vergil signed the Articles of 1536 ;* and in that of 1547 the declaration for the Communion in both kinds.†

veritate, expoliti." The following appears as a preface at the back of the title-page to this and the succeeding folio editions.

" Elogium Anglicæ Historiæ.

" Paucis ante annis, Polydorus Vergilius Vrbinas edidit historiam suam Anglicam, in qua primum arte conficienda, deinde ordine digerenda, dein de oratione vestienda, quanquam et omnium ferme opinionem expectationemque et atque adeo seipsum superavit; attamen cum ille in suis de rerum Inventoribus libris demonstraverit, nullam olim artem quæ futura esset excellentior, intra suum stetisse initium, quod nihil prope sit simul et inventum et perfectum, ex eo voluit eam ipsam historiam regustare, polire, locupletare, id quod biennio post, hoc est, anno MD.XXXVI. primum, deinde etiam LIII. naviter fecit, salva tamen ac incolumi illa prisca integritate majestateque veritatis historiæ. Quare optime Lector accipies hoc opus perfectum, quo abhinc sexcentos, ut vetus ille dinumerandi modus usitatus doctis usurpetur, annos, non aliud in eo scribendi genere, haud forsitan temere dices, latinius elegantiusque compositum fuisse : atque istuc est tibi testatum, quo posses merito gaudere seculum nostrum tandem aliquando elocutione latina passim pure emendata plene florere. Quapropter in hac equidem parte vel ipsa Anglia non minus felix censenda est, quod talem rerum suarum gestarum scriptorem primum habuerit."

* Burnet's Hist. of the Reformation, fol. edit. i. 436.

† Ibid. ii. 102, iii. 360.

In the interim between these two years affairs of busi-
ness called him to Italy. How long exactly he remained
there we are not told, but it was for some time. The
fact of his departure is stated by himself in the pro-
œmium to his twenty-seventh Book. Up to that time he
had been in the constant habit of marking events as they
occurred. When he returned, his health failed ; and,
perhaps, in that perilous day for churchmen, his courage.
He says " secutus est Henricus eo nomine octavus, numero
vero Regum vigesimus septimus, cujus res gestas usque
ad trigesimum regni ipsius annum perscripsi, qui post hac
octo regnavit annos, cum ipse id temporis in Italiam re-
vocatus fui negotiorum causa, ubi perdiu mansi : at simul
ac inde reverti in Angliam, interrupta jam serie rerum
publicarum, quas in dies singulos annotare prius solebam,
non statim post idem mihi institutum tenere per valetu-
dinem incommodam licuit."

In 1550 the infirmities of age requiring a warmer cli-
mate than that he had so long been pleased with, he
sought and obtained a licence from King Edward the
Sixth to return to his native country : to remain there for
life at his pleasure : and, at the same time, to retain the
rents and profits of the archdeaconry of Wells, and of his
prebend of Nonnington, in the Church of Hereford,
" without incurring danger, penalty, or forfeiture."* The

* See the Append. Num. V. Newcourt says he sold the perpetuity of

letters patent state expressly that the indulgence thus af-
forded to him was in consideration of his literary merits.
He likewise retained till his death his prebend of Oxgate
in the Cathedral of St. Paul.*

Polydore did not take immediate advantage of his licence, for in 1551 we find him still in London, receiving
the further bounty of the Crown. In the Council-Book of
that year, Nov. 1st, there is the entry of a warrant to the
treasurer and chamberlains of the Exchequer to deliver to
" Polydor Vergill in way of the Kinges Majesties reward
the sum of one hundred marks :" and on the 9th of November following another warrant to the Exchequer to
pay to " Polydore Vergil in way of the Kings reward the
sum of three hundred crowns, after five shillings the

---

the house at Wells at this time, which belonged to his archdeaconry.
Burton assures us he was a benefactor there " in beautifying the choir of the
Cathedral Church of Wells with fair arras hangings (which are there at
this day, 1636) ; wherein, in many escocheons, are his Arms ; viz. Argent,
a laurel tree vert, supported with two crocodiles proper ; over which, in a
winding label, a scroll is written,

        ' Hæc Polydori sunt munera Vergilii ;'

underneath, in a strait scroll,

        ' Sum Laurus virtutis honos pergrata triumphis.' "

        Nichols's Hist. Leic. vol. iii. pt. i. p. 538.

    * " 1555, 13 Decemb. Magister Johannes Braban clericus collat. ad
preb. de Oxgate in Eccles. S. Pauli *per mortem Polydori Vergilii*" Reg.
Edm. Boner. Episc. Lond.

d

crown."* No intervening entry occurs to show that the one superseded the other; they stand as separate gifts. The following short letter to Sir William Cecil, the original of which is preserved in the Lansdowne MS. N°. ii. art. 66, relates to the later gift.

" Optime Cecilli. S. Initium jungendæ amicitiæ tecum occasio hæc facit. Heri enim adivi ad illustrem Northumbriæ Ducem, mei negotii causa, qui statim petiit an accepissem schedulam a consilio regio subscriptam de dono Majestatis Regiæ dato. Respondi intellexisse me a domino Privati sigilli custode eam esse signatam. Tum ille inquit, Mane domi, ipse namque ad te illam mox mittendam curabo, si non potueris commodo tuo ante habere. At ego ne immodestus viderer, hodie bene mane me ad Regiam contuli, quia etsi heri te convenire studui uspiam, tamen non potui, sed accidit, ut tu paulo ante de cubiculo tuo exiveris. Quare nunc mitto ad te famulum meum Polydorum Rosse, cum his literis meis, cui rogo, velis eam ipsam schedulam ad me dare, quo possim tempore suo rem meam peragere. Siquid vero tibi tuisve ministris inde debeatur illud libenter persolvam. Vale, et me ama. Ex ædibus nostris x. Novemb. 1551.

Tuus POLYDORUS VER-
GILIUS, manu mea."

Addressed,
" Domino Cecilio, Secretario Regio."

These presents, in all probability, were to provide for the expenses of his journey ; and in those days must have been more than sufficient. He retired to Urbino ; and there, to the close of life, continued to devote himself to learned pursuits.

* Harl. MS. 6195, p. 16.

He is stated to have collated the first impression of Nicolo Perotti's " Cornucopiæ " with a copy in the Duke of Urbino's library, and to have corrected its errata.

Honiger obtained his Notes on Horace, and included them with those of other commentators in his edition of that author, printed in folio, at Basle, in 1580.

A manuscript List of English Bishops, by him, is also referred to,* but whether it still exists, or at what period it was compiled, is unknown to the editor of the present volume : though he suspects it is not impossible that it may be only the original of the List of Bishops of the several Sees from early time, printed at the end of the Index to the later editions of Polydore Vergil's History.

His last composition that we are acquainted with, is a Latin letter of congratulation to Queen Mary the First, upon her accession to the English Throne, dated August 5th, 1553 : without the mention of place, but, doubtless, from Urbino.† The original is preserved among the Harleian Manuscripts in the British Museum.‡

Peter a Sancto Romualdo, in the Continuation of Ademar's Chronicle, p. 326, asserts that Polydore Vergil died

---

* " MS. among the English Ecclesiasticks, commended by Stapleton," Princ. Doctr. lib. xiii. c. 7. Wharton, Angl. Sacr. vol. i. p. xiv.

† See it in the Append. Num. VI.

‡ MS. Harl. 6989, fol. 149. The same Volume contains an earlier letter of Vergil " Edovardo Lælio, Regis Angliæ apud Cæsarem Oratori." Lond. 19 Oct. 1526.

in 1562 ; but his biographers generally place his death in 1555 ; and they are confirmed in the correctness of this latter date by the Registers of the Sees of Bath and Wells, of Hereford, and of London, in all of which it appears that those who stepped into the archdeacon's preferments succeeded in that year " *per mortem* Polydori Vergilii."

FEW writers of the English Story have met with such harsh treatment as Polydore Vergil. Sir Thomas Pope Blount in his " Censura Auctorum," and Bayle in the Notes to his " Historical and Critical Dictionary," have taken pains to enumerate the charges brought against him for deficiency in judgment, for partiality, and for gross falsehood.

The truth is that Polydore Vergil's attainments went far beyond the common learning of his age. The earlier part of his History interfered with the prejudices of the English. He discarded Brute as an unreal personage ;* and considered Geoffrey of Monmouth's History an heterogeneous mixture of fact and fable, furnishing comparatively little which could be safely relied upon as history.†

* " Cæterum Livius, Dionysius Halicarnaseus, ac plerique alii qui diligenter de antiquitatibus Romanorum scripserunt, nunquam hujus Bruti meminere. Neque illud ex Britannorum annalibus prodi potuerat." Polyd. Verg. ut supr. lib. i. p. 17.

† " At contra quidam nostris temporibus, pro expiandis istis Britonum

Hence Leland's defence of Geoffrey, printed in the " Collectanea," where it fills no fewer than nine octavo pages, " Codrus, sive Laus et Defensio Gallofridi Arturii Monumetensis contra Polydorum Vergilium :" followed by his " Assertio inclytissimi Arturii, Regis Britanniæ," first printed in 1544.*

Sir Henry Savile, in the dedication of the " Scriptores post Bedam" to Queen Elizabeth, was the next who assailed Vergil. He was little to be attended to, because a foreigner ; " homo Italus, et in rebus nostris hospes."†

maculis, scriptor emersit, ridicula de eisdem figmenta contexens, eosque longe supra virtutem Macedonum, et Romanorum, impudenti vanitate attollens : Gaufredus hic est dictus, cognomine Arthurus, pro eo, quod multa de Arthuro ex priscis Britonum figmentis sumpta, et ab se aucta, per superductum latini sermonis colorem, honesto historiæ nomine obtexit. Quinetiam majore ausu, cujusdam Merlini divinationes falsissimas, quibus utique de suo plurimum addidit, dum eas in latinum transferret, tanquam approbatas et immobili veritate subnixas prophetias vulgavit." Ibid.

* Lelandi Collectanea, edit. 1774, vol. v. p. 2.

† " Nam Polydorus, ut homo Italus, et in rebus nostris hospes, et (quod caput est) neque in republica versatus, nec magni alioqui vel judicii vel ingenii, pauca ex multis delibans, et falsa plerumque pro veris amplexus, historiam nobis reliquit cum cætera mendosam tum exiliter sane et jejune conscriptum." Rerum Anglic. Script. post Bedan. fol. Lond. 1596.

Nicolson gives a comment on this passage, which shews that he had not looked into Polydore's History to form an opinion for himself. " Some," he says, " have fancied that the severer character which Sir Henry is here pleased to give of this author, might chiefly be applied to the History of Henry VIII. and that a great many passages in that reign may be darkly or falsely represented by him, by reason of his being unacquainted with the

Paulus Jovius charged him with administering flattery
to the English; he says the French and Scotch writers
had made the same complaint; and adds that he had introduced into his History the names of inconsiderable
captains.*

Humphrey Lhuyd, without adducing the slightest evidence, stigmatised him as a malicious detractor.†

English tongue ; which could not but very much obstruct his knowledge in
modern transactions.   Other things, say they, have fallen from him under
a borrowed light and colour, out of the respect he had for Queen Mary,
and his great inclinations to serve the interests of that princess."   The
slightest investigation of Polydore's History of Henry the Eighth's reign,
however, will evince the futility of these remarks.

* " Conscripsit Historias rerum Britannicarum, ea fide ut Scotis et Gallis
sæpe reclamantibus, alieno potius arbitrio quam suo intexuisse multa in
gratiam gentis existimetur, quod in recensendis minorum Ducum nominibus,
tanquam gloriæ avidis plurimum indulserit."   Pauli Jov. Elog. cap. cxxxv.
p. 279.

† " Cum ante paucos annos in Polydori Virgilii Itali, et Hectoris Boethii
Scoti historias Britannicas incidissem quorum ille nominis Britannici
gloriam non solum obfuscare, sed etiam Britannos ipsos mendacissimis suis
calumniis infamare totis viribus conatur: hic vero dum Scotos suos e
tenebris eruit, quidquid unquam aut Romani aut Britanni laude dignum in
hac insula gessare, hoc totum illis attribuit insulsissimus scriptor."   Lhuyd
Descr. Angliæ, fol. 6.   Other passages, equally calumnious as relating to
Polydore, are quoted from Lhuyd by bishop Nicolson, Hist. Lib. edit.
1776, p. 57.   Such as " Homo ignotus et exterus."—" Vir perfrictæ frontis "
—" Invidia et odio tumens "—" Infamis homunculus"—" Os impudens"—
" Delirans Urbinas."—Nor ought anything of this, he adds, to be attributed
to an over-boiling of honest Humphrey's Welsh blood, *if the other matters*

Owen reviled him in an epigram,

> " Virgilii duo sunt: alter Maro : Tu Polydore
> Alter, Tu mendax, ille Poeta fuit."

Caius, in his Treatise " de Antiquitate Cantabrigiæ," makes a heavier charge. He mentions it not only as a thing reported, but found to be certainly true, that Polydore Vergil committed *as many of our ancient and manuscript historians to the flames* AS WOULD HAVE FILLED A WAGGON, that the faults of his own work might pass undiscovered.*

La Popliniere, in his " Histoire des Histoires," improves even upon this; he says, Polydore caused all the histories to be burnt, which *by the King's authority* and the assistance of his friends he could possibly come at.†

Against these charges Polydore Vergil was ably defended, more than two hundred years ago, by Burton, already mentioned, in a manuscript written in 1636, which

---

he is accused of be true.   Nicolson evidently, himself, doubted the truth of the charges.

* " Fama percrebuit, atque etiam cognitum et compertum certo est, tot historias nostras, vetustas et manuscriptas immani scelere igni commendasse, quot ne plaustrum quidem posset capere et sustinere, arbitratus, ut credo, se ejus generis omnes solum habuisse : aut veritus sibi vitio dari, quod secutus legem jampridem librorum veterum castigatoribus datam (ut ipse de se ait in præfatione in Gildam) nonnulla resecuerit, quæ scriptores prodiderunt." De Antiq. Cantabr. 4to. Lond. 1574, p. 52.

† La Popliniere, Hist. des Histoires, liv. ix. p. 485.

has been since printed by the late Mr. Nichols in his History of Leicestershire. His words are these:

" Upon the first coming of Polydore, King Henry VII. imposed on him the penning of the English history from the first beginning to that present time ; wherein, as himself saith, he spent twelve years' labour together, but yet finished it not. After some discontinuance, he set upon it again, and performed it in 1533 in the 25th year of King Henry VIII. to whom he then made dedication of the same ; a work of great labour and like reading, but much carped at by John Druse* (who wrote a book against him), Jo. Leland, Richard White, Jo. Lewis, Humphrey Lluid, and others; not, as I conceive, for any just cause, but for that he, being an alien, should be graced with such a matter of charge, which most properly had belonged to a native of the land. The chief matters they charge him with are, first for that having taken the substance of the beginning of his History all out of the works of Geoffrey of Monmouth, yet unthankfully (imitating therein William of Newborough) lashing at him ; next, for that in many places he pitcheth somewhat smartly upon the antiquity of Britain ; thirdly, for that he doth seem severely to censure some of those Kings which he treateth of ; lastly, that, having gotten many old manuscripts together, by whose help he compiled his book, after his conclusion of the same, he set fire on them all.

" For the first and second, it is well observed by many of great reading and judgment, that Geoffrey of Monmouth hath somewhat hyperbolically extolled the praise and antiquity of the Britons, and interlaced many passages of his own device, and drawn down a series of descents, but with what truth the just and true chronology of time, upon good examination, will soon discover ; so that Polydore doth not upon the matter impeach the antiquity of Britain, but the fabulous inventions of the said Geoffrey. To the third,

---

* This is a mistake for Price. The title of the work is " Historiæ Brytannicæ Defensio, Joanne Priseo Equestris Ordinis Brytanno Authore." 4to. Lond. 1573.

those Princes which opposed the Pope's proceedings are indeed by him cen-
sured, those that gave way are applauded ; but that is to be attributed to the
time, and to the circumstance, as whose agent he was, yet whoever shall
peruse what he hath written shall find that many things he did not approve,
though instituted by the Pope's authority, but held them impertinent and
novel, as the inhibiting of marriage to spiritual men, the ordination of
festival days, examinations, kneeling to pictures, creation of Cardinals and
religious orders, and such-like.*   Lastly, for his destroying of manuscripts,
I could never yet be drawn to believe it, neither is it probable, for that,
unless he had had all the copies of each kind together, that by one act they
might all have finally perished, he would never have attempted such an
enterprize ; and certain it is, by Leland's Collectanea, that almost in every
Abbey (himself setting down a catalogue of all manuscripts which he saw in
each place) there was variety and store of copies, not only of the chiefest
writers, but almost of the meanest chronologers and historians.   But, whatsoever they have said, this I may truly say, and can make good, He was a
man of singular invention, good judgement, and good reading, and a true
lover of antiquities."†

Gale in the preface to his " Scriptores," and Bishop
Nicolson in his English Historical Library, have joined in
later times to give currency to another charge, that of
shipping manuscripts for Rome.   Gale says the vessel
loaded with them went from Rochester Bridge.‡   He is

---

* Bale, De Script. Britann. Centur. xiii. says the same : " licet in ple-
risque scriptis suis veræ Religioni superstitionem prætulerit, pie nihilominus
Christianorum ministrorum conjugia defendebat, pièque statuarum cultum
damnabat, cum quibusdam aliis Romanensium Rabbinorum imposturis."

† Nichols's Hist. of Leicestersh. vol. iii. pt. i. p. 538.

‡ Gale, Script. xv. fol. Oxon. 1691. Præf. ad lect.   " Certe si famæ
receptæ et inveteratæ credere liceat, unus Polydorus Virgilius quæstor tunc

e

"said to have borrowed books out of the public library at Oxford, without taking any care to restore them : upon which the University, as they had good reason, declined lending any more, till forced to it by a mandate, which he made a shift to procure from the King. In other places he likewise pillaged the libraries at his pleasure, and at last sent over a whole ship-load of manuscripts to Rome."[*]

But neither the proof nor the probability of this have been established: and it is not a little singular that so many of our good antiquaries and historians should, like sheep, have leaped after each other in gross error.

Taylor, too, in his History of Gavelkind, 4[to] Lond. 1663, pp. 83, 84, says, Polydore "*laboured to disparage the* BRITISH ANTIQUITIES, and not only so, but under the patronage of King Henry, having power to search all Records, *is reported to have seised the most antient thereof (that were in being) in the Treasury of* LANDAF, *and to have destroyed them;* something of which nature I have also seen ; for in a Register book, compiled by St. Thomas de Cantilupe (bishop of Hereford) I found three leaves cut out ; *which, by a constant and confident tradition of the Registers of the Diocess of Hereford,* in whose custody that Book was, *it is averr d that this was done by Polydore.*"

apud nos Pontificius, navem istis spoliis onustam a ponte Rhoffensi Romam misit."

[*] Nicolson, Engl. Hist. Lib. edit. 1776, p. 58.

This again is Welsh ; even Herefordshire, up to the time of Henry the Eighth, was frequently if not usually considered as a Welsh county.

Had there been any truth, or evidence in support of the Oxford story, Antony a Wood would have been sure to have ferretted out the facts : all *he* says in his History of Duke Humphrey's Library is, "That several scholars would, upon small pledges given in, borrow books thence : which pledges, being not half worth the books that were borrowed, were never restored. Polydore Vergil, as tradition tells us, borrowed many after such a way ; but at length being denied, did, upon petition made to the King, obtain his licence for the taking out of any manuscript for his use (in order, I suppose, for the collecting materials for his English History or Chronicle of England), which, being imitated by others, the library thereby suffered very great loss."*

Even Burnet has a fling at Polydore, but it is for his character of Wolsey only. He says, " Neither Erasmus nor Polydore Vergil made their court dexterously with the Cardinal, which did much intercept the King's favour to them ; so that the one left England, and the other was but coarsely used in it, who has sufficiently revenged him-

* Wood's Hist. and Antiq. of Oxford, edit. by Gutch, 4° Oxf. 1796, vol. ii. p. ii. pp. 918, 919.

self upon the Cardinal's memory."* Yet who is there
that has studied the history and correspondence of Wolsey's time but sees the corroboration, in every part, of
the portrait which Polydore Vergil has drawn ?

Wharton, in the Anglia Sacra, has given a character of
Polydore very different from Savile, Gale, and Nicolson.
He calls him " Vir undequaque doctissimus, et Anglicanæ
Historiæ peritissimus."

THE compilation of Polydore Vergil's History occupied
the labour of twenty-eight years before it was presented
to King Henry the Eighth. It was the first of our histories in which the writer ventured to compare the facts
and weigh the statements of his predecessors ; and it was
the first in which summaries of personal character are
introduced in the terse and energetic form adopted in the
Roman classics. In choice of expression, and in the
purity of Latin style, Polydore Vergil exceeded all his
contemporaries :† and the numerous editions of his work

---

* Hist. Reform. Oxford edit. vol. i. pp. 20, 21.

† His Address to the Reader at the end of his History apologizes for
the necessity of using a few terms unknown to classical latinity.

" POLYDORUS VERGILIUS LECTORI S.

" MONITUM te, optime Lector, volo permulta verba minus Latina, longo
usu, non item ratione, jampridem in consuetudinem quotidiani sermonis
venisse, sic, ut velimus nolimus, ea interdum usurpare cogamur : cujusmodi

in the sixteenth century sufficiently shew the estimation

--sunt Dux et Comes, olim officii tantum, at summæ nunc dignitatis vocabula.
Item comitatus, pro regione ; cancellarius, pro sciibarum ; abbas, prior, pro
monachorum præfecto.   Ista paucula (nam cætera facile declinavimus) cum
legendo in ea incideris, non mini vitio des, sed atque adeo nostris temporibus,
quæ ita quondam barbara facta sunt, ut nondum ejusmodi nævis purgari ad
unguem potuerint. Vale."

/   If the reader can endure another specimen of Polydore's Latin, let him
peruse the following short notice of the last moments of Queen Catherine
of Arragon, and his translation of her letter to the King :

" At Catherina sexto post die graviori morbo affecta, cum animo præ-
sentiret mortem adventare, ancillam non indoctam jussit binas scribere-
literas eodem exemplo, unas ad regem, alteras ad Eustachium, quas ipsa
dictavit, in hæc verba :

' Domine mi rex marite semper charissime, Salve.   Jam advenit hora
mortis meæ, in quo temporis puncto, amor facit ut te paucis admoneam de
—salute animæ tuæ, quam debes cunctis mortalibus rebus anteponere, neglecta
præ ea omni corporis cura, propter quam et me in multas miserias, et te
ipsum in solicitudines plures conjecisti : sed hoc tibi ignosco, ac Deus tibi
ignoscat, tam velim, quam precibus piis oro.   Quod superest, commendo
tibi filiam communem nostram, in quam quæso, officium illud paterne totum
conferas, quod ego a te alias desideravi.   Præterea precor summé, uti ancil-
las meas respicias, easque suo tempore bene locare nuptiis placeat, quod
—multum non est, cum non sint nisi tres, et dare meis ministris stipendium
debitum, atque in unum etiam annum ex tua gratia, benignitate, liberalitate
futurum, ne deserti vel inopes esse videantur.   Postremo unum illud testor.
Oculi mei te solum desiderant.   Vale.' "

It is true that we know of no English composition now remaining in
Polydore's hand-writing ; but, after the reading of this beautiful translation,
who will be so bold to assert, or who will believe the assertion, that Polydore Vergil was ignorant of the English tongue ?   The length of his residence in this country alone repudiates the supposition : and his History shews
it was impossible that he could be ignorant of it.

in which his contemporaries held him.*   Locked away in a language unknown to the common reader, his History has suffered disparagement in later times.   Even Lingard, the best of our modern English Historians, scarcely quotes him.

Thus far, as regards the Latin History.   In the Catalogue of the Library of Henry the Eighth, in the 34th year of his reign, transcribed from a book in the Augmentation Office by the late Mr. Thomas Astle, and by him presented to the British Museum,† "CRONICA POLYDORI" occurs. It was, no doubt, the presentation copy to that monarch : but this Manuscript is not forthcoming now.   It had ceased to be found in the Royal Library when Casley formed his catalogue.

The Manuscript Translation from which the Three Reigns here prepared for the Camden Society have been selected, has the signature of LUMLEY on the first page,— and could not, therefore, have formed any part of the Royal Library previous to the time of James the First, when Lord Lumley's Books and Manuscripts, which had been purchased for Henry Prince of Wales, merged into the Royal Collection. ‡

---

* Even Lhuyd acknowledges the popularity of Polydore's History, " Sed cum in memoriam revocarem, Polydorum Virgilium, *cujus opera in omnium manibus sunt* "—p. 69.

† Addit. MS. Brit. Mus. 4729.

‡ Dr Birch, in his Life of Henry Prince of Wales, pp. 161—163, says,

The volume itself, MS. REG. C. VIII. IX. (once in two books), at present forms a folio of some size, in a hand of the latter part of the reign of Henry the Eighth. To the end of the reign of Henry the Sixth the writing is uniform and beautiful; the work of a scribe. The two last reigns are in a coarser hand, with numerous interlineations, marginal additions, and changes of expression, like an author's copy, prepared for fair transcription. The Translator, it may be conjectured, might not have lived to the entire completion of his task, as the Volume comes down no lower than the death of Richard the Third, leaving the reigns

"The death of John Lord Lumley on the 11th of April 1609, without leaving any issue, gave the King an opportunity of gratifying the Prince's love of books, and making a noble addition to the Royal Library.

"King James I. enriched the Bodleian Library at Oxford at the expense of his own, giving a warrant to Sir Thomas Bodley, under the Privy Seal, for the choice of any books, which that gentleman should like in any of his houses or libraries. But His Majesty very amply supplied the place of them by the purchase of Lord Lumley's library, which contained not only his own collection, but that of his father-in-law, Henry Fitz-Alan Earl of Arundel, who had lived in the reign of King Henry VIII. when, upon the dissolution of the Monasteries, he had great opportunities of collecting manuscripts, many of which, as well as of the printed books in the Royal Library, have the name of Arundel and Lumley written in them.

"King James, having purchased Lord Lumley's library, ordered it, at the suggestion of Mr. Newton, to be reposited, together with that of his predecessors, in the palace of St. James', where the Prince resided, for the use of his Highness; and Mr. Patrick Young, son of Sir Peter Young, his Majesty's tutor, was appointed keeper of it."

of King Henry the Seventh and King Henry the Eighth untouched.

The Translation is free, and of a thorough English character, evidently made by a person powerfully acquainted with the language into which he rendered his author, and well versed in the colloquial phrases of the period. Who he was we have yet to learn; but this must be said, that in elegance of expression he rivals his author. As a specimen of language alone the whole Work is worthy of publication.

Polydore's History during the reigns which form the present volume is indispensable to fill a chasm of near seventy years in the dark period to which they bear relation ; and it is important to know that he wrote this portion of his work whilst many of the persons alluded to in the events of the reigns of Edward the Fourth and Richard the Third were alive, and who communicated with him.*

* See pp. 185, 209.

APPENDIX.

Pope Leo X. to King Henry VIII. in favour of Polydore Vergil whom the king had imprisoned.

[MS. Cotton. Vitell. B. ii. fol. 164.   *Orig.*]

LEO · PP̃ · X^s.

Charissime in Christo fili noster : salutem et apostolicam benedictionem. Commendavimus alijs nostris literis Majestati tuæ dilectum filium Polidorum Verginium, hujus sanctæ Apostolicæ Sedis in regno isto subcollectorem ; qui quidem in carcerem tuo jussu conjectus est, pluresque jam in eo menses detinetur : hortatique sumus te, pro tua in eandem sedem atque nos reverentia, proque nostra in te paterna dilectione et charitate, velles eum liberum facere.   Cujus quidem rei, cum nihil dum actum abs Te intelligamus, has ad tuam Majestatem literas dandas duximus ; quibus etiam atque etiam id ipsum abs te attente atque enixè requirimus, tum etiam ut Collectori domum quæque ablata ex ea sunt mandes restitui, neque patiaris ut ad te frustra totiens de eadem re scripsisse videamur.   In eo præterea Majestas tua nobis gratissimum faciet, si dilectum filium nostrum Hadrianum Cardinalem Batoniensem, tuæ Majestati deditissimum, resque ejus omnes fovebis, tibique ipsas nostro nomine commendatas facies.

Datum Romæ apud Sanctum Petrum, sub annulo piscatoris, die tricesimo Augusti, M.D. xv., Pontificatûs nostri anno tertio.

P. BEMBUS.

Carissimo in Christo filio nostro Henrico
Angliæ Regi Illustri.

Num. II.

The Cardinal Julio de Medicis to King Henry VIII. in favour of Polydore Vergil.

[MS. Cotton. Vitell. B. ii. fol. 165. *Orig.*]

Serenissime ac invictissime Rex et Domine Domine mihi colendissime, humillimas commendationes. Nisi scirem qua promptitudine reverendissimus Dominus meus Cardinalis Hadrianus in causa Collectoriæ se gesserit, ut Majestatis vestræ voluntati satisfaceret, quave fide et servitute in eam semper fuerit, minus audacter fortasse scribere quam nunc facio pro Polydoro ejus servitore, quem non sine molestia in carcerem conjectum intellexi. Nam quum reverendissimus Dominus Cardinalis omnia fecerit quæ ex eo petebantur, et Dominus Andreas possessionem Collectoriæ acceperit, et omnia acta transacta jam sint, proinde Majestatem vestram plurimum rogo nè permittat talem Cardinalem et Servitorem suum tantam pati indignitatem, ejusdemque Servitorem sic diutius detineri, quem quantum magis ex animo possum commendo vestræ regiæ Majestati, et supplico ut dignetur mandare quod liberetur. In quo faciet Sanctissimo Domino nostro rem valde gratam : mihi gratiam singularem : et ipsum Dominum reverendissimum non mediocriter consolabatur. Et felicissimè valeat vestra regia Majestas, cui me humillime commendo.

Bononiæ, iij. Septembris M.D. xv.

Excellentissimæ vestræ regiæ Majestatis,

humillimus ac fidelissimus servitor

Ju. Cardinalis de Medicis.

Serenissimo ac invictissimo principi et
Domino, Domino mihi colendissimo,
Domino Henrico Angliæ, &c. Regi.

Num. III.

Polydore Vergil to Erasmus, 3 June, 1523.

[Erasmi Epist. fol. Lugd. Bat. 1706. Append. Epist. cccxxvi.]

Reverendo Domino Erasmo, amico charissimo, Polydorus Virgilius,
S. D. P.

Mi Erasme, salve. Nudiustertius noster Zacharias salutem mihi tuis verbis nuntiavit, significavitque te meorum libellorum famæ profuisse, ac de me postremo quæsivit, an illud scissem. Ego ad ea respondi, me certum habere studium erga me tuum, et id esse, ut perinde tu mei, ut ipse tui et amantissimus et studiosissimus sum. Postea heri ille duxit ad me puerum tuum, a quo particulatim intellexi, quonam pacto tecum ageretur, id quod summæ mihi fuit voluptati : nam quod vivis, quod vales, illud maxime ex republica nostra litteraria est, cum perspicuum sit, naturam te omnium unum ad eam locupletandam peperisse. Quod tua in me officia continenter confers, ago gratias, ita respondes amori, ita jus necessitudinis, quæ jampridem mihi tecum intercessit, naviter servas. Ego itidem facio, qui tuæ maximæ laudis haudquaquam detrectator exsisto, id quod testatur Epistola nostra ad nostrum Cuthbertum Londinensem Episcopum, cui nuper duas sacrorum adagiorum centurias dedicavi. Scripsi item, postquam hinc proxime discessisti, ad te litteras, easque nostro Moro dedi, sed quia nihil responsum est, postea mihi eatenus tacendum putavi, quoad usu veniret, ut uspiam una essemus, quod tandem aliquando fiet. Interim si tibi usui esse possum, utere Polydoro tuo, qui te etiam pecunia juvare cupit, cujus rei cum post hac periculum feceris, spes non fallet, uti de puero tuo scire poteris. Vale. Londino, 3 Junij, anno 1523.

Saluta, quæso, meis verbis Joh. Oecolampadium, si istic agat, et nostrum Beatum Rhenanum.

Num. IV.

Erasmus to Polydore Vergil, 24 *March* 1527.

[Ibid. Epist. dcccliv.]

Erasmus Roterod. Polydoro Vergilio S. D.

Quo non penetrant linguæ fascinatrices? Quas nos, mi Polydore, non
alia ratione melius ulcisci possumus, quam ut amicitiam, quam isti rescissam
vellent, vinculis quam arctissimis adstringamus.   Videbis Homilias tibi
dicatas, nunc rursus excusas cum dignitate, quo magis etiam urantur, quos
cruciat nostra concordia.   Quod sedulo agis εἰρηνοποιον inter Leum et me,
pro isthæc animo Christus tibi referet promissam beatitudinem.   At præ-
scribit ille parum æquas pacis conditiones.   Ostendat ille quæ perperam
scripserim in ipsum, ego vicissim ostendam quæ ille perperam scripsit in me.
Tum post mutuam palinodiam coeat amicitia.   Verum, hoc esset non sarare
gratiam, sed renovare simultatem.   Optimum fuerit μὴ μνησικακῆσαι, sed
illa Græcorum αμνηστίᾳ prorsus omnium veterum injuriarum abolere memoriam, ac scripto quopiam amico testari positam esse simultatem, et animos
Christiana junctos concordia, quod factum est inter Jacobum Fabrum ac
me.   Quod mihi cum tot portentis dimicandum est, agnosco feroque fatum
meum.   Cum summis mihi pulchre convenit.   Clemens Septimus bis jam
misit ducentos florenos, nihil non pollicens.   Cæsar nuper ad me scripsit
amantissime cum suo cancellario.   Regum, Cardinalium, Ducum, Episco-
porum literis honorificentissime scriptis habeo plena scrinia.   A multis
veniunt et munera nequaquam vulgaria.   A tenebrionibus velut a cimicibus
ac pediculis mordeor: nam his nec Cæsar nec Pontifex potest imponere
silentium.   Tuti sunt suis tenebris.   Sed nihil aliud efficiunt nisi quod
traducunt seipsos.   Nos rectum clavum tenebimus usque ad extremum vitæ
terminum : de eventu viderit Christus, hujus fabulæ choragus.   De libello
excudendo egi cum Frobenio, respondet se paratissimum, ea lege qua excudit
Adagia.   Bene vale, patrone magne.   Basilea, 24 Martij, anno 1527.

Num. V.

The Warrant for Polydore Vergil to depart the Realm, A.D. 1550.

[Pat. 4 Edw. VI. p. 5, m. 14. Rym. Fœd. tom. xv. p. 234.]

Edwarde the Sixte, &c. to all and singuler to whom, &c. greting. Whereas our trustie and welbelovid Polidorus Virgilius hathe made humble sute unto us that, he being bourne in the partes of Italie, and having servid our grandfather King Henry the Seventh, our father King Henry th' Eight, of most noble memorie, and us, by the space of forti yeares and above, in writing and putting fourth in print divers notable Workes and Stories, may be licencid to departe oute of this our realme to visit and see, nowe in his old age, his said natyve countrey, and there to make his abode during his pleasuer, and also quietly, without interruption, to have, hold, and enjoy the profits, rents, and commodities of th' archdeaconrie of Welles in the Cathedral Churche of Welles, and the Prebend of Nonnyngton, in the Cathedrall Churche of Hereford, which the said Polidorus now enjoyith and holdith within this our Realme.

We let you wit that, by the advyse of the lords and others of our Privy Counsail, in consideration of the long, painful, and acceptable service heretofore done by the said Polidorus, of our grace especial and mere motion, we have lycensed, and by these our letters patents doo license the said Polidorus Virgilius, not only to pass out of this our realme, and to inhabite and dwell from hensforth in the said partes of beyond the seas, during his lief, at his pleasuer, but also that, by vertue and auctoritie of theis our said letters patents, the said Polidorus Virgilius, at all tymes from hensforth during his said lief, may be absent and nonresident from his said archdeaconrie of Wells and the said prebend of Nonington, without incurring any daunger, penaltie, or forfaiture for the same, and shall and may, by hymself, or by his sufficient proctour or assign, receyve, take, levye, and enjoye, all and singuler the rents, profitts, commodities, and revenues perteyning or belongyng to the said archedeaconrie and prebend, and to either of them, during his said naturall lief, and the same to convert to his oun use, profitt, and commoditie, any use, custom, ordinance, or prescription of the said church or churches whereunto his said archedeaconrie and prebend doo apperteyn, had or made to the contrarie, or any act, statute, ordinance, provision, or proclamation heretofore had or made, or hereafter to be made, within this our realme to the contrarie hereof in any wise notwithstanding.

Wherfore we woll and commaund all and singuler our officers, ministers, and subjects, to whom in this case it shall apperteyn, to permyt and suffer the said Polydorus Virgilius peasably and quietly to enjoy the hole effect, tenour, and purport of theis our Letters Patents, upon th'only sight of the same, without any manner of lett, impedyment, or molestation to the contrarie hereof, as they and every of them tender our pleasuer and good contentation in that behalf.

Provided always that the tenths, first fruyts, dismes, subsidies, and other devoyers due or to be due unto us or our successours, kings of England, and all other duyeties lawfully accustomed to be paid and born to any other person out of the said archedeaconrie and prebend, be from tyme to tyme duly born and supportyd of the revenues and proffits of the same as apperteyneth ; and further that the said Polidorus doo, or cause to be done, all and every such thing and things as by the laws and orders of the realms, already establyshed or hereafter to be establyshed, he shall be bound to doo or cause to be done by reason of the said archedeaconrie and prebende. Although expresse mention, &c.   In witnes wherof, &c.   Teste Rege apud Westmonasterium secundo die Junii.

PER BREVE DE PRIVATO SIGILLO.

NUM. VI.

Polydore Vergil's Letter to Queen Mary I. upon her Accession to the English Throne.

[Harl. MS. 6989, fol. 149. *Orig.*]

Salve Regina, Virgo, Maria brevi futura renascentis Regni genetrix. Namque scire licet Angliæ regnum ab initio septem habuisse reges, et eos tam diu inter se conflixisse, donec ad extremum potestas ad unum pervenerit. Postea secuti sunt reges, qui illud ipsum potentia, autoritate, nomine, opibus, legibus auxerunt, item religione, literis nobilitarunt, templisque passim atque alijs ædificijs ornarunt, sic ut ei non alterum ferme par foret, cum vicissitudo rerum cum mutatione temporum, pervaserit in animos quorundam multo infirmiores, qui a religione in primis aberrantes, remoto Dei metu, non dubitaverint facere contra rempublicam conjurationem post homines natos longe exitiosissimam. Sed ecce Deus Optimus Maximus vocavit te ad imperium, salutemque populi in tua tutela ac præsidio esse voluit. Quare, electissima prudentissimaque Regina, tibi persuadere debes, hanc esse divinam dexteræ excelsi mutationem, et tibi occasionem datam, quomodo posses regnum tuum undique quassatum, bonis vel moribus ac institutis spoliatum in pristinum reducere statum, quamprimum errata, delicta, peccata hactenus per licentiam commissa pie, modice, severeque emendando, corrigendo. Ex quo profecto deinde in omni memoria seculorum, merito diceris tanti Regni nova et sola genitrix fuisse. Quippe illud ipsum parvo sane negotio efficies, si a principio delegeris consiliarios, viros graves, modestos, prudentes, qui studio reipublicæ commoda quærant. Porro si princeps optimus sit, et malos habeat consiliarios, nihil omnino, uti divinus Plato ait, bene sperandum est de republica, quia unus bonus facile a multis potest depravari. Contra si malus sit qui regnat, et probos habeat circa se principes viros, nihil procul dubio est desperandum, quoniam unus itidem ad bonitatem et virtutem deduci potest a plurimis. Hinc igitur, Regina sanctissima, satis constat oportere regem habere domi suæ senatum et consilium ex optimis quibusque viris constitutum : id quod si Majestati tuæ similiter facere libuerit, certe quidem tu ut justitiæ cultrix et in summa atque sempiterna gratia apud Deum temet, et in magna gloria apud cunctos mortales laudabiliter pones. Vale. Ego vero homo senecta jam ætate volui te Dominam sicut servus literis salutare, officij causa, quod deinceps coram sæpius præstabo. Die 5 Augusti 1553.

Ejusdem M^{tis} T.

Servulus POLY. VERGILIUS.

THREE BOOKS

OF

POLYDORE VERGIL'S HISTORY.

HENRY THE SIXTH.

THE XXIIJ^{TIE} BOOKE OF POLIDORE VIRGILL OF THE HISTORIE
OF ENGLANDE.

ALTHOUGH the Englishe affaires did seeme somewhat weakned
by the death of king Henrye, the noblemen neverthelesse determined to renew the warres with valiaunt courage, and to make
preparation, as well at home as abroade, of all thinges that might
be necessary for forthwith as oportunitie did serve. Humfrey duke
of Glocester returned againe into England, and, assembling the
nobilitie, made relation what his brother king Henry had geven in
charge upon his death-bed, and in what estate the Frenche affaires
did stande. After that the nobles had conceaved all thinges, it The duke
was agreed, that the government of the realme should be com- made Pro-
mitted to the duke of Glocester hymself, according to the kinges tector.
commaundement, who tooke upon him that charge; and to
thintent he should not at any time afterward repent eyther of
deede or direction, as a man mindfull of others and forgetfull of
himselfe, he beganne to governe with high commendation, and to
provide for, place, and prepare all thinges apperteyning to the
honor of the realme, and profite of the common wealth. At the
very first he had speciall care to this, that Henry his nephewe

CAMD. SOC. B

might be trayned up vertuously, and did procure him to be committed unto Katherine his mother, whom he had brought into England with him a litle before, and did use reverently with all frendshipp and curtesie. And so having established civill and private causes, he beganne afterward to prepare with like diligence whatsoever was needefull for the use of warres. And making forthwith a levie of souldiers, whomsoever he thought meete for the warres eyther in Englande or in Fraunce. Then he commanded to be in readynes with all furniture, and appoynted over them centurions, and other captaines, skilfull of martiall discipline, that, when occasion should require, they might be readie. After

A parlia- these thinges, he levied, by authoritie of parliament, a great masse
somoned of money to support the necessary charges of the warres, so that there should not be want of any thing to the hinderaunce thereof.

The duke While that the duke of Glocester disposed matters thus in
regent of Englande, on thother side of the sea John duke of Bedford, whom
Fraunce. as chiefe directour of all actions they called Regent of Fraunce, with Phillipp duke of Burgoigne, provided with like care for all thinges that were necessary, but principally he labored to bring under subjection Charles the Dolphin, even as king Henry had

Charles the purposed in minde. When as loe, Charles the king departed
rrencne
king diethe. this life, by reason of whose death there chaunced great chaunge of thinges in Fraunce, which was so commodious for the Dolphin's affaires, as that it seemed God himselfe had speciall care for the conservation thereof; for right manye of the nobles of Fraunce, who before that time, partly fearing the English puyssance, and partly afrayde least the breache of their allegeaunce might turne to their owne displeasure, had holden with king Charles, after that they knewe the king was deade, did no more regard at all by what maner or meane (so that by one or other) they might expell the Englishe nation, recover ther countrey, and unite themselves againe to their owne people. And so at one instant they went to

the Dolphin, submitting themselves and all that they had to his
protection, which when the duke of Bedford, being regent, and
the duke of Burgoigne did perceave, they both disposed garrisons
to fitt and covenable places, and gathered their armie togethers
all at once; and calling their noblemen unto them, the regent The re-
—made an oration, admonishing them not to falsifie their fayth, and gentes ora
that they should neyther be authours, ne yet suffer young king nobilitye of
Henry to be defrauded of his graundfathers kingdome, by enuye Fraunce.
of moste false and forsworne men; nor the enemitie betwixt
England and Fraunce, nowe for a good while since extinguished,
to be againe renewed; and howe that they should call to remem-
braunce that the kingdome of Englande and Fraunce was by eter-
nall league and consent of minde become, of twoo, one of the
goodlyest kingdomes that ever was, and of late so established as
that no humane force was able to withstande it. And though they
had receaved some detriment by warres, yet they might within
short time turne the same to their benefite, if they wold honor,
obey, and love Henry their king, and determine resolutely to persecute his enemies, and so should be the best to serve their liege
lorde valiauntly and faythfully with all diligence. After this H.6 crown-
oration ended, Henry was proclaymed King of Englande and ed Kinge of
Fraunce by common consent of them all, and the lordes there France, and
present were commaunded to sweare homage unto him, and the homage
residue throughout the whole realme were bounde to take the same him.
othe. When these thinges were thus done, they sent for their
forces from all partes, and furnished themselves with all thinges
to the renewing of warre. Likewise in Englande he was proclaymed king by the name of Henry the Sixt, and all thinges were
done in his name, that so the honorable stile of a kingly maiestie
might be bruted amongst the people. As for the Dolphin, he
was at that time in Poyctiers, who upon intelligence of his father's
death was in minde partly sory and partly glad: sory for the

death of his father, but gladd that the government was so commed
unto him, whereby being advaunced to the title of a king he conceaved good hope of habilitie easily to defende the same: and
therfore calling togethers the noble men and chiefe of his faction,

he nameth himselfe king Charles the Seventh, and commaundeth
by edict that he should be generally so called; and so lifte up with
an assured confidence, once at the last to expell his enemies out
of the countrey, he maketh preparation for warre with greater
courage than before. There was forthwith even at the beginning
litle skirmishes made upon both parties, as occasion did serve,
thone to invade the other upon the sodaine. But within a while
after, when their armies were on eyther syde assembled, their
dealinges was as in puissaunt warres moste hott and perillous; for
Charles saylyng (as the common saying is) with a prosperous
winde, intermitting no delaye, wherby himself might casually be
weakened and his enemie made stronger, gathered a great armie

within fewe dayes, taking on hande sodainly to beseige Meulane, a
towne in Normandie, situate upon Seyne, and wanne it forthwith,
killing all the Englishemen that were in garrison there, not one
lefte alive; which when the duke of Bedforde understoode, he sent
to recover the towne Thomas Montacute earle of Salisbury, a man
for hawtines of courage and valiancie rather to be compared with
the auncient Romanes then with men of that age, and John
Lucenberg, who was generall of the horsemen to the duke of

Burgoigne, with a choice company of souldiers. They besieged
the towne, and, because Charles had lefte slender supply there,
they wonne it by assault quickly, and upon the Frenche garrison
used suche severitie, as that not one of all escaped. After which
happie exployte, the earle of Salesbury departed with part of his
armie into Champaigne, whereof he was lieftenant, and within a

fewe dayes after besieged Sens, a towne of Brye (which is all that
part lying betweene the rivers of Seyne and Marne), and winneth

it by assault, killing all that were lefte for the tuition therof, and _{Sens wone}
amonges them Gwilliam Marine, their chiefe captaine. The _{y th of Salesbur}
Parisians in the meane time perceaving king Charles to increase
in forces dayly, and conceaving hope thereupon that they should
returne within a while under his dominion, which was their
greatest desire, to thintent that they should not be suspected unto
thinglishe partie of treason the meane while, untill that the matter
should fall out according to their heartes desire, sent therfore
ambassadours into England unto king Henry to require ayde; unto _{The Pa-risians}
wnom, after great thankes geven for their dutifulnes, aunswer was _{sent am-}
made that they should continue their obedience and loyaltie to the _{bassadors}
king; for there should neyther ayde nor succour want unto their _{succore.}
citie, so that they would not be negligent in their owne behalfe,
nor yeelde unto the enemy.

Also in the very selfe same yere, which was the yere of our salvation 1423, and the first of king Henries reigne, Humfrey duke of _{Humfrey}
Glocester maryed Jacobine princesse of Bavaire, who had been _{Glocester}
maried to John duke of Brabant as yet living; which matter _{maryed th}
made men greatly to mervaile, that the duke of Glocester would _{the duke of}
needes, contrary to all law and right, mary another mans wife; _{Burgoyne.}
but the duke of Glocester more esteemed the contract and mariage
of so riche a ladie then any admiration or rumour of people. But _{The regent}
John duke of Bedford, Phillip duke of Burgoigne, and John duke _{princes}
of Britane mett togethers at Amiens, and renewed the league _{confirmed a firme}
amongst them, with these further conditions: That every one _{league.}
should mutually ayde another, altogethers, defende king Henry
by force of armes, and deliver him from all injurie. That league
was confirmed with a new affinitie, for Joane sister to the Duke of _{The duke}
Burgoigne was placed in mariage to the duke of Bedforde, who at _{married to}
that time was unmaried, whom he upon dissolution of that treatie _{the duke of}
tooke with him to Troys, and there did celebrate an honorable _{sister.}
mariage, from whence he returned to Paris.

In the meane time certaine citizens there, who obeyed the

A plot layd Englishe government against their willes, seeing the duke of Bed-
ha
traved Paris ford so farre absent, determined to receave king Charles into the
to the towne, and, thinking that so profitable occasion was not to be
slipped, they gave him intelligence of their practise, and appoynted
a day when he should repaire to the gates; but their perillous
pollicie prevayled not, but was to the destruction of the devisers
thereof; for the duke of Bedforde came the while, sooner then the
conspiratours weened; and being informed of the conspiracie, did
punishe them that were giltie of that offence. After that, conceaving thereby howe the citizens were affected, the duke tooke order
with all diligence and carefulnes, for fortifying of the towne, disposing of watche and warde every where, preventing the subtilties
of the Frenche, leaving nothing unprovided for on his owne behalfe, reposing on their behalfe no confidence at all.   While this

Crauantum. was a doing king Charles besieged Cravaunt, whither came forth-
The with the earle of Salesburye, and William Pole earle of Suffolke,
men dis- with four thousand souldiers, and joyning battaile, did kill, discom-
comfited at
Cravante. fite and chase the Frenchemen, whereof two thousand were slayne,
Bucanus. and four hundred taken, amongst whom was the erle of Bowhan,
Constable of Fraunce, who was soone raunsomed, and returned
againe to the warres. After this fortunate successe, the earle of
Salsbury understanding that the Frenche men had in the meane
Laudunensi time certaine pyles in the territory of Laonnoys, did hasten thither,
and with like good fortune recovereth all the sayde holdes. On
Compendio. thother side, at the very same time, the townes of Compeigne and
Croteio. Crotoy, which is in the countrey about Turwan, did yielde unto
the Frenche men; but the comming thither of the Englishe was
suche terror unto the garrisons there lefte, as they were quickly
recovered also. While this stirre was in Fraunce, the duke of
Glocester having mustered for the making out of souldiers in
Englande, sent ten thousand well furnished with armour and

weapon to the duke of Bedford unto Paris, who were committed
to the government of the earle of Salisbury, and of Robert Willoughbie, a man of noble birth and great forecast, and of William
Pole. Himselfe had in his retinewe a thousand eight hundred 10,000 sol-
horsemen and eyght thousand footemen. With these forces the diers sent
duke of Bedford, removing from Paris, marched into Normandie, England.
to se if he could any where provoke Charles to any indifferent
conflict; for, so longe as he was unvanquished, himselfe thought his
owne affaires woulde never be in very good case. But when his
enemy would no where discover himselfe, the duke besieged the
most strong castle of Yvers, being upon the frontiers of Normandie. Yveres be-
There was within the same a great bande of choyse souldiers, who wone.
defended themselves valiantly; but the duke casting a great
trenche and rampire about the same, and assaulting it with mynes
and engines, forced them to yeeld within fewe days after that it
was first begoonn to be besieged. Charles at that time laye at
Towres, who, being certified that Yvery was besieged, seemed not *Turomilus.*
to make great accompt of the matter; but partly trusting to the
naturall strength of the place, and partly to the force of the garrison within the same, was busied onely about the levying of an
armie, whereby he might be able with equall force to encounter
his enemie in open fielde. And therfore, when he had gathered a
more large number, he sent the duke of Alanson to relieve the
towne, commanding him that, if occasion did serve, he should not
refuse the fight. The duke marched forward with all speede, and,
perceaving before he did approche the place that the castle was
yeelded, therfore chaunging his purpose, he diverted to Vernoill, Vernoylle
wanne it by assault, and killed the most part of the Englishe garri- recovered
son; the which towne, being well fortified, was geven unto him by Frenche.
Charles, for that he had a good while before claymed the same to
be parcell of his inheritance. After that the duke of Bedford had
intelligence hereof, he marched to Vernoill without delay, in good

arraye of battaile, and in the same order came even to the very
tentes of his enemies. The Frenche, somewhat appalled by reason
of the sodaine arrivall, tossed the matter amongst themselves what
best were to doo. The most part were of minde to tarrye in their
tentes till they might see what their enemies would take on hand;
for being well experienced that often-times before they had been
vanquished, when as they joyned battaile with the Englishe men,
they were loth to fight hand to hand ; but when they sawe their
enemies armie approche nigher and nigher, taking to them hart of
grace, with howling and rejoycing, as their maner is, they take
wepon in hand, and set themselves in array before their tents.
The battaile was begonn with shott, but, when the shott ceased,
they marched forward, and drawing their blades mutually, ranne
together with great cryes. The fight was forcible and continuall,
and so throughly maintained of both parties that harde was it to
judge whither the victorie would incline. The slaughter was great
on eyther partie, the stirre was equall, and the maner of fight likewise. Where moste daunger was, there was every man with lively
courage most readie to resist and repulse; so the battaile continued more then foure howres in equall balance. All this while
the duke of Alanson rested not to pray and exhort his soldiers not
to quaile, nor to suffer their enemies, even now at the poynt of
flight, to be conquerours. But the duke of Bedford was no lesse
provident and painefull to go from place to place, to encourage his
souldiers to enforce the fight everye where; who at the last perceaving the Frenchemen, being faint with labor and travaile, to be
more feeble in fight then before (for such is the nature of the
Frenche, that they are not able to abide a long battaile, that to
make their enemies afraide, they will geve a prowde bragge readily,
but not accustomed to mainteyne the same out afterward), then,
therefore, with might and main he assailed them, and all his whole
armie folowing him, did with such force invade thenemie, as that

A greate
Katle wone
by the duke
at Vernavll
rd

first he caused them geave grounde, and immediatly drove them
headlong to the flight.   There was killed in that battaile five
thousand French men, whereof the chiefe were therle of Boughan,
admirall of Fraunce, and John Steward, a noble man of Scotland, Many no.
who, as we have before mentioned, came to the ayde of Charles, Scotlande
and tenn Frenche noblemen more that were of government, and slain in
had charge.   There were taken about two hundred, and amongst batle.
them John duke of Alanson; but the report is, that there were
killed and taken fifteen thousand.   Of thenglish partie there were
wanting two thousand, partly horsmen, partly footmen.   The
Frenche men receaved this discomfiture in the yere of our salvation 1425, and the thirde of king Henries reigne.   1425.

The duke of Bedford, after thobtayning of so honorable and
great victorie, incontinent kneeled downe upon his knees, holding up his handes, and yeelded unto God immortall thankes for so
great a benefite, and for a certaine space weeping for joy, he
prayed devoutly, afterward givinge the Frenche men leave to
depart he received againe Vernoill, and, placing therein a garrison, Vernoille
returned unto Paris.   But the earle of Salisbury went to besiege by the
Mountes, a most rich and stronge towne; the citizens whereof, English.
although they were in great terror, both by reason of the sodeine Mounts be
approche of thenemie, and also of the name of Salisbury, which wonne.
was very famous, as well amongst his enemies as his owne people
and countrimen, yet their care and preparation was great to defende themselves, insomuch that the towne was furnished within
throughly with a multitude of most valiant souldiers.   Thenglish
earle placed his tentes as nere the towne as he possiblye might
without annoyance of his people, and did so shake and batter the
walles with brazen peeces, which the Italians call bombardes, the First
use whereof (being begonn but in the yere of our Lorde God 1370,* begin ing
                                                                    of gones,
* All the Latin Editions of " Polydore Vergils History," and his book " de Inven-   1370.
toribus Rerum," say, M.CCC.LXXX.—ED.

as in the IIth booke of the Inventours of thinges, the 11th chapter, is declared) was not so well knowen before that time to the Frenche men, that within fewe dayes a great part of the walles about the towne was beatt downe to the grounde. Upon the sight whereof thinhabitaunts of Mountes, wythout hope of reliefe which unto that day they had expected, having obtained leave for the garrison of souldiers there safely to depart, yeelded the Towne.

St. Susanes And the same being strongly fortified and furnished with souldiers, William earle of Suffolke was made captaine thereof, and the armie was conveyed to St. Susannes, a towne within the same region, of great renowme. One Ambrose Delore was captaine thereof, a notable and famous man of warre, and had there with him a great crewe of souldiers. After that the earle of Salesbury had well viewed the situation and nature of the place, he made all thinges ready to geve thassault at that part where the towne seemed to be least fortified ; ladders were laide too, and at the first showt and assault they attained almost to the topp of the walles, but the townesmen with the Frenche garrison, who durst not issue out of the towne to skirmish with the enemy, begann then to make resistance, and repulsed the force in all that they might. The assault was continued that day and often afterward, with great bloudshed and slaughter on both sides ; but thinhabitantes were neverthelesse earnest in fight. As soone as the earle of Salesbury sawe and understoode howe that in such maner of bickering he could nothing prevaile, he withdrewe his souldiers into their tentes : and first environing the wall with trenche and diche, afterwarde gave commandement that such as had charge of the great shott shoulde laye their ordinance to the weakest places, and so day and night batter the wall ; which was done without delay, so that within fewe dayes there were made large breaches therein ; wherwithall

The castle of Mayone takene. Delore was put in terror, so that he yeelded the towne, paying for the safe passage away of him and his, two thousand crownes, which was to depart without armor, every man with one onely garment.

After that, the earle of Salesbury tooke the castle of Maion, and
divers other townes, partly by force, partly by composition. In
the meane time the fame of this geere was spread over all Fraunce,
by reason whereof some were stricken in feare, some in heavines;
but in England, upon the receit of letters of victory, which the
duke of Bedford sent very often, all men did leape for joye, that
their governors in warre and captaines had vanquished in plaine
field, and had gotten so many townes at once; wherefore the lordes
of the counsaile tooke order with Henry Chicheley, archbishop of
Canterbury, that he should appoint publike prayers to be made
forthwith, whereby it might appere that they did rather ascribe
those victories to God then to their owne forces. During that
time also, king Charles, having received so many discommodities
altogethers, thought not to omitt any care necessary as towching
his owne affaires, but gathered newe supplye of soldiers on every
side, and principally demaunded ayde of James king of Scottes,
which he did not only not denye, but immediately sent Robert
Patillok, a bolde and hardie gentleman, with a company of valiant
souldiers, to joyne with Archebold, although that the duke of
Glocester, governor of England, did repine much therat, and
dealt with king James by ambassadours, that he would not take
on hande to doo contrary to the league which he had made a little
before with king Henry: but frendshipp prevailed more then
justice with the Scottish king.

Whilest that the English affaires had prosperous successe in
Fraunce, the duke of Glocester and Jacobine his wife passed the
seas, and tooke from John duke of Brabant Mounts, the most
famous citie in all Henault, and all other possessions whatsoever
the said John helde, as in the right of his wife Jacobine, which
dealing the duke of Burgoigne Phillip, who was a patrone of the
duke of Brabantes cause, tooke in evill part: and not mistrusting
but that the duke of Glocester would, for the old good-will and
frendshipp betwixt them twoo, yeelde to that which was for his

Mena,
a e II
s me
Chron.
e
Juliez.

Publicke
pra res
made
throwe
g
for the
good suc-
altogethers.
France.

The Kinge
of Scotts
joynes
with the
Frenche.

The duke
of Gloster
tooke
Mounts in
un
right of his
wiffe.

honor.   He therefore dealt with the duke by letters, admonishing
him to leave off that wicked enterprise, affirming openly, that it
was as dishonorable an offence to enter upon and holde another
mans possessions, as to pollute another mans bedd.   But the duke
of Glocester was so farre from giving eare to the wholsome
councell of his frende, as, whether it were that he were blinded
with love or with covetousness, he boasted that he would defend
with armes the possession of those places which he had taken from
the duke of Brabant.   Who when as he was within short time after
called againe into England of necessitie, about divers weightie
affaires, left the said Jacobine in Henault with a great number of
souldiers, to defend her owne possessions against the duke of Brabant.   But after the duke of Glocester was departed, then loe, the
duke of Brabant made warre against the woman, wherewithall,
when they were both well wearied, the matter was at the last deferred to Martin the Vth, bisshop of Rome.   As soone as he had
examined the cause, he gave sentence, as concerning the mariage
with the duke of Brabant, and by his authoritie denounced the
contract betwixt Jacobine and the duke of Glocester utterly voyde.
And the matter so ended, Jacobine did sticke unto her former
husband, and that not altogethers against the will of the duke of
Glocester, as whom right and reason had ruled, and the impor-
tunacie of the woman had begoon alreadie above measure to make
wearie.

The bishop
of Rome
gave sen-
tence
against the
maryage ot
the duke of
Glocester
and his
wyffe.

During this time, Edmond duke of Somerset, who was liefte-
naunt of Normandie, repaired St. James Towne, which had been
rased long time before, adjoyning upon the Britans, and fortified
it with a strong garrison.   This Edmund succeeded in that earldome
unto his brother John the first duke of Somerset, who dying lefte
behinde him one onely daughter called Margaret, who (as shalbe
spoken of otherwhere) brought forth unto Edmund, erle of Richmonde, king Henry the Seventh, and John the first earle begott
the saide second John and Edmond his brother, which first earle

(as we have before declared), Richard the Second made marquise Dorsett, because he issued from John duke of Lancaster, his uncle, begotten of Catherine his third wife. Hereof I thought good to geve warning, that the saide Margarete had no wronge, though she succeeded not John her father in the earldome of Somersett; for, by reason of an auncient custome in England, dukes and earles have their titles of dignitie of the counties, within the which oftentimes they have no possessions nor patrimonie; but their revenue consisteth of lands and possessions which they have other-where; wherefore, it maketh litle matter who succeede in those titles, which the Kinges maiestie at his pleasure bestoweth as he list upon them whom he maketh dukes or earles, as before in the 19th booke I have explaned. But we have digressed sufficiently.— *foot*

While that the fortune of warre was in this sort variable, the duke of Britaine, remembring howe that in times past the Englishmen had geven attempt to gaine soveraigntie in the earldome of Britany, and fearing presently that when the Frenche should be conquered they would cast an eye to his earldome, determining with himselfe to drive away and remove the contagion of such disease imminent, as he untruly suspected, revolted unto king Charles, whom that matter much encouraged, being for the evill successe of late attemptes in some terror. Wherefore, for the duke's cause, he made his brother Arthure, whom the state of England had created earle Arthure, of Richmonde, who also presentlye with his brother had revolted, brother to the E of admirall of Fraunce: which charge the earle of Boughan of late Britany had, who was killed at the battaile of Vernoile. The duke lived ma E. f Richmond. not longe after, and lefte behinde him three sonnes, Fraunces, Peter, and Gyles: Fraunces succeeded his father; but I will returne to Arthur. He by reason of his newe office, desirous of renowne, thought he should doo very acceptable service to the French King if he might winne the towne of St. James, and cast out the English St James garrison; wherefore, gathering togethers almoste twentie thousand de Beneon.

men, he besieged the towne, and began to assault it couragiously. The Englishmen suspecting no such matter, were troubled with this sodaine attempt, and did hardly defend the gates: but by litle and litle taking heart of grace, and consulting together, they begann to make resistance; and in the meane time, part issuing out at the castle gate, which is towarde the walles, and part sallying out of the towne otherwhere, made head, and gave charge upon thenemy before and behinde. Then the Frenchemen disordered with this sodaine alarme, being out of hope that it was preignable by assault, some ranne away, some were killed, and some drowned in a lake or diche nigh unto the town. And so Arthure, omitting the seige, returned to the campe which was harde by, whether also many of his company had before withdrawen themselves out of the chase. The night folowing the Frenchmen were in great chafe for evill handling of this matter, every one putting the blame thereof to other (for the state of warres is such, that in victorie cowardes will boast and bragg, but upon a discomfiture the very best souldiers shalbe burdened with dishonor), so that a mutinewe rose sodainly thereof, and every man forsooke the campe and departed, though that Arthure did earnestly require the contrary, especially because they should leave their ordinaunce unto thenemy. But Arthure, very sorowfull that so great an attempt should fall out so evill, thinking by some valiant exploit to put away the dishonor of that shamefull flight, marched from thence with all speede into Angeow, and every where as he went wasted, destroyed, spoyled, and tooke one or two townes, with which furious fact all the rage was sodainly appeased. About the same time the duke of Bedford departed into England, partly to remove certaine privie grudges from amongst the noble men proceeding upon envy, which were fitt to be speedily layde apart, partly to levie a newe supplye of souldiers. Soone after his arrivall he called the Councell togethers, and, when the differences amongst the nobilitie was throughly examined,

The duke of Bedford ur into Eng- land.

those who were found to be in fault, were by just desert, and by
most honorable assent of the whole borde, rebuked that they should
in the time of forreyne warres, for revenge of private injuries,
stirre the people at home to sedition and uprores; at which time,
most principally of all other, it was every mans part to upholde
unitie of minde and concorde. He after exhorted them to defend
with all their devoire the dignitie and high reputation of king
Henry, under whose fortunate government at that time all Fraunce
was in a maner subdued to the English empire; whose wordes so
moved the noble men which mutually hated one another, that by
and by they agreed, and by authoritie of parliament a great levie
of men was appoynted to be made; which matters brought to pass
according to his desire, and the state of the common wealth re-
formed, as the matter and time required, the duke returned into
Fraunce with as much celeritie almoste as he came from thence,
accompanied with a multitude of choyse souldiers, whereof he
made chiefe captaine John lord Talbot, a man amongst men of John Lo.
reputation in deede esteemed both for nobilitie of birth and Talbott
haultines of courage, of most honorable and high renowne, who Fraunce.
was afterward conqueror in so many sundry conflictes, that both
his name was redowted above all others through Fraunce, and yet
—contineweth of famous memory universally at this day. There
folowed the duke, Henry, both bisshopp of Winchester and cardinall of St. Eusebius, sonne to John duke of Lancaster by his
thirde wife, called, by reason of the place where he was born,
Beauforde, a man of great providence and sufficiencie, who most of
all other supported the English affaires, being often in distresse,
with councell and treasure. The duke of Bedford, a little after his
return into Fraunce, had intelligence by espials, that Montarge,
which is a towne within the territory of Orliance, was without garrison, insomuch that it might easily be surprised: whereupon he
sent thither part of the retinew which was at Paris, and the whole

supply which he had brought out of England under the government of Richarde earle of Warwicke, who tooke as great journeys as he possibly might untill he came to the towne: but, understanding that the same was furnished with men more strongly than the report had been, would not assault it, but, encamping himselfe nigh thereto, besieged it rounde about. These doeings came quickly, what by common report, what by messages, unto the eare of Arthure, admirall of Fraunce, who perceaving the matter to require diligence, and that himself could not at that time relieve the towne, sent forthwith Stephen Hyre, a Frenche knight, with most part of his armie, to raise the siege. After that the saide Frenche men were come thither, they, trusting to their multitude, wherein they did muche exceede, set upon their enemies campe, and breaking the trenches thereof after great slaughter, put the English men to flight. I finde written of some authours that there was 1500 English men either killed with the sword, or drowned in the next river that runneth into Yon, the bridge which was over the same being broken with the swey of people that thronged over the same. But at that time it seemed there could not happen to the Frenche partie anye thing so joyfull, which was not intermingled some other way with heavines: for at the very selfsame season Nicholas Browgh, sent by the duke of Somersett to annoy thenemy within the boundes of Britaine, (who, as we have a litle before shewed, had yeelded themselves to the amitie of the Frenche,) departed, sending out his horsmen all abroade, by whom the forrow was so mainteyned every waye, without resistance, as that all villages and buildinges every where were burned, great bootie was driven from all places, townes of small strength were taken, and the inhabitantes of the same eyther killed or ledd away captive to be raunsomed. The saide boundes being in this sort wasted and destroyed, Nicholas retyred unto the armie in Normandie with huge bootie, and without any wounde receaved by himselfe, or any of his retinewe.

Borthus.
Nicholas
Browghe
revolts
to the
Frenche.*

* Such is the side note.—ED.

This discomfiture of their confederates did somewhat appall and diminish the loftines of the Frenche, not without cause, being otherwise verye haultie for the late victorie, whom on thother side, againe, the returne of John duke of Alanson did greatly encourage : for he, being taken the yere before at the battaile of Vernoille, was let home out of England about the same time, paying for his raunsome a hundred thousand crownes.

While that these thinges were done otherwhere, thinhabitantes of Mayne were solicited to revolt, for the chiefe men in the citie, who long before grudged at the government of thenglish nation, when they understoode that the Britains refusing the amitie of England had submitted themselves to the protection of king Charles, supposing that his side would shortly prevaile, resolved to receave the Frenche men into the towne. And having devised the mean and time, howe and when to execute their intent, they discovered by moste secret messengers their privie conspiracie unto the chiefe captaines of the Frenche armie, lying in campe not farre off, who, upon so good oportunitie gotten, commended greatly the citizens, and promised to be readie in time, laboring them, neverthelesse, with all faire speeche and promise of rewarde to hasten diligently the performance of that which they had determined. When the day came, the Frenche captaines drew nigh secretly in the night, and, geving signe of their arrivall by a blase of fire, approached the towne. The watch of the citie which was upon the walles, awaiting their comming, espied the fire afarre off, and gave the same signe againe : then was the fire put out on both parties, and the Frenche men presently proceeded to the gate. The conspiratours within came also sodenly unto the gates ; they killed the watch sleeping in their beddes, and opened the gate. The Frenche men entered with their footmen, commanding their horsemen to stay, that, as occasion should require, they might have the field open freely to ride at their pleasure : then they let goe their souldiers every where

Mayne was revolted and by treason gotten.

to kill thenglish men. The stirre and noyse was such, as in a towne sacked is accustomed; but what the matter meant, not one man did certainly conceave, except only a fewe that were of the conspiracie; the rest of the citizens beleeved that the English men were risen up to sacke and spoyle the towne : the English, againe, thought that the sedition was by meane of some treason wrought by the townsmen. William earle of Suffolke, lieutenant of the place, awaked with the first tumult, after that he understoode by the crye of his people, who being absent that night by chaunce from their warde, were killed every where through the towne, that the Frenche men were lett in, fled quickly, with the garrison which he had, into the castle, which is situate at the gate called commonly the gate of St. Vincent, and from thence sent speedie messengers unto John lord Talbot, who lay at Alanson, with letters, to demaund and earnestly praye him of reliefe. The lord Talbot, after he had read the letters, repaired thither with an armie of light harnessed men well appoynted, sendinge worde before to the lieftenant that he would come to relieve him by and by, and praying them all not to be dismayed. In the meane time the Frenche men rove like rulers in the towne thus taken, and fearing nothing, became so ydle and carelesse, as though there were no daunger imminent from thenemy : for they fell to refresshing of themselves after their great travaile susteyned, and thought they had the Englishmen so shutt up in that turret whereinto they were fledd, that they would not possibly attempt any warlike practise, but would incontinent treate for the safetie of their lives. Howbeit, the lord Talbot tooke great journeys, and was forthwith at hande, who being receaved of his countrymen in at the gate which they did enjoy, entred the towne, and even as they looked for, so they founde all thinges without order or care, as in prosperitie is accustomed; no warders before the gates, and the same wide open; the vanquisher roving, and onely rejoycing for the

The earle sente to the Lo. Talbot

Mayne is re red ag aine by the Lo.Tal-bot.

libertie of the citie, and slaughter of the enemy. By that occasion was the town taken againe of the Englishmen. Thus were
the French conquerours killed every where, and had not so
much leysure, as eyther to assemble togethers, or yet to arme
themselves; wherefore every man, for safetie, fledd to the gates, but
finding them kept by thenemy, they were sodenly in despaire to be
saved by flight, and therefore begann then to crye for mercie;
whereupon the lord Talbot proclaymed, that every man should
disarme himselfe, and that the unarmed should be forborne, and
the armed onely killed. So the Frenchmen conceaving hope of
life, cast away their weapons, and yeelded to their enemy : part of
them were killed, and part committed; which exploit having taken
fortunate effect, the lorde Talbot departed to Ponthoyse, and took Ponthoyse
it. But earle William, the lieftenant, made inquirie upon the con- take y
spiracie of thinhabitantes of Mayne, and punished such as were Talbot.
founde to be principalls therein.

Seing that the English affaires had at that time such prosperous
successe, Thomas Montacute conceaved advisedly good hope to
winne Orleaunce. That is a most mightie citie, which of olde
time was called *Geneve,* scituate upon the river of Seyne, in that *Genebum*
part of the countrie which sometime was termed the Gawle Celtyk. beseegede
But because the scituation of the place was naturally of passing by he E.
strength, he thought good to conferre thereupon with others, burye.
though himselfe were thonely man by whose prowesse thenglish
nation was universally much more terrible to the French men,
uppon whom the whole state of the common wealth of England
did depende, as appered plainly afterward when he was dead:
and therefore might have ordeyned and done many thinges after
his owne fantasie, for he was a man alwaye of most ready witt
and mature judgement, valiant to enterprise great matters, and in
greatest daunger pollitike; neyther body nor minde would ever
yeeld to painfulnes nor travaile; by reason whereof there was none

in whom the men of warre had more confidence, nor under whom
they durst so well attempt any daungerous exployte. Wherefore,
after that deliberation had bene a pretie space of so weightie a
cause, though the matter was thought hard, and of most great
difficultie, yet for because he, measuring the same according to the
hawtines and forces of his minde and body, thought it but easie to
be atchieved ; all men, therefore, did alowe his opinion ; wherefore
thearle, full of good hope and courage, having provided all thinges
needfull for the besieging of the towne, accompanied with William
earl of Suffolke and the lord Talbot, conducted his armie towardes
Orleance, and encamped himselfe not past a mile from the same :
then he drewe neere and viewed the site therof, the walles, and
what part seemed strongest with wall, water, or warrier, which
when he had perfectly viewed, seing no souldiers abrode without
the gates, he approched even to the walles.   Here he tooke counsell upon the naturall situation of the place ; for there was a bridge
upon the citie of Leyre, whereby victuals were continually brought
out of the countrie into the towne : there were also certaine other
lesser townes not farre off, standing upon the water side, which
also relieved the towne with necessaries.   These did he first bring
in subjection, and fortified with garrison.   In like maner also he
caused the bridge to be kept with watch and warde : moreover, he
erected in longe circuit about, certaine fortresses, furnishing them
with men and artillerie ; afterward, derivining a trenche from fort
to fort, he environed the towne, and planting his ordnance in convenient place, beganne to annoy the same.   On thother side, those
of Orleaunce, a litle before the comming of the enemy, prepared
all thinges necessary for their defence ; they burned the suburbes
of the towne, they spoyled the countrey rounde about of all kinde
of victuals and forrage, gathering the same into the towne.   And
when they saw their enemies to have compassed the towne, then
they planted ordinance against ordinance, they made rampires and

countermures all alongst within, least by reason of any breache
that might happen to be made in the walles, the Englishmen might
enter ; they also prepared number of men sufficient to defende the
walles, whereof they made captaine Stephan Hyre, and John the
bastard sonne of Charles their duke, taken a fewe yeres before at
the battaile of Agincourt, and as yet remayning prisoner in Eng-
lond. And so the English earle approched the walles, and begann
to geve thereunto very sharpe assault. There was dayly skirmishing by reason of the citizens sallying sometime out of the
towne, otherwhile fighting from their bulwarkes and towres of defence ; but the Englishmen so placed their archers, whereof the
number was great, that right many of the towne were wounded,
and the terror of that shott was great. While this adoe was of
eyther side, king Charles sent Lewes duke of Burbon to ayde
them of Orleaunce with an armie of men well appoynted ; he
hearing by the way, that certaine bondes of English souldiers
should bring from Paris into the campe great store of victualls, determined to set upon them unwares, and chaunging his purposed
journey, marched towardes them : John Fastolf, captaine of the
said companies, had intelligence of his comming, by meane of scurryers, and forthwith caused the cariage to stay, araying his men in
order rounde about the same. That done, he sent forth his horsemen, and receaved the charge of thenemy approaching with such
courage and withal made such slaughter, as that the Burbonian
retired of his owne accorde, with the losse of more than two hundred of his men; who proceeding to Orleaunce, got harde entrance _{The duke}
with a very fewe. But John Fastolfe, marching at ease, came unto _{of Burbon}
the campe with the said victuals, voyde of all hinderance or lett. _{Orleance.}
The newes thereof brought by messengers into England, made
there a double joye : for at the same time, which was about the
eyght ides of November, Henry being but a childe of eyght yeres

H. 6
crowned
King in
England,
1429.
age, was with great solemnitie after the auncient custome crowned, which was the yere of our salvation 1429.

Thus the siege of Orleance continued the more part of winter, with great perill, many woundes, and much slaughter : for the Englishmen, in cruell assaultes, did every where eyther kill or wounde many of their enemies. Againe, the towne valiantly de-fending, requited them the like ; when, as in the meane space, the chaunce was, that the earle of Salisbury, loth to tarry longer, and desirous to winne the towne, one day early before sonnrise, began to viewe the same againe more earnestly then he was wont, out at a certaine windowe of buildings which he had in an high place, to thintent he might espye where to geve commodiously a newe as-sault ; which he thought mightily to assay as one inflamed with desire eyther to winne the towne by force, or to cause it yeelde. While that he was busied in this order, and by the space of 60 days did vehemently annoy the citizens, behold even sodenly —eyther an yron or stone pellett, shott out of a brasen peece with great force right against the place where he stoode, did strike and breake thone side of the windowe, and drove certaine shilvers thereof into his face, wherewithall he was so wounded as that he dyed thereof two dayes after.   He lefte one Alis, his onely daugh-ter, very like him in conditions, vertue, and honor, whom, as we shall hereafter shewe, one Richard Nevill took to wife.   But howe great losse tne common wealth sustained through his untimely death appered evidently incontinent.   Truely from that day forth the English forrain affaires beganne to quaile ; which infirmitie though the English nation, as a most sounde and strong body, did not feele at the first, yct afterward they suffered it as a pestilence and sicknes inwardly, by litle and litle decaying the strength : for —immediatly after his death the fortune of warre altered, as here-after shalbe declared in place convenient ; wherefore the death of

The E. of
al   ye
slaine in
a windowe.

Alis, d. &
heire to the
ᴇᴀ ᴏᴊ ᴊᴀᴌᴏᴊ-
bury,
ᴀᴛᴠᴇᴅ to
Richard
Neville.

the earle was much lamented of all the captaines in generall, who, neverthelesse, after that they had performed all thinges for his buriall, mainteined the siege and sought to atchieve that which the earle of Salesbury had in mind determined, which was, by what meane they might eyther take the towne by force, or, at the least, compell the citizens to yeelde. William Nevill, a valiant and expert man of warre, was principally carefull and painfull in this matter: he did continually annoy the enemy, and caused his souldiers more diligently to keepe watch in the night, to mainteyne fight on the day, exhorting, fighting, and bearing out all disadvauntage with great magnanimitie. Neyther did the residue of captaines omitt any thing which they thought meete for subduing of the towne. By which meanes finally it came to passe, that those of Orleance, almost despairing of reliefe, began to consult amongst themselves concerning the geving up of the towne. After that severall opinions were uttered touching the avoiding of that daunger, many did accompt and esteem it as a most high dishonor, and as evill as the utter destruction of the towne, to submitt themselves to thenglish men, cool frendes to the French nation: on thother partie, they feared the victory of thenemy, for that thereupon are wont to proceede both many mischiefes, and some-time indeede very tyranny, wherefore they supposed, that it was as well the part of unwise men not to beware hereof, as the con-senting or yeelding to abide thother was to be attributed to a ser-vile inclination. But when they sawe the matter brought in great distresse, both to avoide slaunder and miserable fate, they ad-judged one thing most fitt for their purpose, and that was to sub-mitt themselves, and all that they had, under the protection of Philip duke of Burgoigne, because he was descended from the most auncient stocke of the kinges of Fraunce, and for that, as every man had conceaved opinion, the matter would so fall out in the ende, that he would once at the last forsake the English amitie.

This resolution being allowed, and the duke of Burgoignes minde herein by secret messengers knowen (which was that he would fafourably receave them, so that the duke of Bedford should like thereof) they sent ambassadours to the duke at Paris; who, after their ambassage heard, called the councell togethers, and declared what condicions of peace they of Orleance did offer. Some thought tne yeelding upon those condicions was to be admitted, to thende that so great and riche a citie might by this meane be withdrawen from the partie of king Charles. But the duke of Bedford, and the better part of councellours thought it would be a foule, perillous, and detestable example, if a towne so longe besieged, and nowe almost taken for and in the name of king Henry, should finally come under the subjection of any others than the king-himselfe: for truelye, others would readily folowe their example of Orleance, and therefore such conditions were not to be graunted unto. This sentence tooke place, and thambassadours were aun-swered, that the warres were kept for king Henry: and likewise tne victory ought to be his. With this aunswere the duke dis-missed thambassadors: but upon litle occasion commeth often great alteration, for two mischiefes fell out thereupon. First the duke of Burgoigne, angry in minde, supposed that the English men did envy his renowme, and therefore even then begonn to be evill affected towardes them. Secondly, the Englishmen were forced afterward to leave the siege.

While that those of Orleance treate by ambassadours with thenemye for peace, king Charles gathereth forces on every side, and with faire promises seeketh to alienate the nobilitie of Fraunce from the amitie of England. Also he carefully prepareth victuals which he might send to the besieged Orleances, at which time there was brought unto him a cetaine damosell of thage of twentie yeres, or thereaboutes, a damosell so called for that she had pre-servyd her virginitie, who was endowed both with singuler witt,—

Ambassa-dors sent r- leance to e o Bedford, with condi-submis-

Theambas sadores e refused.

Orleance with victu-ales by the l a woman.

could also foreshewe thinges to come; who, when she came before the king, being apparailed as then after the common sort of other men, because she would not be knowen, is reported to have saluted him as foloweth : "O King, be of good cheere, and feare not, for you shall overcome your enemies, and that by the conduct of me, and shall at the last restore your countrey to thaunceient libertie, if that you shall not thinke it unworthie for your kingly maiestie to use the helpe of a woman." King Charles, who greatly feared his afflicted state, gave credit readily unto her speeche, and conceaved very good hope, as one persuaded that the damosell had receaved some inwarde revelation from God, and the rather because she had saluted him by the name of King, when he was not apparailed as a king. But there was another matter also, which caused his hope : for the damosell demanded a sworde, which, as she saide, was revealed unto her to hange in the church of St. Catherine at Towres, amongst thauncient offeringes there; whereat king Charles mervailing, made searche for the sworde, and, finding it, caused the same to be brought to the damosell, and the rather to make proufe of hir vertue then that he had great confidence of any notable exploit to be atchieved by a woman, he committed to her in charge a bande of souldiers, and part of the victuals, wherewith she might go to relieve the towne. The damosell, so armed, led, as captaine, all that company to Orleance, and whether it were that she deceaved the watch, or that she went invisible by divine power, so it was, that in the dead of the night, she passed through the middest of her enemies into the towne, and brought in the victuals without hurt of her people. In the meane time, the Englishmen, assuring themselves that the citizens were not able long to abide the siege for want of corne, did not presse them so earnestly as before, and were more negli- - gent in their watch ; but when they knew that Joane, a damosell, had conveyed in victuall, though they had in contempt the

-woman who was become a souldier, yet in great rage, for the
reliefe which was sent, they determined much more sharply to
assault thenemy; and therfore the captaines exhorting their
souldiers, once at the last, after so great toyle, to receave the fruit
of victory, promised great rewarde to them that first should scale
the walles. After proclamation wherof, sodenlye they flye from
all partes unto the wall, they fill it full, contending both with shott
of all sortes, and also with weapons, to expell thenemy from defence thereof, continuing thassault in that order without intermission. Although thenemies were throughly affearde of this newe
affray, yet they were not slacke in their owne cause, nor utterly
discouraged, for John the bastard signified to king Charles by
poste, howe the citie was in great distresse for lacke of corne, and
that thenemy was so earnest upon them, as no man's force was
able to withstande; wherefore the matter was in such extreme
daunger as ear longe it would hardly fall well out; howbeit, to prevent the chaunce thereof, rested in his diligence and ayde. These
thinges knowen, king Charles sent with all haste possible both
supplye of men and plentie of victuall, which French force was
conducted to Orleance, and incamped welnigh two miles from the
towne. From thence they gave intelligence to the damosell at
Orleance of their comming; they admonished and required her to
choose out a company of trayned souldiers, to meete them the
next day, and to procure their safe entrance into the towne, which
after the Englishmen had permitted them to doo, who supposed it
should be for their owne availe to suffer many enter into the
towne, wherein famine did reigne alreadie, the Frenchemen all at
once issued the day folowing out of the citie thicke and threefolde,
and so set upon the next fortresse with might and maine continually, that, after great slaughter on both parties, they tooke and
burned the same. Then with greater courage they assault another
much bigger. Here, because the force of the defendantes was

well great, the fight was more vehement. The Frenche, who did
exceed in number, environing it round about, gave eger assault on
every side. The English for defect of fortification, which beganne
nowe to be broken, were in distresse every way, and hardly able
to holde out, neyther yet the very lorde Talbot, who was not farre
off, and helde the thirde fortresse, was able to relieve them in this
extremitie of conflict, being afeard, least by his absence that fort
also, whereof he was captaine, might be lost; wherefore the
English men, pressed a good while with all these difficulties, at the
last were driven from their place; and yet araying themselves in
forme of a triangle, sodenly they withdrewe to the lorde Talbot in
the thirde bastile. The lorde Talbot without delaye sallyed foorth
against the multitude with a number of souldiers well appoynted,
and putting his enemies in great terror he both comforted his
owne folkes, delivering them from feare, and repressed thenemy,
insomuch as that they retyryd hastily within the walles. The
Englishmen made the lesse slaughter, because the bastile, wherein
they receaved the first brunt of thassailantes, was not stronge.
Not long after, the lorde Talbot called the counsell togethers, and
declared to them very many causes for the which he thought that
the siege of a towne so long assaulted, and, as it were, by divine
providence defended, was eyther to be utterly forsaken, or to
another time to be referred, when as they might with better lucke
geve newe attempt, least otherwise they should consume the time
wherein; when winter was ended, they might proceede to warres
more necessary. This opinion was allowed generally of all men,
not so much for liking as for necessitie; and so, upon signe geven
to remove, they withdrewe to Magdune. Upon whose departure *Magdunum.*
those of Orleance were sodenly replenished with all joy and mutuall gladnes, for that they had escaped so great daunger. Wherefore,
referring the benefite thereof to God, publique prayer was appoynted for sundry dayes togethers, they gave prayse to him in all

holy churches, beseeching him of universall victorie. Here truly
we may see that he sometimes getteth to litle who coveteth too
much.   Indeede thenglish men might have overcommed; but
esteeming the yeelding of Orleance greatly to their dishonour, if it
had been made in other sort than they demaunded, they neglected

The seege
retyred
from
Orleance.
the victorye, as though it had been theirs alreadie; but afterwarde,
they were so farre from gayning of the towne, as that meere necessitie made them desist from their enterprise. But the Frenche tri-
umphantly rejoysing for the repulse of thenemy, determined in no
part to omitt that good oportunitie of dealing in their owne cause,
and therefore, forthwith they made rodes through all the territory
of Orleance, to thintent they might recover againe such townes as

Gargeum.
thenemy held with garrison : First, they went to Jargeaux, and
within fewe dayes tooke it, killing there more then two hundred
Englishmen, and taking fortie prisoners; howbeit, of their owne
retinewe were wanting also three hundred.

But the lorde Talbot, whom we have before mencioned, anone
upon his breaking up of the siege of Orleance to have gone to
Magdune, after that he had fortified the towne with garrison,
marched to Lavalle, where he pight his tentes harde by the wall,
and having well viewed the scituation of the place, with great exhortation to his souldiers, so fiercely assaulted the same, as that

Magdune
taken by
the lo.
Talbot.
three days after his arrivall there he tooke bothe the towne and
castle; but the townesmen, whose froward obstinacie was deemed
woorthy of smart, he punished severely. The Frenche men, on
thother side, after the recovery of Jargeaux, marched with all their
forces, under the conduct of the damosell aforesaide, unto Magdune,
and incamped under the wall; which thing once knowen, the lord
Talbot, and John Fastolfe, with an armie well appoynted, made
haste thither to relieve their frendes ; whereof, after that Arthure
constable of Fraunce had intelligence by espials, he without more
adoe, calling to him the damosell, and John duke of Alanson,

marching forward with all force, to stopp their passage, pight his
tentes at Patay, a towne unto the which he thought his enemies
would repaire, and placed his horsmen in order of battaile before
his tentes, to geve charge upon thenemy approching, and to geve
the first onset, while thenglish men marched forwarde in their
voyage, espying a farre off the cavallery of Fraunce, they suspected
some traine to be made for them, which was to be avoyded; wherfore they stay, and commande their footmen to empale themselves
round about with stakes, after their accustomed maner; but the
cavallery of Fraunce came upon them with so great speede, as
having no leysure to put themselves in readines to fight, they were
forced to fight a field with horsmen.   In this place, when as the
conflict had continued more than three houres, thenglish horsmen,
oppressed with multitude, were put to flight.   But the footmen,
having spent almoste all their arrowes, marched forth close togethers, with their swordes drawen, and by helpe of some part of the
horsmen, came safe to Magdune.   At the first encounter was Great
killed about a thousand Englishmen, a hundreth were taken, slaughter
                                                              made of th
amongst whom was John lorde Talbot.   Of the Frenche partie English,
were slaine more then six hundred souldiers.   But after it was lo Talbot
spred abrode through Fraunce that the lorde Talbot was taken, by taken.
and by every man had opinion that thenglish partie was the
weaker, insomuch that many townes at one instant revolted to the Many
Frenche, for all men generally were ravished with flagrant desire t wt
                                                              revolted
to recover libertie.   Then, finally, they hoped for good lucke, then from the
had they confidence that God would deliver from troubles the ng s
common wealth of Fraunce, which seemed even now to advaunce
it selfe, for as much as God, pleased by prayers, is wont to relieve
the afflicted.

When king Charles was advertised of this victory, then, finally,
he conceaved in minde and assured opinion of restitution and
libertie, who had been hithertowarde of such noble courage as in

his moste adversitie he did never dispaire, wherfore nowe the earle of Salesbury being deade, and the lord Talbot captive, two of the most excellent captaines amongst all his enemies, the magnaminitie of his minde was much increased ; and therefore, to beginne withall, he determined to goe unto Rheins, that winning that towne he might there, according to the maner of his auncestors, be with accustomed ceremony annoynted King, to thintent it might be apparant to all men that even as he called himselfe, so was he in deede, and so to be called, a King, as well by due consecration as by right.   And so with a huge armie, under the conduct of the damosell or virgin aforesaide, whom as an oracle he consulted in all his affaires, passing through Champaigne, he marched to Auxer; there, when as he approched, ambassadours came out of the citie to meete him, promising that they would willinglye obey his commaundementes, so that it might please him to spare them for a few dayes, wherein they might knowe (for duties sake) whether thenglish men would relieve them or not.   Charles, because he would not offend the good minde of the citizens towardes him by any unlawfull fact, graunted their desire, and entrenching part of his armie not farre from the citie, garding also the same sufficiently, that the townes men should not beguile him, he conducted the residue thereof unto Troyes.   This being the chiefe towne of all Champaigne, he assayed within fewe dayes to besege, which in the ende was yeelded unto him upon permission of thenglish men who were placed there in garrison to depart.   In like maner did those of Chalons, where, placing a garrison, he passed the river of Marne,

Rheines
revolted
to Kinge
Charles,
and then he
crowned
Kinge.

and besieged Rheins, which he recovered easily; for the citizens could not well beare thinglish government, and were therefore not willing to abide the siege; but for that they should not be reported to have betrayed the towne, they opteyned of king Charles libertie for thenglish garrison safely to depart.   When king Charles had receaved the towne, he was there annoynted after the use of his

auncestors, unto whom the cities of all that faction had sent their
chiefe and principall personages, as oratours, who forthwith assembled joyfully to salute him, protesting that they nowe at the last
understood Almightie God to have pitie upon the miseries of
Fraunce, and to have restored unto them the libertie which they
had receaved longe since from their auncestors. Thinhabitantes
of Auxer also, after the prefixed day, seeing the Englishmen did
send no reskue, submitted themselves to his obeysance.

In the meane time, the duke of Bedford had deep consideration
as touching all partes of the realme, and perceaving the taking of
the lorde Talbot to be muche hinderance to his affaires, insomuch
that certaine cities, voyde of all feare, made no doubt to alienate
themselves, and many mo dayly affected to revolte, he to prevente
the daunger hereof, determined by all meanes possible to procure
king Charles to the fielde, that the event of victory (whiche by
Gods helpe he assured himselfe upon) might keepe the people
which he had yet left in obedience and feare. And so departing
from Paris, he marched towardes king Charles, who a litle before
was gone from Rhems to Dammartine; and taking certaine principall townes by the way, which he also furnished with men, had
made there his abode, meaning to corrupt the Parisians with payment or promise. The duke of Bedford approched, and pitching
his campe upon an hill, sent out his horsmen to provoke, stirre
upp, and egge thenemy both with weapon and worde to fight.
King Charles at that time also had no doubt but he might cope
with his enemye in plaine fielde; but when he understoode by
espialls that the duke was egall unto him, both in number and
force, he resolved it better to absteyne, without daunger, then with
hazard to joyne battaile, least by temeritie he might interrupt and
trouble the prosperous successe of his proceedinges. Wherfore
some skirmishing there was by the horsmen betweene the two
campes, and nothing els. But when king Charles sawe the

earnest desire and livelynes that thenglishmen had to fight, suspecting least by his tarying occasion would fall out that eyther he must fight against his will, or els shamefully to keepe within the trenches, he raysed his campe about midnight, and removed, which thing when it was knowen, very early in the morning, the duke of Bedford could hardly hold back his men from pursuing thenemy; but he stayed them upon great discretion, because he would doo nothing rashlye.   And so dispairing that it was possible to entice king Charles to the fielde, he returned to Paris, purposing to augment his armie, that when as possibilitie might be geven afterwardes he might also with greater force assaile him.

Warre preparapa a-
rainste h
Bohemy-
by t
bushoue of
Rome.At this very time the Bohemians, who are of a sect different from other Christians, because they obey not the bishop of Rome, partly for defence of their owne heresie, partly (as it chaunceth) moved with envie against other nations, beganne to keepe warre against their neighbours, whereof, after notice was geven to Martine the Vth., bishopp of Rome, he anone sent legates intoGer many, to move the devout and Godly princes unto warres against the Bohemians, as enemies of Christian religion.   Also he made

The bu-
)p
Winchester
the Popes
n e
into Ger-
manye.Henry cardinall of St. Eusebius and bisshopp of Winchester, legate who should come out of Englande to that warre, with a certaine force of men.   He commaunded him withall to levye by his authoritie the tenthes of all spiritualties, for the mayntenance of religion.   This Henry imparting the Popes commandement to the Kinges councell, and they resolving that nothing was thereunto to be preferred, did levye the money, and gathered no small number of souldiers (although that so sundry impositions were neyther daylye paide, nor so many musters of men made, without great hurt to the common wealth).   And so, furnished with all thinges, purposing shortly to journey thorough Germany, he came to the sea shore, and the souldiers beganne to take shipping, when as the while letters were sent from the duke of Bedforde to the duke of

Glocester, requiring a newe supply of men. The duke of Glocester was greatly troubled with this message; for neyther any other force of men was readie which he might transport, neyther did the time, wherein by reason of the warres against the Bohemians there had been so lately a levye of souldiers, serve at that instant to gather yet againe a newe armie, especially seeing the matter required great haste; who therefore of necessitie made no more adoe, but earnestly requested the bisshop of Winchester that he would first goe with his armie unto the duke of Bedforde, to ayde his owne countrymen in the battaile which the duke of Bedforde was to fight with his enemy; and from thence, having therein good successe, whereof he had no doubt, that he might proceede to the Bohemians. Henry, though he were sory that his journey was hindred, yet because he would not faile his owne nation and frendes, passing thocean, went to Paris to the duke of Bedforde. *The bushope of Winchester, beneshed for his journey ie many, was command- first into France.*

In this meane while king Charles, advertised from his horsemen, whom he had sent abroade all over to feele the mindes of the people, and to move them to revolte, that Campeigne and Beavoys were well affected towards him, greatlye coveting to be delivered from the dominion of thenglish nation, and therefore readie to open him their gates at his comming, if that they might so doo without ieopardie of their lives, marched therfore with an armie of light and lustie souldiers to Campeigne: whereof when knowledge was had, the duke of Bedforde, having his forces augmented with the great supplye which Henry the cardinall had brought, marched also forwarde towardes thenemy, to thintent he might allure him to some indifferent fight, but he was scarce come within the territory of Senlis, when king Charles entered Mountpillioll, which is betwixt Champeigne and Senlis, where getting a covenable place, he encamped his armie, not meaning to conduct his men out of that place upon small occasion. These thinges were by and by reported by espialls to the duke of *Siluanectum. Piliolum.*

Bedford, who, bringing forth his armie into order of battaile, approached nigh to thenemy, and offred battaile: but the French men kept within Mountpellioll; their horsemen skirmished nowe and then a litle without their trenches, but they would assay nothing els: for king Charles considered howe much force fortune, which is to meane the sodaine and unlooked for event of some casuall thing, yea of least moment, is of in battaile, who was therein perfectly taught and instructed by detrimentes before often receaved. Moreover, when he understoode that manye and great cities of Fraunce did with evil will suffer the government of thenglish nation, and were readie upon oportunitie to revolt, he hoped, without battaile, to expell thenglish men in short space utterly out of all Fraunce: and this, as he adjudged, was the very cause why the duke of Bedford, as a wise man, not ignorant of his owne decaye, desired so much to trye the whole matter at once in battaile. Wherefore taught therein by experience of the causes aforesaide, he was fully resolved in minde, no where to adventure battaile, but in as much as necessitie should constraine him, and that deemed he would be hereafter most for his profite. The duke of Bedforde, who had the Parisiens in gelousie, because they did all his commaunde- mentes in such sort as might well appere to be against their willes, neyther yet much trusted in the duke of Burgoigne, the cause whereof we shall hereafter declare in convenient place, when he sawe his enemy of purpose to deferre the fight, returned to Paris. Then Henry the cardinall legate to the Romane bisshop, with his armie which he had brought before out of Englande, went forth his voyage against the Bohemians xlv^tie dayes after that he entred Fraunce: whither when he came, finding the warres all over very hott, he begann valiantly to ayde the christian cause to thuttermost of his power, and taried in Bohemia by the space of certaine monthes, so long, untill that he was revoked by the pope, with other legates; and the cardinall of St. Angell called Julian Soesa-

The Car-
Winchester
departeth
u
France into
Germany.

rine was sent to that warre with great forces. And so the said Henry, after that he had served honorably in that holy warres, returned safe home.

King Charles, after the duke of Bedfordes departure, receaved into his obedience Campeigne, Beauvays, and Senlis, the citizens yeelding thereunto of their owne accorde : of which fortunate successe though he much rejoyced, yet he had no hope of habilitie to exterminate the English nation, before he should seperate the societie of them and of the Burgoignion, which in the ende he trusted would once come to passe. And therefore he first assayed by often messengers to purge himselfe unto the duke of Burgoigne of his fathers death, and to admonish him, that nothing was further from all righteousnes and pietie, nothing more undecent, then to deale against his comhabitauntes, against his countrey, or for revenge of private iniuries to joyne with their auncient and perpetuall enemies. After that he begann busily to treate of pacification, to offer high and large condicions of agreement, to promise more then he was able to performe, insomuch that the duke of Bedforde did easily understande his whole drifte, wherefore he, much troubled in minde with deepe and weightie considerations, seing the English affaires greatly decaye, determined to provide for one thing especially what adversitie soever should befall, which was to meane, that if all the holdes which king Henry his brother had woonn in Fraunce, could not be retayned. kept, and defended, yet that Normandie, so longe by his auncestors possessed, might not be lost, according as king Henry himselfe, in the last wordes that ever he spake, had commanded to be done. Wherefore committing the government of the citie of Paris to Lewes Lucemburge, bisshopp of Turwine and chauncellor of Fraunce, leaving also for defence thereof no small garrison, he went into Normandie, whither after his comming he called specially unto him the chiefe of every citie, and first rehearsed unto them the benefites bestowed alway by his

King Char[les] [la]boured to drawe the Duke of Burgoigne on his p[art].

The Duke of [?] fortefied Parris and Normandy.

auncestours upon the Normans, the restitution of their priviledges
and lawes, and also thauncient stocke of the Norman dukes, from
whence the kings of England were descended ; afterward he exhorted every man by name, that they would with hart and hande
be very carefull and earnest to preserve peace, and not to breake
their allegiance : this if they would doo, then he assured them
they might woorthely hope for at king Henry their kinges hande
all that ever they would demaunde.　While that the duke of Bedforde is dealing in thaffayres aforesaide, newes was brought unto
him that many for feare forsooke both towne and fielde, wherewith
being much moved, he calleth togethers his councell : yea, and
addeth thereunto the captaines of every bonde, requiring them to
saye their opinions as concerning the keeping of the Normans in
obedience.　All men generally thought best, that the armie should
be devided into severall places : and so was one part assigned to
defend the sea coast under the government of Richard duke of
York ; another part was sent to supplye garrisons in cities and
townes ; the third part was committed to Edmonde duke of Sommersett, to be conducted unto Roane.　The duke of Bedford, thus
having ordered his affaires, and severed his forces, himselfe returned to Paris.　The meane while that these doinges were in
Normandie, Charles the Frenche king tooke St. Dionise by
treason, and did spedily furnish it with garrison : from thence he
sent before John duke of Alanson, and the Mayde, that they might
marche apace to Paris, and procure the citizens to revolte, yea, and
if they sawe cause, to take in hande thassault : who marched forth
in square battaile every souldier havynge his buckler, and approaching the wall, was by great slaughter by thenglish garrison
repulsed.　Whereof the duke of Bedforde hearing, came in great
haste to the towne, and with high commendacions, gave thankes to
the citizens, for that they followed not thexample of the Dioni-
sians.　But king Charles disappoynted of his purpose in that

matter, enterprised another attempt : for he sent Ambrose Delore
to Laignie (which is scituate upon the river of Marne) to whom *Latinia-*
uppon his arrivall the citie was yeelded. Not long after he departed *cum.*
from thence, leaving there a garrison, as in a place wherein, being
of itselfe very stronge, he reposed much trust, and made a voyage
into Angeow, at which time thenglish men on thother side wanne
againe by force the towne of St. Denis, assaying also to recover
Laignie : but the Maide, being therein for succour thereof, made
sharpe resistance, and so it was valiantly defended. About the
same time certaine companies of English souldiers who rested
about Roane, under the conduct of Thomas Tirrell, a valiant gentleman, hearing, as they forrowed abroad, spoyling the countrey, that
the towne of Clermont was slenderly manned, assailed the same,
and took it at the first brunt. But because they were so fewe,
that they might not spare men to fortify the same, therefore first
they threwe downe a part of the wall, then sacked the towne, and
returned from whence they came loden with great bootie of all
kinde. Of another side, the Bourgoignians, under the conduct of
John of Lucemburge, marched to Campeigne with a great force of
English men, and environed it with a trenche. But neither the
towne, being throughly fortified and strong, was easily to be gayned,
neyther the siege like to prove to anye purpose, because that it had
been perfectly well victualled before. Howbeit, hoping eyther to
winne it by assault, or compell it to yeelde, they undergoe the
wall, their army being devided in two, and continually, some with
arrowe, dart, and suche like, some with great goonshott, others by
making mines, and others with other almost perpetuall fight molest
the towne, laboring to that ende chiefly that the same might
quickly yeelde, when as loe sodainly Joane the maide, the pro- Joane cap-
phetisse of God, as the common sort termed her, though ignorant ꜰ ᵗⁱⁿᵉ ᵗ
of her owne fate, came to relieve them, and mightily entred the taken by
towne : but soone after when as she sallied out unadvisedly against enburghe.

thenemy, she was taken by John of Lucembrowgh, and sent to the
duke of Sommersett at Roane. •

Joane the
captayne of
was burnt. This maide, forasmuch as she did many notable exploites above
the force of a woman, and in a maner without any skill of martiall
discipline, was suspected of the common sorte to deale by witch-
crafte : wherefore, accused of sorcerie, she was firste straitly examined by the duke of Sommersets commaundement, as towching
the articles of her fayth : afterwarde, because she ware mans apparell, and was verely accompted a witche, therefore was she with
severitie condemned and burnt. But the unhappie Maide, re-
membering, before execution done, what apperteyned to humanitie,
which naturally is bredd in every one, fained herselfe to be with
childe, to thende she might eyther move her enemies to compassion, eyther els cause them to appoynt some more milde punishment. But after being reserved ix. monthes for that cause, and
her surmise founde false, she was burned notwithstanding. This
saide sentence thus pronounced was thought the hardest that ever
had beene remembred, which could neyther be mollified nor mitti-
gated by tract of time. Surely it was of some thought that this
woman thus excited to martiall manly prowesse. for defence of her
country, was woorthy favour, especially seeing there were many
examples of mercie showed in such case, as that principally which
Porsenna King of the Trurions hath left in memorie. For when
as he, upon conclusion of peace with the Romanes, had receaved
pledges, and amongst them Cloelia a virgin, who, conducting a
company of others like, beguiled the watch, and amongst the
middest of her enemies swam over Tiber and fledd to her owne
people, notwithstanding that afterwarde she was by the league re-
delivered, yet he did not punish her, but with great commendation gave her part of the pledges, and sent her home againe. But
I will returne to the matter.

   This was the ende of Joane Puselle, more fitt, as the brute went,

to practise magike than martiall affaires. But the Frenche men
to this day will not heare but that she was sent of God from
heaven to expell thenemy out of their countrey; for they affirme
that she dyed a virgin. After her fall the Frenche failed not in
courage, who both with continuall sallyinges out of the towne,
and also with ofte bickering in plaine fielde, so annoyed their enemies, that, dispeyring to winne the same, they departed of their
owne accorde.

The affaires of England grewe by this meane, from day to day,
through Fraunce, woorse and woorse, which did diversly affect the
nobilitie: for some, very pensife in mind, deemed the distresse of
the present time light, in comparison of that which they forsawe
to be imminent: others thought that woorse could not chaunce
than had alreadie chaunced, for they sawe the forces of thenemy
augmented and their owne diminished: wherefore every man, much
musing with ardent affection, considered with himselfe particularly
whether it were possible to remedie the state of thinges almost
utterly decayed: when as in the end it was resolved, generally, to
be best for the present neede that king Henry should repaire, as
soone as conveniently might be, with a newe armie into Fraunce,
partly to comfort his owne people, partly to keepe under and in
obedience the cankred courage of Frenche men, eyther for feare,
eyther els for favor, seing the yonge king was of so amiable and
lovely countenaunce. Wherefore men were mustered sufficient
for such a voyage, and money was levyed by an imposition or
taske, sett as well upon the clergie as laitie, for to support the
charge thereof; and so king Henry, under the tuition of Henry H 6 re-
the cardinall, transporting out of Englande came first to Roane, paired the
and from thence to Paris. All the whole citie came forth to meete Winchester
him, and with all fortunate signes and shewes of joy and gladnes into
France.
they saluted him as King, an impe of most excellent towardnes and
disposition, though many perchaunce there were, who did all that

honor with holowe heartes : but so it was to thoutwarde appe-
raunce, that that day of the kinges arrivall was there celebrated of
all men generally with great rejoysing, for the whiche an oration
was openly made in prayse of the people, and great plentie of
money, corne, and wine was bestowed upon them.   After that, the
duke of Bedford, assembling the nobilitie, is reported to have

The duke
of Bed-
fords ora-
saide : " Beholde, my lordes, the course of humane causes ; Henry
the Vth was to have been your King, as well by right as by league,
but he deceassing, in a manner before his full and perfect age, hath
lefte a sonne to succeede and enjoye his grandfathers kingdome ;
he is here amongst us : hither is he brought for that cause, that
he may be proclaymed your King, and that both he may knowe
his Frenche people, and they likewise him, who are wont principally among all other nations to esteeme, honor, and both faith-
fully and also carefully obey their King (if I may so say) in the
very steede and place of God.   And though some there be who
take part with Charles, yet the cause thereof appereth to be error
and not disloyaltie ; wherefore, whosoever will returne and acknowledge his dutie, shalbe pardoned.   Therefore it onely resteth
that you will with all loyaltie, as you have hithertowardes diligently done, endeavour your selves from henceforth to keepe and
conserve the people in obedience, whose dutifulnes in this behalfe
shall so well deserve of your King, as that his maiestie will not
denay you anything that shalbe for your utilitie and honour ; whose
thankfull bountifulnes of minde towardes you hereafter you may
measure unto your selves according to the rate and proportion of
your owne simple and well affected consciences towardes his high-

H. 6,
nes."   Thassemble dissolved, king Henry, being of thage of tenne
at Parrys,
yeres, was consecrated by Henry the cardinall in the church of our
anno 1432.
lady mother of God, and the crowne set upon his head, with all
due and accustomed ceremonie.   After celebration of the divine
misterie, the Frenche noble men sware homage to king Henry ;

after that proclamation was made, that all men should be pardoned who would within a certaine time returne into thobedience of king Henry. This was the yere of our salvation 1432.

While these thinges were a doing at Paris, king Charles recovered, partly by force, and partly by treason, the townes of Melun, Corbole, and sundry others; but otherwhere the event of *Meledu* thinges was otherwise. There was a great garrison of Frenche at *num.* *Corboli* Beauvoys, whom Thomas earle of Arundell thought by pollicie to allure into the field : wherefore pighting his tentes afarre off, he layde both footmen and horsemen nigh the towne in a secrete and privie place ; after that he sent out some light horsemen, that might provoke thenemy to issue, which horsemen executing his commaundementes, proceeded even to the gates ; where finding Frenchemen ready to pursue them, they counterfaited flight, drawing the pursuers within daunger of thambush, who were so intrapped and killed downe right, together with the townesmen, who also folowed the chase, whereof part, hearing the great stirre and noyse of horses, conceaved the traine, and hardlye recovered the towne, the residue were slaine. The number of them who were killed is not mentioned of any author, so far as I knowe, which surely is thought to have beene not small. Also, Richard earle of Warwicke had like fortunate successe about the saide time in a conflict with his enemies at Gorney, where many were killed, and three score *gentlemen* taken. The like force of frowning for- *Equites* tune did Rhenate duke of Barry feele about the same time, who by meane of his puissance had greatly ayded king Charles : for Rhenate, who had an old grudge against Anthony earle of Vaudemont, had gathered togethers great forces, and marched withall to surprise the towne of Vaudemont : of whose approche when the Earle hearde, fearing to be compassed about of his enemy, he lefte the retinewe of souldiers which he had, to furnish the towne, and fledd in poste to the dukes of Bedforde and Burgoigne, whose

CAMD. SOC G

part he tooke, requiring them of ayde: and having obteyned the
same, he and Anthonye Tolongone, lieftenant of Burgundie, returned againe with a mayne hoste to relieve his people, sharply
urged by his enemy.   Which when Rhenate understoode, fearing
least as soone as the citizens should perceave their duke with
succours to approche, that both they should issue out of the
towne, and the duke set upon them behinde all at one time ; he
therefore, forsaking the siege, turned his forces against thenemies
that were comming, and commaunded his men to geve the charge.
The fight was mainteyned a while amongst the horsemen, who received the first brunt, untill the footmen drewe neere, who entred
the battaile with such might and mayne, as that the Frenche was
not onely unhable to abide, but were put to flight forthwith.

Reynat
duke of
Barr
taken.

Rhenate was taken with three hundred of his souldiers.   There
was killed about three thousande.   The English had about the
same time no lesse oportunitie offered to have atchieved a prosperous adventure in another quarter also, if they had not un-
wisely omitted the same: for Robert lorde Willoughby, and
Mathew Gough, a valiant Walshman, besieged the castle of St.
Selerine, by nature of the place very strong, and pressed to take
the same by force: on thother side, the garrison within did lustely
defende the place, whereof king Charles being advertised, sent to
succour his people, in all haste, Ambrose Delore, with divers other
captaines.   He, because himselfe was captaine thereof, and that
the garrison who defended the same were of his placing, as one
earnest to ayde his owne, at the first set speedily forward, but
soone after doubting to be compassed about, he stayed at Beau-

Belli-
monte.

monte, minding there to tarie while the residue of captaines appoynted should come thither also, that from thence they might
altogethers proceede against thenemy : but the while of this
assemblie, the English men that were at the siege having intelligence by espialls what their enemies did, determined to encounter

them before thone partie should joyne with thother : and therefore
the better part of the campe issuing without any noyse in the deade
of the night, founde their enemies campe so evil garded, that about
a thousand men were within the trenche or ever any man almost
perceaved; but the slaughter in the very trenche made awaked
thenemy, who, not suspecting the chaunce, were sodenly striken
in such terror and trouble of minde, that no man did effectually
assaye to take armour, or to make resistance : but when the day
appered thenglish souldiers, seeking after spoyle, did not pursue the
chase, but were satisfied with so huge bootie, and busied to cary
away the same, whereby beholde it chaunced that the Frenche
men who were in marching thitherwarde, hearing the clamour of
fighting men, hastened themselves, came upon their enemies unwares, and set couragiously uppon them all laden with spoyle.
The residue also of them who fledd, made head againe and returned. The fray was fierce and cruell of both sides, and longe
continued in equall balance; but in thende thenglish men, oppressed with multitude, gave grounde. Divers of them were taken,
and amongst them Mathew Gough. Many Frenche men were
killed, but mo taken, in the number of whom was Ambrose Delore.
After that Robert L. Willoughby lefte the siege. Surely a chiefe
captaine in warres ought to regard the victory, and nothing els,
which is so harde to be gotten, and so easily lost, as that he
who supposeth him selfe to have it in his hande, may alwaye be
deceaved, and bring himselfe in daunger, before he holde it fast:
or whoso hath it may easily with losse foregoe it againe, except
he have speciall care of keeping thereof: for example, thenglish
men, while as conquerours they sought for spoyle, loste the victorie
alreadie gotten.

But while these two nations of Englande and Fraunce doo thus
fight for superioritie, for soveraintie, yea, for safetie of life itselfe,
by reason of such lowse libertie as warres gave throughout the

Mathewe
Goughe
prisoner.

whole French region, all men were berefte of their riches, holy
treasures were spoyled, Christian blood by slaughter or wounding
was every where shed, the commonaltie cruelly tormented and
punished, matrones were defiled, virgins were rested out of their
parentes armes and ravished, townes were taken every day, dayly
were they sacked, and the townesmen transported otherwhere,
houses and whole streetes were burnt, and finally, no kinde of
crueltie could be devised, wherewith the poore Frenche man was
not afflicted; I omitt an innumerable kinde of other calamities,
wherewithall they were all at once oppressed. To thincrease of
all these mischiefes, the common wealth during this time was
forced to lye without lawe, (which for the most part is silent in
warres,) without all civill government, and justice. Neyther was
England exempt cleere from such injuries, for they sawe dayly the
death, slaughter, and woundes of their felowes and frendes; their
substance was exhaust with continuall exactions; so that the mischiefes were mutuall and common to both sides; the whole occident
did ringe with their outcries, the fame of their doleful state was
spred through the whole earth, wherefore there was no man
living who wondred not with compassion howe these two nations
should be able to abide so long charge and affliction : but chiefly

The Bishop
of Rome
---- ---
legate to
treate of
of all other, Eugenius the fourth, bisshop of Rome, tooke pitie
hereof, who, very desirous to devise some meane whereby this
outragious warre might once have ende, sent Nicholas cardinall of
the Holy Crosse into Fraunce to make attonement betwixt the two
kinges. He, after his comming thither, went first to king Charles,
and explained to him his commission from the Pope : from thence
he did the like to the duke of Bedforde : he persuaded peace,
shewed by demonstration, declared, and by argument well proved
the same to be more apperteyning to the dutie of Christian princes
then warre, who ought to applye all their travaile for the profite of
their people, to mainteyne justice, to rule themselves by reason,

alway to remitt somewhat of their rage, to put up part injurie, which thinges warres would not permitt them to doo. The cardinall endevouring to perswade the two princes to be of this minde, they both gave aunswere, that they were readie to yeelde to all reason. But when the matter was dealt in, they were so farre from agreing to any indifferent conditions of peace, as that they remayned more obstinate in their error; which thing when the cardinal conceaved, dispairing to conclude a perpetuall peace, yet because it should not be thought that he had taken all that travaile in vaine, he concluded a truce for six yeres: where- A truse unto as either partie was hardly drawen at the cardinals request, agreu upon so after his departure they sodenly brake. Some late writers have England mentioned, that the Frenche did first violate the same, who everye for 6 years. where set sore impositions and punishmentes by purse uppon such as were frendes to the English or Burgoinion; whereby it came to passe that the malice of their mindes mutually inflamed, the warres beganne againe more sharplye then before; that was the yere of our salvation 1433.   1433.

But I will returne againe to king Henry. King Henry, within a fewe dayes after he had bene adorned at Paris with the maiestie of the regall diademe, departed to Roane: where while he tarieth Henry the cardinal was revoked againe into Englande, for pacifying an uprore of certaine moste wicked persons, who, under pretence of embrewing the mindes of men with a newe religion, had conspired to disturbe the quiet government and tranquillitie of the realme. The Cardinall conferred with the duke of Glocester as concerning the state of forreine causes beyonde the sea, and assured him, that, as he thought, the Frenche men would shortly breake the trewce, and therefore, that it were meete to make in readines a supply of men and money necessary for the use of warre, which when the duke of Glocester understoode, he called a A parlia- parliament, by decree whereof men were mustered, and money ex- moned by

which
men and
~~~~~~~
were de-
o be
prepared
and a peace
o
with Scot-
land.

acted. During this season, James, king of Scotts sent ambassadours to the duke of Glocester as concerning peace. But because the king was absent, the duke referred that demaunde to the parliament, whereupon, after long debating of the matter, peace was granted, because there was good hope of the continuance thereof, insomuch as the Scottish king was troubled with intestine division, and tnat there was a trewce taken betweene Englande and Fraunce for six yeres. The parliament being dissolved, the Cardinall, with the forces that were gathered, and great store of money that was levyed, returned to the king at Roane. Thither came also the duke of Bedford from Paris to consult what best was to be done. Here the whole matter was referred to councell. Some suspected, that the Frenche men would not keepe and sticke to the condition and covenants of peace, forasmuch as it was apparent, that they almoste all generally were inwardlye incensed with griefe, that Normandie and Paris, and so many goodly townes, were reduced under thenglish empire, and therefore were earnest to persuade that nothing might be remitted pertayning to the warre, least, upon sodaine breache of trewce, they might be compelled with extreme hazarde to take sodaine advise in most weightie causes, all unreadie, both lacking men and money. Againe, this many did affirme, that it was not possible to continue the warre in that order, during so long time of trewce taken, without breache thereof, seing it was a very harde matter to restraine the souldiers hande from evill doing, who should continue dayly in armes for feare of the enemy, and therefore they thought good to fortifie places of most importance with garrison, and to sende the rest of tharmie home againe, during continuance of the trewce. After the matter was thus argued both wayes, the dukes of Bedford, Somersett, and Yorke, allowing upon the former opinion, determined that all thinges expedient for warres should be prepared, that the souldiers should be payde their wages, and that a greater armie shoulde be gathered against all adventures.

Such resolution being made, king Henry returned first to Calis, H. 6. re-turnetne into Eng-land. and from thence into Englande. The duke of Bedforde accom-panied the king to Callis, and there made his abode a fewe dayes; when as the while sundrye souldiers, remembring their accustomed martiall libertie, begann to make ravine and spoyle every where, which after that he knewe, having gotten this litle occasion to mi-nister justice, he caused to be apprehended the authours of this wicked attempt, and punished them with great severitie, thereby to terrifie others, that they might the rather refraine from other mens goodes. And so the duke of Bedforde having delivered the towne of most pernitious people, fortified the same with newe supplye, and so journeyed to Paris, when as in the mean time another matter came in his head : for a fewe monthes before he had forgone Anne, his wife, sister to the duke of Burgoigne, by reason of whose death it fell out that the Burgoignians affection was after more easily alienated from the amitie of the Englishe nation, who, as we have before touched, was moved earnestly thereto for other causes ; wherefore he determined to mary Jaquet, The duke ot Bedforc marved tl E. of St. s daughter. daughter to Peter of Lucembrowgh, Earle of St. Paule, a very noble man ; by reason of which newe affinitie thauncient acquaintance and familiaritie betwixt him and that noble house might be con-firmed by more straite and sure bonde of benevolence. And so departing from Callis, he rode towarde Tirwine, where the earles house was, whom the earle interteyned very joyfully, and gave to him in mariage his daughter Jaquet, which was the thing that he demaunded. And so the duke of Bedford having his desire, after most sumptuous and honorable solemnization of mariage, came with his wife to Paris. The duke of Burgoigne took that in evill part, who, being minded to joyne with king Charles, was sory that the duke of Bedforde shoulde nowe be strengthened by affinitie of the auncient and mightie house of Lucembrowghe, which might stande him in great steede every where. About the same time,

John Tal-
an
somed.

John Talbot, whom we before shewed to have been taken of the Frenche men, at Patay, was raunsomed for a great somme of money, and the restitution to libertie of Ambrose Delore, taken also a fewe monthes before, and so suffered to depart from thenemy, returned into Englande.

While these thinges were done thus in other places, the Frenche souldiers lacking pave, and having amongst them an heape of unthriftes, whom hope of spoyle and delight of warre had withdrawen from husbandrie, and all other dayly exercise of good occupation, begonne first to take prisoners, sometime English men, sometime Burgoignions, as occasion served, and to raunsome them according to their substance : which though it were more unlawful during the truce, yet they feared not to proceede with suche enterprise afterwarde openlye, by reason of which injurye the English men were forced to take weapon in hande againe anone, after six monthes next ensewing the making of the trewce, and by this meane was the warre renewed, which the most part generally supposed and much desired to have been ended, or for longer time stayde. But the Frenche trewce breakers without delay armed themselves, and

St. Valery
o the

tooke the towne of St. Valery, scituate in the mouth of the river Some, upon the frontires of Normandie. Another company, under the conduct of Ambrose Delore, made rodes about the same time into the territory of Cane. On thother partie, thenglish men under the duke of Bedforde beseiged with great force the towne of

Latinia-
cum.

Laigney, standing, as we have before shewed, upon the river of Marne, litle in deede, but environed with mighty trenches and deepe diches, which for because they could not winne at the first assault, they intrenched themselves, and having wonne the bridge, they builded thereupon a towre for defence thereof, and layde to battery on all sides. Againe, the towne manfully defended themselves, yea, and sometime, by conduct of John the bastard of Orleance, who was captaine thereof, they sallyed out, but not without their owne slaughter. There lay thinglish campe certaine dayes, fighting in this order, when as the duke of Bedforde, forced by matter of more great importance, was withdrawen otherwise : who leaving the siege, returned to Paris, least the citizens who were perversely affected might take occasion by his absence to worke some practise the while against him. Anone after his arrivall there, without any tary, he sent Peter of Lucenbrowghe, his father in lawe earle of St. Paule, and Robert lorde Willoughbie, to recover the towne of St. Valery. They, forasmuche as all mens mindes were inflamed with desire of revenge, marched thither speedily, besieged the towne, and buckled to thassault. The Frenche who were within, after a fewe dayes spent in making resistance, hope-lesse finally of any ayde to releeve them, yeelded the towne upon composition safely to depart from thence. Peter of Lucenbrowghe and the lorde Willoughbie, leaving sufficient garrison, returned to the duke of Bedforde conquerours of that exploite ; but the towne, whether it were by contagion of corrupt ayre, or els by reason of old unholesome vyande wherewithall the souldier was fedd, beganne to be sore infected with pestilence, to thintent (as I beleeve) that thinfortunate towne, after so manye overthrowes and miseries as they had nowe twise suffered, firste during the siege of the Frenche, and than that of thinglish people, might be plagued also with that deadlye disease. Moreover, a litle before, the Frenche men had invaded the boundes of Burgundie also, taking certaine townes and towres, and some thereof rasing to the very grounde. And while that the Burgoignians labour to recover the same, the duke of Bedforde sent the lorde Willoughbie and Thomas Tirrell, with certaine bandes, to make helpe speedily unto their frendes. They setting forwarde in all haste, after that they were entred the terri-torie of Laonoys, mett by chaunce with a mayne hoste of enemies, and encountring therewithall, put them to flight, whereof they killed clx, and tooke some, whom they killed afterwarde. Theng-

St Valerye recovered ag.....

Laudu-
ne use.

lishe men after this proceeded on their purposed journey, and joyned with the Burgoignions, who, their forces thus united, recovered quickly all the saide places.

In this meane time, the lord Talbot having mustered a number of able men in Englande, transported into Fraunce with a great armie, and arrived at Roane, where, after he had refresshed his souldiers, he went from thence unto Paris to the duke of Bedforde, whose arrivall, a wonder is to speake, how much it encouraged his owne frendes, and appalled his enemies: for he was accompted an especiall good captaine in the warres, and his approved pollitique government there was woorthely fearfull to the Frenche, and to his owne nation full of assured hope and confidence. This lorde Talbot, after he was directed by the duke of Bedforde as touching his proceedinges and enterprises, marched forward with an hoste well appointed to besiege the towne of Beaumont, which at the first push he wanne by assault; he subdued also the holdes adjoyning with like successe. Amongst these matters the earle of Arundell beseged the castle of St. Selerine, whereof he was conqueror three monthes after that he had laide siege therunto, killing the garrison that was therein. From thence he came before the towne of Silly, the citizens whereof, being in terror by reason of the slaughter lately made at St. Selerines, gave pledges by and by upon promise to deliver the towne within thirtie dayes, except they should be reskewed the meane while by king Charles, and sent forthwith certaine men to king Charles, who, advertised thereof, commaunded Arthure, with certaine ensignes, to goe forthwith to succor the Syllyens. After they did once appere, therle of Arundell rendred to the towne their pledges, and offered the Frenche men battaile in a fitt place for the same not farre from his tentes, which he had chosen out a litle before thapproche of thenemye. Arthure, though he were willing to fight, yet perceaving the Englishmen to have taken such grounde as was not meete for his multitude, would not advaunce forth against them, but the night folowing, having releeved the towne with part victuall and part garrison, returned from whence he came. After his departure, thearle of Arundell wanne the towne by force, and departed into Normandie spoyling the countrey all the way as he went, and subduing divers castles of Mayne and Angeow. Thither also repaired the lorde Willoughbie, and Thomas Tirell out of Burgundie, conquerours, as we have before remembred, who tooke by the way a very stronge towne called Louviers, and furnished it with garrison.

Louerium.
Louviers
taken
by the E.
of Arur
delle

About this time, a huge rowte of rurall Normans, inhabiting upon the sea coast, whether they were thereunto labored by the Frenche men. or that they were desirous of alteration. which the common sorte of people greedily gapeth after, armed themselves, expelled garrisons by force, and tooke certaine holdes, crying out every where, to persecute onely the Englishmen. Hereupon truely may we conceave, that it is more possible for thethiop to chaunge his colour, as the common saying is, then for them who inhabite Fraunce to beare great good will to thenglish nation : for indeede the Normans were subject long to the King of Englande, and well interteyned, who nowe forgetting dutie, but no poynt of envye, were not afeard to ryse against their chiefe lorde and soveraine. This multitude thus stirred up, tooke their way first towarde Cane, that there, increasing in number, they might consult upon the body of the matter. In which meane while the dukes of Soommerset and Yorke, hearing of such uprore of commons, and advised of their proceedinges, sent against them without delay the earle of Arundell and lorde Willoughbie, with six thousand archers, and a thousand three hundred light horsmen, to let and stopp their passage by all meane possible, so that they might not be able eyther to runne and range abrode, neyther yet to goe forwarde. The earle of Arundell, diverting somewhat out of the way,

The Normanes rise
............you
against
H. 6.

premised the lorde Willoughbie with part of the horsmen and two thousande footmen, to lye in ambushe some where nigh the way, to intrapp the multitude approching ; he, as he was commaunded, so placed himselfe secretly, and advertised the earle of the place where the ambush was layde, whereby he might understande when to geve the signe of invading, which when the earle of Arundell knewe, he folowed the rowt behinde, as one driving a hearde of deare into nettes, and after that he perceaved the retchlesse multitude draw nigh to thambush he made a signe incontinent, whereupon the lord Willoughbie gave charge on them before and himselfe behinde, all at once ; with which sodaine accident the ruralls, all agast, helde up their handes, and casting away both weapon and armor, prayed to spare their lives ; with whose piteous prayers, the earle of Arundell, moved to compassion, caused the souldiers to cease from bloudshed, and taking them specially whom he supposed to have been practisers of that comotion, suffered the residue to depart safe home ; but yet there was a thousand men killed even at the first encounter, before the souldiers could be reduced againe unto their ensignes. So this stirre appeased, and so great rage by good rule and government forthwith restrained, there were strait inquisitions thereof made, and all that were giltie were condemned and put to death. In the meane time, the Frenche men, under the conduct of Peter of Rokeforde, tooke from thenemy Diep and some other townes of small strength. But the earle of Arundell, after so many notable and honorable exploites, not longe after assayed one other, which was his last attempt that ever he made. The castle of Gerbory, in Beauvois, was scituate upon a place of great strength, but whether it were by force of man, or by antiquitie of time, it was nowe almost levell with the grounde. Because this place stoode very aptly to expell the sodaine incursion of thenemy, king Charles had geven Stephen Hyre in charge to repaire the saide castle, which when the

The Normans yeld and submit themselves.

Deepe and some other townes lost to the Frenche.

earle of Arundell understoode, by and by he came out of Normandy into Beauvoys with too slender force of men to interrupt and let the building thereof. The Frenche men stirred with the sodaine approche of thenemy, left the place to the workmen, and arming themselves in haste issued forth. They gave a sore charge upon the English men approching, who abode and bare it out a while; but when the earle of Arundell fell from his horse sore wounded, then casting themselves in a triangle, and omitting somewhat the fight, they were forced to retire. The earle of Arundell, thus wounded, dyed not long after, a man of singular virtue, constancie, and gravitie, whose death in so tempestuous tormoiles exceedinglye appalled the courage of his nation. But the Frenche men, after the departure of thenemy, made an ende of the worke which they had begonne. The death of Thomas earle of Arundell chaunced in the year of our salvation 1434, and the twelfth yere of king Henries reigne.

The very selfsame yere the towne of St. Denis was twise taken, once of the Frenche men by treason, and againe of thenglish by yeelding. Also Corbelle, Vicenes, and Meulane were brought under the subjection of Fraunce; for townes which for the most part were voyde of walles laye so open to the spoyle, that thinhabitantes, who were able to performe nothing by constant obedience, did alway yeelde to the first assailants, as ofte as the garrisons there placed would permitt them so to doo, least they should otherwise suffer thextremitie. Whereby it came to passe that nothing was fuller of troubles than Fraunce, nothing more subject to spoyle, nothing more beggerly. Neyther was the souldier in much better case, who, though he were gladd of spoyle, yet was he killed every where, during the while that eyther King laboured to keepe the chiefe cities of his faction in obedience. Wherefore, the people of eyther partie begann now to wery with bloudshed; now was so many discommodities done, by both sides, that every

Marginal notes:

The E. of Ar wounded to deathe and Beauvoys.

1434, the f 4 6,

St. Denis twi takene.

Vicencias.

man generally did lament himselfe to be thus oppressed, tormented, and utterly destroyed; every man was vexed with most
deepe dolor, every man afflicted and muche broken with sorrowe;
wherefore those who were of most perverse and obstinate disposition were thereby inclined to peace. Hereunto also they
were urged by want of all thinges; for the fieldes lay every
where wasted and untilled, the principall cause whereof was,
because men were compelled for savegarde of life not to ere the
grounde, but of necessitie to serve in warres. And so, constrained
thereto by manyfolde mischiefes, neyther partie was unwilling of
peace; but thone thought it dishonorable eyther to demaunde it
of thother, or yet to yeelde thereunto. Wherefore it was needfull
that Eugenius the pope should be the author and arbiter of so
great an attonement, who finally might by his authoritie, counsell,
and perswasion, wrest out the wepons from the handes of these
most invincible conquerours, and of other warriers who never
would cause sounde the retraite, never would heare of abstinence;
which saide Bisshop was broughte in good hope of pacification,
especially for because the fame was, that Phillip duke of Burgoigne
grewe wery of that he had done; for he at the beginning, desirous
as well to revenge his fathers death as to mainteyne his owne preheminence and dignitie, shewed to the English nation all the
frendshipp he could, not supposing that he should, by reason of
this league with the king of Englande, be constrained to offende
against the common wealth, which he ruled as then at his owne
direction and pleasure, neyther that he should depart from that
preheminence, so longe as he should agree with Englande; but
when it fell out afterwarde otherwise then he had weened, forasmuch as the king of Englande used nowe the government by
right of inheritance, and challenged all sutes, lawes, peace, and
warres, to be in his power, whereof the duke had had a litle before
good experience, when in the treatie for geving up of Orleance

the same was denyed to be yeelded in his name; then lastly he determined to returne into the way from which he had strayed, and both to stand and holde with his owne nation, as soone as he might have any honest pretence so to doo, whereby he should not be reported to intangle himselfe with newe perillous practises, nor to contribute any such against thenglish people. Wherfore Eugenius, the Romane Bisshopp, having intelligence that all men were thus generally affected, made as it were an assured accompt of peace, and sent as soone as might be Nicholas the cardinall againe into Fraunce, who anon upon his comming thither, appoynted the meeting to be at the towne of Arras, whither came *Ad urbem* ambassadours from king Henry; Henry cardinal of Winchester, *Atrebatium.* and Henry archbisshopp of Yorke, William earle of Suffolke, and John earle of Huntington, as chiefe in commission concerning *A treatye* that treatie. Also the French ambassadours; the archbisshop of *at Arras.* Rhemes, the duke of Burbon, Arthure earle of Richmonde, and divers other gentlemen of woorshipp. The Burgoignion also sent his ambassadours; the bisshops of Liege, Cambray, and Arras, with many other woorthie personnages of honorable estimation. In this great assemble, after muche reasoning, Nicholas the cardinall, a man of an approved judgement, was made by all their consentes umpire in the cause. He againe required every mans opinion, to thende he might judge uprightly. The English ambassadours demanded that the Frenche king might be declared to holde of the king of England. Againe, the Frenche of thother faction would have the kingdome of Fraunce free, and not to holde of any other. Nicholas, esteeming it no time then to geve judgement as concerning the title and right of the crowne of Fraunce, proponed openly suche lawes of league as for the present state of thinges he adjudged indifferent for both parties. But both parties refused them. And so, without any conclusion in the matter they came for, thassemblie departed. But thereby grewe that the Burgoignions and Frenchemen begonne to treate of trewce, and to talke of peace betwixt them twaine; which Phillipp himselfe, duke of Burgoigne, had, for many causes before mencioned, desired in his heart longe before. And so peace was concluded upon these maner of condicions: that king Charles should depart from, unto *Perona.* the duke of Burgoigne, the townes of Amiens, Corbie, Perone, St. Quintines, Abbevile, and the counties of Artois, Pontieu, and *Bononi.* Bullonnoys, besides sundry other places adjoyning upon Burgundie, which had been of the dominion of his auncestours. Many other thinges promised the Frenche king, which he could not afterward performe; for he durst not denye the Burgoignion any his demaundes, as one who thought himselfe forthwith fortunate if with such an adversary he might be able to conclude a peace, though not honorable, and as he would desire, yet necessary, and in respect of the present state very commodious, which was to his great advauntage after, as he conceaved even then that it would prove. Moreover, when as they chaunced to meete within fewe dayes after, it is reported that king Charles did salute the duke in this sort: ' I wish you good fortune also, nowe finally at the last I finde myselfe voyde of feare, and delivered from great cares, for that you, the mightiest prince in Fraunce, next to the king, and of all other men in that nation best accompted, are returned againe to your countrey, according to our desire; for this saying of the Gospell was fixed ever in my minde : Every kingdome devided against itselfe shalbe destroyed. O Lorde, howe much was I affearde, least that should have happened by our dissension. But nowe the matter is safe, when you will joyne with me in carefulnes to repell thenglish men, our common enemies, with all diligence out of Fraunce, and that care you will have, as I trust. Assure yourselfe I am readie to shewe you any honorable pleasure that I can.' Hereunto the Burgoignion aunswered, that he would indevor himselfe not to fayl of his dutie in any poynt.

When the league was made, the Burgoignion made more haste The duke of
of nothing then speedily to dispatche ambassadours to king Burgundie sent ambas-
Henry into Englande, to let him understand that he was wery sadors to
with that longe warres, and the dayly complaintes of his subjectes, treate of
which from day to day receaved greater and greater damage of the peace be-
Frenche, who lamented and openly complained, that he was the veen H 6. & the kinge
onely man who releeved, enforced, and armed the English nation of France.
against his owne countrey, and that was more carefull to retayne
them in the lande of Fraunce, then to restore king Charles, his
cousin of bloud. Finally, that he was constrained to make peace
with king Charles ; and, forasmuch as king Charles offered very
indifferent and honorable conditions of peace, therefore he willed
them to exhort king Henry in his name to agree to that league.
But indeede the Burgoignon, whose owne conscience accused him
of woorthie and notable reproche, sent that ambassage, rather to
avoyde blame, to thende that thereby he might wipe away the note
of that fowle fact, because he was reported tretcherously and
traiterously to have revolted from thamitie of Englande, then that
he desired greatly in heart any good to thenglish affaires : when
thambassage was hearde, all men there present were so kindled
with the shamefulnes of such dealing, as that they could not holde
in their anger, nor moderate themselves therein, nor yet refraine
from speech, but called the Burgonion a traitor, a false and craftie
man. But after that this breache of league and fidelitie was bruted A great tu-
abrode, they proceeded from brawling to blowes ; for the common- mult aised in Lon on
altie, stirred togethers by reason of this unthankfull message, be- against the
ganne so farre forth furiously to invade all kinde of Flemminges gs for the
then being in London, as that many were wounded, many killed, falshod of the duke of
before the multitude could, by open proclamation, be appeased. Burgundie.
The kinges gratious goodnes was willing that his subjectes should H. 6. his
refraine from shedding of innocent bloud, and himselfe the meane r to the
while aunswered thambassadours, that they should admonish the Burgoyne ambassa-

dores.

duke from him, not to become enemy to thenglish people without
cause, but rather with reverence to continue olde amitie, which
better was then newe warres, and that he should not be so unad-
vised as to chaunge certainties for uncertainties; therfore he would
wish him take good heede, least otherwise he should intermingle
the florishing state of his dominions with the causes of king
Charles almost desperate, and so should rashly revolt from prosperitie to adversitie. With this aunswere thambassadours were
dismissed; but in the meane time king Henry determined to
make the duke some such busines, as that entangled therewithall
he shoulde the lesse be able with his forces to ayde the Frenche
king.   And therfore he sent forthwith secret messengers into
Flaunders, to stirre up with money the heades men of cities to
innovations, whereunto they were wont of their owne naturall
disposition to be much inclined. The messengers did their devoir,
and, for olde acquaintance sake, first assayed the Gantays, but
they nothing prevailed, for those people sawe apparently that the
forreine affayres of England would dayly decay. These thinges
were done in the yere of our salvation 1435, which yere was
famous by the death of John duke of Bedforde, an exceeding good
man in time of peace, and in warres most valiant, who dyed of
sicknes at Paris in the woorst time that could be for the common
wealth.   His corps was caried to Roane, and buried in the chiefe
churche there.

John duke
f ed   de
died aud
buryed at

After the duke of Bedforde, being regent of Fraunce, was dead,
all thinges fell to nought, so as it might well appere that they
lacked a Regent, for then the Frenche people, almoste voyde of fere,
enterprised, not onely to revolt, but openly to take armes against
thenglish.   And so even at that instant chaunced great alteration
of thenglish affaires.   Howbeit thenglish men did not faint and
geve over their cause, but by generall assent committed the chiefe
and principall government to Edmonde duke of Sommersett and-

Richard duke of Yorke, in which two all their whole hope was The dukes
reposed.   They sent forthwith Robert lord Willoughbie, to Paris, of Somerset and Yorke
for succor and ayde of the towne : but king Charles, advaunced made Re-
with such fortunate successe, after his forces were augmented by France.
ayde of men from the duke of Burgoigne, sent Arthure, admirall of
Fraunce, with a good part of his armie to besiege St. Denises, St. Denes
hoping verily after the gayning of that towne to bring in subjec- taken by the
tion Paris also : Arthure did as he was commaunded, he marched Frenche.
speedily to St. Denises, and within fewe dayes tooke it by force ; Parish-anes muti-
after which attempt happily atchieved, he proceeded to Paris, of nied against
whose comming, after that the citizens understoode, supposing the lishe and
time to be nowe come when as they might safely revolt, they set submytted Paris to
sodenlye with great furie upon thenglish people, and all at once, the kinge of
as well men pursued them with weapon through streetes and crosse France.
wayes as women from windowes and batelmentes of their houses
cast downe stones and hott water upon their heades.   Robert
lordé Willoughbie was within with garrison, as is before shewed,
who, contending awhile to appease thenvyous people, when he sawe
himselfe not able to withstande, fled into the towre, which is right
over against the church of St. Anthony.   In the meane time
Arthure, perceaving an uprore to be through the whole towne, approched the gates, and finding them set wide open very early in
the morning by the citizens, entered, and by and by assayed to
assault forceably the place which thenglish men helde, who defended themselves a fewe dayes valiantly, because they hoped
uppon reliefe from the dukes of Sommersett and Yorke.   But the
dukes made them no helpe, not knowing that they had drawen
themselves to that streight, by reason that thenemy so occupied
and kept all passages, as that they could have no certaine intelligence : for the rumor of revolt was so vehement, as that they
thought verily the lord Willoughbie, with all the garrison, eyther
taken or in so huge tumult and rage of people to be slaine.   Wher-

forc the lorde Willoughbie, hopelesse in the ende of ayde, yeelded the place by composition, and repaired with his men safe to Roane. And so Paris, the chiefe and principall citie in all Fraunce, was recovered againe by the Frenche, fifteen yeres after it had been brought in subjection of thenglish nation, which was the yere of our salvation 1436.

1436.

After the losse of Paris was divulged abrode through Fraunce, then generally almost all thenglish people utterly forsooke the townes beyonde the seas ; they thought, esteemed, and assured themselves to have from thenceforth no certaine place of refuge in any thereof; no further courage, no policie, nor any sufficient force of armie ; which opinion surely, amongst all other men tooke first place in the minde of Phillipp duke of Burgoigne : for that he at that time, muche moved that king Henry had a little before labored the Gantoys and other Flemminges to rebellion, marched forth with a huge and perillous armie to waste and spoyle thenglish boundes. He came to Callis, he besieged it, and with all his forces assayed to winne it, and at the same time, deviding his armie, gave assault to Guynes, a towne adjoyning : but the townesmen fortified against thenemy, not onely with munition and men, but much more by nature of the place, defended themselves with great magnanimitie, which thinges when the Burgoignion understoode, esteeming that he must goe another way to worke for the compelling of them to yeeld then he had begoon withall, drove this onely drifte, to debarre them of all victuall and supplye, whereby he should by famine force them to yeelde : and so placing his souldiers all over in stacions, he occupied the whole shore : he beatt them with goonn, dart, and arrowe, day and night, that not a man durst peepe over the wall to annoy his enemy, or yet to make defence. While as the Burgoignion continued the siege in this sort, the duke of Glocester, with an armie furnished in all poyntes, made haste out of Englande to succour his people. When the duke of Burgoigne hearde of

Callis be-
seeged by
the duke
of Bur-
goyne.

his terrible approche, and that he lay upon thother shore awayting The duke o Bur- o ſne bearinge of d e of Glosteres arrivall at Call raised his seege.
the winde to transport, he was past hope of gayning the towne:
and so in the dead of the night, forsaking the siege, drewe home-
warde. The duke of Glocester was at Callis well early in the
morning, and issuing to the tentes of his enemies, gott great praye:
for they, fearfully forsaking their stations, had lefte part of their
cariages of fine force. Afterwarde with armie well arrayed he
proceeded to spoyle the confynes of his enemy, and entering thereunto he wasted all thinges with sworde and fire; he tooke every
where great bootie, and he did not onely destroye the fieldes, but
set fire also upon castle and towne. Thus allured with spoyle, he
marched further forwarde, and with light assault he annoyed
townes, into the which the rurall people were gathered for feare.
So finally raging even unto St. Omers without any encounter, he The duke of Glostere in to Eng- land A truce concluded H 6 and the duke of Burgoyne, yet in his wyves name it went.
returned with great bootie, first to Callis, and from thence into
Englande. After these thinges there was, by persuasion of frendes,
a treuce treated betwixt king Henry and the duke of Burgoigne
for a fewe yeres: which were in the ende concluded with the wife
which Phillipp had the same time, for he had three; and of the
last called Isabell he begott and lefte behinde him his sonne
Charles. All thinges afterwarde betweene the king of England and the Burgoigne were (by report) done in her name:
which may be thought to have been done, for that neyther it
shoulde be saide that the king of Englande did beleeve the Burgoignion, whom he had approved not long before to be disloyall,
nor that the Frenche king should have any cause to conceave
suspition when he should understande that the trewce was taken
not with the duke but with his wife, which her husbande was
bounde by no lawe to observe.

During that time, dyed Henry archbisshop of Yorke, unto The deathe of Henry, archebus- shop of Yorke.
whom succeeded John Chemp, in order of bishopps the fiftie.
About that time also dyed Katherine, king Henryes mother, who

Katherine
ther died
at this
tyme
Owen Te-
ther mar-
ried e-
rine the
widow of
had by her
3 sonns.

Two earles
created.

Owene Te-
hedded.

Henry
arl
Richmond
borne.

Richard E.
ar
wick
diethe.

Lewes the
g
Fraunce his
sonne mar-
ryethe the
Kynge of
t
dau hter

of Scottes
by

racye.

was interred at Westminster, in the sepulchre of her predecessors. This woman, after the death of her husband, king Henry the Fifth, being but yonge in yeres, and thereby of lesse discretion to judge wnat was decent for her estate, married one Owen Tyder, a gentleman of Wales, adorned with wonderfull giftes of body and minde, wno derived his pedigree from Cadwallider, the last king of Brittons, of whom she conceaved and brought forth three sonnes, Edmonde, Jaspar, and the thirde, who was a monke of the order of St Benet, and lived not longe after, and one daughter, who was made a noonne. Afterwarde kinge Henry made Edmond earle of Richmonde, and Jaspar earle of Pembroke, because they were his brothers on his mothers side. After the death of queene Katherine, the saide Owen was twice committed to warde by the duke of Glocester, because he had been so presumptuous as by marriage with the younge Queene to intermixe his bloudd with tne noble rase of kinges, and in the ende was beheaded. This Edmonde, earle of Richmonde, begott of Margarete, daughter unto the duke of Sommersett, a sonne called Henry, who, as otherwhere in place convenient shalbe declared obteyning the kingdome, was nominated king Henry the Seventh. The very selfsame time Richard earle of Warwick dyed at Roane, his body was brought into Englande, and buried in a newe churche at Warwicke: also James, king of Scottes, intermaried with king Charles by placing his daughter Margarete to Lewes, the saide Charles his sonne, and so king James, forgetfull of the league which he had made a fewe yeres before with king Henry, as opportunie served, mustered out a newe supplye of men to goe to his armie, which lay as yet at Carleil, and was withall aboutward to make warre of Englande, when as he was sodenly taken by the way; for Gualter, his uncle, earle of Atholl, a factious man, and that aspired to the kingdom, made a conspiracie with certaine desperate rebelles, and caused the king to be killed upon the sodaine at St. Johnston, which was—

which was no hurt to Englande : for, seeing that king James was
a passing valiant man, thoccasion serving, as chaunced afterwarde,
he would undoubtedly have scourged England cruelly during the
factious stirre and division betwixt king Henry and Edwarde.
James, his sonne, the second of that name, succeeded his father,
who, even from the beginning entangled with civill sedition, was
rather offensive to his owne people then to thenglish, which we
will speake of at large and more aptly afterwarde. Nowe was come
the seventeene yere of king Henries reigne, which was of our salvation the 1439, when at Westminster, besides London, a par- 1439.
liament was called, for the right and fitt establishment of thinges A parlia-
concerning as well civill government at home, as the warres abrode, Westmin-
in which parliament was argued, provided for, and enacted many ster.
thinges necessary for the warres, and no small number of such
statutes as were requisite for the state of the common wealth :
amongst which this was one, that it should not be lawfull for mer- Marchant
chauntes straungers to sell their merchaundises brought into the strangeres
realme to any other then Englishmen, to thende they should not to sell to
thereby engrosse and gather into their handes thonely trade thereof, any heare
which lawe is observed at this day as very commodious for the lishemen.
commonwealth.

In the meane time king Charles, after he had brought in subjection Paris, and many other places within two yeres before, nowe
was he in full hope easily to recover Normandie ; for from thence
he had intelligence that the countrey was geven somewhat to
sedition, wherefore he sent Arthure admirall of Fraunce, and with
him John duke of Alanson, with a mightie armie into Normandie.
They with great speede came to Avranches, and besieged it forthwith. That towne is situate upon an hill in that coast of the
country which butteth upon the British ocean, fortified with high
walles, and parfytely well manned. When thenemy had continued
siege before the towne a longe time, beholde, upon the sodeine,

John lorde Talbot, and Thomas earle of Dorchester, with an armie
well appoynted, came and encamped themselves as neere the enemies as could be, meaning to provoke them to battaile. The
Frenche were so farre from taking that offer, as that they fortified
and kept themselves more straightlye within their trenches, which
when thenglishmen understoode, removing from thence about a
mile and better, they choose out a place not very commodious for
themselves to fight in, thereby to make their enemies lesse afearde.
But when they could not allure the Frenche to the fielde by that
meane neyther, they tooke up their tentes, and in the view of
thenemy entered Avranches; from thence they issued, and perceaving the French without feare to be scattered more lously
abrode, put them to flight, and the passages being debarred they
mett with many, whom they slewe in the encounter. At the same
time another hoste of Frenche men, running rashly a forowe, even
to the walles of Roane, were discomfited by Thomas Tirrell.
Emongst these matters, when as king Charles, notwithstanding
so many overthrowes, litle doubted that it was possible to interrupt the prosperous course of his proceedinges, yea, dayly looked
for better successe, beholde, an huge storme hanging over his
head, so miserable, so wicked, and so fowle, as the woorse thereof

Lewes Dol-
f
France
conspired
g ns.
king
Charles his
could not chaunce. For Lewes, king Charles sonne, a yonge
man of monstrous disposition and frowarde condition, seeking
soveraintie before his time, conspired with such like as himselfe
against his father; the heades of which faction were John duke of
Alanson, and another John, who not many yeres before had succeeded to Lewes his father, both dukes of Burbon; and gathering
an armie, tooke upon him the government of the realme, to rule all
thinges, not according to his fathers direction, but after his owne
fantasie; which thing when king Charles knewe, though he were
wrapped in wonderfull dolours, exclaiming that he was borne to
miserie, for that, as though it had beene but a small matter to

have fought, thus, many yeres within his owne native soile, with straungers, with his owne subjectes for defence of his royall state and dignitie, he should nowe also be forced to fight for soveraintie with his owne sonne. Yet, being a man of readie witt and great courage, as one acquainted with adversitie, he was not utterly dismayed; but supposing it best to stay the beginning, before any violence should be used against him, he called togethers his trustie noblemen and councellers, he deliberated with them howe to shoonn so great a daunger. The better part thought that it was not to be avoyded with warres, but with good councell and lenitie. Wherefore, first of all, letters were sent in the name of king Charles every waye to the cities, straitly charging and commaunding that no man should geve eare to his sonnes commaundement; then was pardon promised to all the conspiratours; lastly, grave and wise noble men dealt earnestly with Lewes and the dukes for reconciliation of peace; and gave plaine demonstration, that to contende nowe for the crowne in suche time as was never more troublesome, was nothing else but utterly to overthrow their countrey, which by forreyne enemies was almost destroyed alreadie. By this pollicie and persuasions, it came to passe that the conspiratours layde armor aside, and were receaved anon into the kinges favor. And so this pernitious enterprise, which was like to have overturned the whole state of the common wealth, was stayed before ever it was put in practise.

The Dolmytted to his father.

Thenglish men hearing the while of this civill discorde in Fraunce, renewed the warre with greater courage, and, having recovered a few fortes before lost in Normandie, were nowe making haste to besiege Paris, when, as besides report of reconciliation betweene Lewes and his father, newes were also brought that king Charles was gone to besiege Ponthoyse. John lorde Clifforde, a notable expert man of warre, defended the same with a great garrison of souldiers, whereof when intelligence was had, the duke

The kinge of France tem e the wynyng of Ponthoyse.

CAMD. SOC. K

of Yorke and the lorde Talbott, with a maine hoste of choise souldiers, marched thither, and, pighting their tentes nigh unto their enemies, offered the battaile; but king Charles, trusting to dispatch the matter without fight or hazarde, refused the fielde, and, leaving part of his army to continue the siege, removed his campe; whereof intelligence had, the duke of Yorke was also advertised that the garrison within the towne was of force sufficient to defende itselfe, and supposing, therefore, that it should not be needfull for him to rest there any longer, purseweth thenemy, and sendeth before the lorde Talbot with horsemen to espye a place where he might by anye meane allure the king to battaile; but the king could not be drawen thereunto in that place neyther; and so the duke with great spoyle returned to Roane. Emongst

A treatye of peace at Calys, but not effected. these great troubles of warre. there was, by meane of letters sent from tne pope to and fro oftentimes to both the kinges, another treatie of peace dealt in at Callis by ambassadours of both sides, which when it could not be concluded upon, the matter was re-

The duke of Orleance released out of wheare he had conty-ᴜᴜᴄᴜ ᴢᴏ yeares. ferred to another time. About that time was Charles duke of Orleance brought to Callis to be the chiefe maker of that peace, who dealing like an honourable good man, when there was no fault in him to the hynderance thereof, was at the last lett home, twenty-six yere after that he had been taken in the battaile of Agincourt. He was all that while deteyned captive because he was not able to paye his raunsome, and yet in the ende was not delivered without money neither. In the beginning of the yere folowing, the dukes of Yorke and Sommersett, who wanted no good will, spared no travaile, nor were negligent in any poynt touching their charge, conferring togethers about the warres, resolved that best was to invade in divers places, to thintent that when thenemie should be urged to make head against every particular invader, the force of the warres should be layde off from the boundes of Normandie (for the which they were afearde) unto

such time as some happy event might alter the present countenance
of frowning fortune; which device truely, considering the time, was
allowed of all the residue as very provident. And so in the beginning of the springe Robert lorde Willoughbie was commaunded
with a great crewe of souldiers to spoyle the territorie about
Amiens. Also John lorde Talbot was sent with another companie
to besiege Diep. Themselves the meane time prepared to destroye
the boundes of Anjow. When the lorde Willoughbie came unto the
borders of Amiens, because there should no signe of invasion
appere, which is chiefly understoude by raising of fire, he therefore forbadd the burning of villages, whereby it chaunced that the
horsmen came upon the pesantes, fearing nothing, before ever they
could flye into townes, and killed of them many thowsands. The
Frenche garrison, who lay in the holdes adjoyning, assembled
upon thalarme made by reason of the great noyse of rurall people,
and set forwarde to encounter thenemy: they joyned battaile, and
the same was for a while mutually mainteyned with great courage;
but at the last the Frenche force, daunted with the death of their
felowes that gave the first charge, turned the backe, whereof part
were killed in the flight by thenglish men, part spoyled in the
way by thearle of Saint Paule, who ayded thenglish. More then
six hundred souldiers of Fraunce were killed with the sworde in
that conflict. And so the lorde Willoughbie, loden with huge
praye, returned after this fortunate exploite into Normandie.
Also the duke of Sommersett drove away great bootie from the
cities of Britaine. During which season the lorde Talbot mightily
besieged Diepe, where was dayly skirmishing on both sides; he The lo.
pight his tentes upon an hill, and made generall thereof William Tal_eott
Poyntes, a carefull man of his charge; himselfe defended certaine Deepe.
bastiles. Nowe was the siege prolonged a great while, when in
fine king Charles sent, to releeve the towne, Lewes his sonne with
a maine armie. He anon upon his arrivall there tooke on hande

to assault the bastiles, where was a cruell conflict. At the first
ioncke many fell on both sides, and many also were sore wounded;
every man ranne to and fro for his advauntage, removing then-
signes hither and thither; thone laboured to holde thother
straite within the bastiles, thother to repulse and keepe afarre
off thenemy. At the last they came to hand strokes; then was
about the bastiles a sore fight; but in thende thenglish men
being expelled, withdrewe themselves into the campe, and so, out
of hope to gayne the towne, they raysed the siege, and retired to
Roane.

Thenglishe
from St.
ies.

A truce
for 18
monthes

England
d France.
H. 6. ma-
ryed Mar-
g re da.
to the duke
of Anjou
e
of Sicily.

A parlea-
o-
moned.

In this meane time, king Charles assailing by force the towne of
St. Selerine, was there of thenglish powere put to repulse. While
tnis stirre was abrode otherwhere, Phillipp duke of Burgoigne
made warre to Peter of Lucenbrowgh, earle of St. Paule. because
he yet stood and helde of thenglish partie, whom the duke easily
overcame, and caused, contrary to his fayth and promise geaven unto
the duke of Bedforde, to joyne with king Charles, which affeebled
no litle the force of Englande. Nowe forasmuch as during this
time the English affaires were nothing iocunde, and the French
successe also brought unto themselves slaughter, mayhame, and
many mischiefs, there was yet another treatie of peace betwixt
the two kinges, which, when it could not be concluded, a trewce
onely was taken for eightene monthes. Thus the rage of warre
ceased for a while, and king Henry tooke to wife Margarete,
daughter to Rhenate duke of Anjow and king of Sicily, a yonge
lady exceeding others of her time, as well in beautie as wisedome,
endeued with an hault courage above the nature of her sexe,
according as her noble actes (whereof we will treate in place convenient) have manifestly declared. During this season also certaine English captaines returned into Englande, desirous to see
their countrey, children, and wives, and also for the preparing of
newe supplye to fill upp the bandes of their olde armie. And so

not longe after kinge Henry held a parliament, wherein many and
divers consultations were had as concerning preparation for warres,
which in the ende every man thought meete to be foreseene, insomuch it was apparent that the Frenche king was wholly bent, immediately after the trewce ended, to renewe the same, wherefore
it was enacted, that money should be levied, and souldiers mustered : but the meane while to gratifie the people, a priviledge was
graunted, that when a quarter (which is a kinde of measure) of An Acte
wheate is solde for 6s. 8d., rye for fowre, barley for three, and not for trans-
above, that it should be lawfull for every man to bye and transport corne.
those graines beyond the seas, so that it were not to the kinges
enemies. This Act was afterwards confirmed by king Edwarde
the Fourth as profitable for the common wealth.

These thinges thus ordered, such provision was made for the
establishment of the realme as that it might appere the king from
thenceforth would have more care for the common utilitie then for
any one mans profite. Lastly, it was enacted, that certaine noblemen
should be exalted in honor at the kinges pleasure, whom I finde to
have been Humfrey Stafforde, and Henry, sonne of Richarde, of
whose ende we have before remembred, earles of Warwicke, whereof Creatyon
—thone remayned earle of Warwicke, thother was created duke of of earles.
Buckingham ; also Thomas earle of Dorchester, and William earle
of Suffolke were both twaine made marquises : but William not
long after was created duke. Also John earle of Huntington was
made duke of Exeter. I finde moreover, that John lorde Talbot,
who had so well deserved of his countrey, was made earle of
Shrewsbury. In that assemble the duke of Gloucester, foreseing An oratyon
·within himself that in continuance there would be alteration of made by
the duke of
thinges which would appall the courage of men very much, made Glostere.
a long oration, persuading all men to endevour themselves dutifully
for defence of the common wealth, because he knewe assuredly
that thenemies sought time and oportunitie to beguile and deceave,
wherefore he thought it not meete to tary unto thende of the

trewce shoulde approche.   These thinges did the duke instill into
the heades of thaudience, rather to suppresse the presumptuous
boldnes of some, whom I suppose he conjectured would inces-
.santly seeke his death, then for that he mistrusted the Frenche
fidelitie, who, weried with continuall bloudshed, were as loth a
good while before as thenglish men were to have the like any
longer.   But good councell could not profite perverse and wicked-

1445.   mindes.   This was the yere of our salvation 1445 ; in the which
Henry   Henry Chicheley, archbisshop of Canterbury dyed, xxix. yeres after+
h echeley
died.   ne had sitt in that see.   This sage fatner, perceaving well that the
dispositions of men were by learning principally holpen to attaine
unto, and reverentlye embrace vertue, had more care of nothing
then to procure that his countrymen of Englande might become
learned ; wherefore he builded two colledges at Oxforde, wherein
he placed two companies of schollers studious of learning, and gave
possessions for the reliefe of them that should applye learning ;
All Souls   thone whereof was dedicate to the memorie of All Soules, thother
S
Bernards   to St. Bernard , as two sure pillers of all vertues, the exercise
college in   whereof is at this day fervently frequented in these two houses,
erected by   insomuch that neyther labour nor expence of the founder hath
Henry   been spent in vaine.   To this Henry succeeded John Stafforde,
Chicheley.
in order of bisshops the three score and one.   But let us come to
the civill dissensions.

Civil dis-   While that the trewce continued, though there lacked nothing at
ce   )r
grewe in   home for the which men needed to be continually carefull in
England.   minde, yet, by meane of a woman, sprange up a newe mischiefe
The au-   that sett all out of order.   King Henry was a man of milde and
thores co-
menda-   plaine-dealing disposition, who preferred peace before warres,
cione of   quietnes before troubles, honestie before utilitie, and leysure before
H. VI.
busines ; and, to be short, there was not in this world a more pure,
more honest, and more holye creeture.   There was in him honest
shamfastnes, modestie, innocencie, and perfect patience, taking all
humane chances, miseries, and all afflictions of this life in so good

part as though he had justly by some his offence deserved the same. He ruled his owne affections, that he might more easily rule his owne subjectes ; he gaped not after riches, nor thirsted for honor and worldly estimation, but was carefull onely for his soules health ; such thinges as tended to the salvation thereof he onely esteemed for good ; and that very wisely ; such againe as procured the losse thereof he only accompted evill. On thother side, Margaret his wife, a woman of sufficient fore--cast, very desirous of renowne, full of policie, councell, comely behaviour, and all manly qualities, in whom appeared great witt, great diligence, great heede, and carefulnes : but she was of the kinde of other women, who commonly are much geven and very readie to mutabilitie and chaunge. This woman when she perceaved the king her husbande to doo nothing of his owne head but to rule wholly by the duke of Glocesters advise, and that him- self tooke no great heede nor thought as concerning the govern- ment, determined to take upon her that charge, and by litle and litle to deprive the duke of that great authoritie which he had ; least she also might be reported to have litle witt, who would suffer her husbande being now of perfect yeres to be under another mans government.   And so this Margarete labored soone after to bring to passe that which she had purposed.   But after that this woman had once enterprised the matter of her owne will and disposition, there were forthwith a companye readie to sedition, prompt to use violence, and very meete to make mischiefe and slaughter ; who, seeking to stirre upp envie againste the duke of Glocester, did urge forwarde, exhort, and perswade her, to looke into the reve- newes of the Crowne, to call for an accompt thereof, and so should she well understande that the duke had used the same, not for the common wealth, but for his owne private commoditie.   The king of Sicile also did no litle egge on his daughter Margarete, that she and her husbande should assume the government. With these persuasions the queene incensed, taketh on hande with her

[margin notes:] Queen Margarets amb tion towards the Glosters governe-

The duke Gloster doi ages looked

husband king Henry to rule the realme. And though the same
could be accompted nothing els but (as the olde proverbe is) to
till the grounde with an oxe and an asse, yet did she with great
haultines undergo that charge, who firste of all other thinges did
not onely cleere sequestre the duke of Glocester from dealing in
publike affaires, but also afterwarde thought him unworthie to be
protected from thinjurye of his enemyes : for not longe after divers

noble men conspired against the duke, and appeached him of
sundry criminall offences, but principally for that he had caused
certaine condemned persons to be executed more greevously then
the lawe of Englande appoynted : for the duke being a severe man,
because he was skillfull in the lawe which is called civill, and
caused malefactors to be sharply corrected, procured thereby
against himselfe the hatred of ungratious people, who feared due
punishment for their mischievous and naughtie factes. What
shall we say, that even at this day the common lawyers, when
their pleasure is to find some detestable fault with the civill lawe,
which the more they be ignorant of in that the more they hate it,
bring forth this example of severitie, as though sharpe punishment
of offenders stoode not with the profite of the common wealthe, and
as though greater fault did not require greater torment. Notwithstanding that the duke answered such matters as were laide
against him with great commendation, yet, because his death
was alreadie determined, he nothing helped his cause, saving
that he was somewhat lesse greeved in minde, when as hearby
it fell out that he neyther knewe of his condemnation nor
prefixed time of death : for the conspiratours were affeared least it
should cause some uprore amongst the people, if that a man so
well beloved of the comminaltie should be put to death openlye,

and therefore determined to execute him unawares. And so a
parliament was sommoned in the kinges name to be holden at
thabbey of Bury, whither at the day appoynted repaired the noble
men, and among them the duke of Glocester, who was taken

—sodenly the night folowing and stranguled, the woorst example that
ever was hearde of ; all his retinew were committed immediatly: but
after he was killed, never one of them suffered, onely divers of them,
to aggravate their reproche, were brought to the place of execution,
and straite waye pardoned. The dukes corps was had to the abbey
of St. Albones, and there interred. By these pernitious practises
of his enemies was this noble duke overthrowen, xxv. yeres after
that he had governed this lande. Thus may we see that (as Cicero
saith) to them which be in authoritie, neither court, the chiefe
helpe of all men, neyther house, the common refuge of every man,
no nor bed, wherein we are to take our rest, is voyde from the perill
of death. But it seemeth, that the title of Glocester geven unto
earles and dukes for honors sake hath been fetall, and foreshewed
the destruction of them who should enjoy it, forasmuch as, before
this Humfrey, Hugh Spencer, and Thomas of Woodstocke sonne to
Edwarde the Thirde, thone earle, thother duke of Glocester,
ended their lives by miserable violence : also, after them, king
Richard the Thirde, duke of Glocester, was slaine in battaile within
the realme ; so that the title thereof may as well be applyed pro-
verbially unto unfortunate personages as sometime was Seianes
horse. But againe to the matter. After that the rumour of the
dukes death was spredd abrode, many were sodenly astonied with
feare, others utterly abhorred the fact, so much was it thought to
all men an outragious and extreme crueltie. But surely the common wealth sustained thereby most losse, the stay whereof depended upon no man so much at that very time as upon him
alone, which was apparent by the event of matters folowing : for
surely after the shamefull slaughter of this duke good men forsooke the court, in whose places succeeded such for the most part
as, seeking themselves for the soveraintie, opened the gate easily
to newe factions and division.

The yere folowing, which was the 1447 of our salvation, dyed

The duke
ter mur-
thered
The dukes
followers
con-
...ed
yet none
die , b t
ardoned
A good
sayenge of
Cicero.
The au-
thores ob-
servacion
of the tytle
...ces-
ter.

Henry the cardinall bisshop of Winchester, who was the onely man by whose high wisdome and puissant wealth king Henry might have been so supported that, all feare sett aside, he might without doubt have continued in perpetuall peace at home. And

yet it was thought that William Wainflete, who succeeded him in tne bisshopricke of Winchester, was able to supplye the great losse which king Henry had susteyned by reason of his death : for that man, because of his upright administration of justice and prudence, was long time lord chancellor of England. Amongst many of his notable deedes this one was above the residue most excellent : that he, to thende his countrey might more and more daylye abounde with learned men, builded at Oxforde a college for suche as shoulde be geven to learning, in a very fitt and large place, and gave thereunto possessions, the revenewes whereof might mainteyne them with sufficient livelyhode : the woorke was dedi-

cated to St. Mary Magdalene, that like as that good woman refreshed sometime the feete of Christe with sweete oyntment, so (she being the patrones of that place) good wittes might be there –fed perpetually with the heavenly licoure of learning, which of them there is doone with diligence. But as touching the parliament which was appoynted for the woorking of the saide wicked traine, after the horrible murther committed, there was in the same no matter debated woorthie of memorie, save that William

marquise of Suffolke was made duke, who was increased with that dignitie because (as after was manifest) he had beene the principall contriver of that develish devise, to kill the said duke of

Glocester. He was chief author also that a sore subsidie was set upon the people, whereat all men rather inwardly grudged then openly withstoode, because they longed to be out of that place where such heynous attempt had been perpetrate and done : for when as the better part of noble men thought themselves nowe berefte of free speeche in parliament, all, by and by, partly oppressed with dolor, partly having brought to passe their practises, departed home, and so thassemble was dissolved.

While this stirre was in Englande, Francisce, an Arragonoys, a knight of Normandie, of singular vertue, and very serviceable, who had alway taken part with Englande, tooke, by stealth, from Francisce duke of Britaine, and spoyled the towne of Foun- *Fulgeras.* giers, adjoyning upon Normandie, and very riche with the wealth of the olde inhabitauntes : after which damage receaved, the duke advertised Charles the Frenche king of thinjurye done unto him ; and, because the trewce yet continewed, besought the king to demaunde againe of thenglish men that which the Arragonoys had thus reft, contrary to right, for that he was on his side. When king Charles had heard the dukes complaint, he dispatched, forthwith, ambassadours to the duke of Soommersett, requiring restitution of Fougiers, and of the spoyle taken during the trewce. Whereunto the duke of Soommersett aunswered, that he liked not of thattempt, because it was done both without his and the kinges commaundement. But if king Charles would sende ambassadours to Loviers, *Louerium* he would likewise sende thither some grave personages to treate of restitution : thambassadours mett at the place, and conferring togethers, adjudged that Fougiers, with the goodes, was to be restored, and the damages to be recompenced : which to doo Frauncisce denayed, and laide many reasons for his defence. Finally, when the Frenche ambassadours demaunded againe the goodes and possessions of their confederates ; and the Englishe affirmed, that it was not in their power to restore that which another man helde in possession ; and moreover, to avoid blame, promised, that if the Frenche king would require the premisses of the saide Fraunces by force of armes, they would not defende him : the meeting brake up without redresse or conclusion made. In the meane while the Frenche men, who, according to their hott and

fierce nature, kest in minde as well howe to be revenged of that
wronge as by what meane they might procure restitution unto their
confederates, tooke, by treason, Pountlarche, letting goe thenglish

The truse
et
England
and France
garrison, who, fearing no such matter, were surprised upon the
sodaine. And thus was the trewce broken, and warres begonne
againe. And yet because the dealing therein caried the color rather of injurie apert, than of any subtill sleight, the duke of Soommersett beganne to demaunde of the Frenche king restitution of
Pountlarche, not by armes, but by ambassadours ; but he aunswered that Pountlarche should be restored, so that Fougiers were
restored to the duke of Britaine. Howbeit, king Charles his drift
appeared shortly afterwarde, who, when he understoode the state
of England, after the death of the duke of Gloucester, to be voyde
of councell, and to burne with sedition, conceaved in minde, that
within short while he should be able to recover Normandie :
wherefore he determined not to slipp any part of that good lucke
and oportunitie, but to take time while time served. Wherefore
he devided and sent out his forces three severall wayes all at once,
and the fame of his former successe somewhat furthering the vic-

Mantenses.
Lexouiū.
torie, he brought into his obedience within fewe dayes, by composition, Mante and Lysieux, though not without losse of some of his
souldiers. The which exploite fortunately finished according to his
owne desire, king Charles, advauuced both in courage and force,

Vernone.
Vernon be-
gec
the
Frenche.
with earnest affection also of the armie, assayeth to winne by
assault Vernon, where, though thinhabitauntes were much dismayed with this sodaine attempt, yet, trusting to the garrison and
hoping of reliefe, they encouraged one another, and made resistance a good while with great valour : but after that ayde was dif-
ferred, contrary to their expectation, and longer than any of them
would have weened, they were forced to covenant with thenemy,
that if reliefe were not sent before a day certainly prefixed, so that

the English garrison might depart with bag and baggage, they
would yeeld. At whiche instant the duke of Soommersett came,
upon knowledge whereof king Charles raysed his siege.

Thus when as the warre so sodenly renewed before thende of
the treuce, then the whiche a greater mischiefe could not have
chaunced, was of itself matter ynough to trouble the heades of the
English captaines, besides that also the sodaine revolting of people
hindered them so, as they were not able to relieve their afflicted
state : for surely, while they prepared to succoure one citie, three or
foure, folowing fortune, fell from them to thenemy. The cause
wherof sprang especially for that the same was alreadie spreade
over all Fraunce, that since the death of the duke of Glocester
the people of Englande were, by factious division of the nobility,
diversly affected, and that William of a marquise lately made
duke of Suffolke, with divers others, who (as afterwarde plainely
appered,) were principall procurers to murther the duke of Glocester, did so molest, oppress, and with innumerable discommodities afflict the commonaltie of Englande, for thexacting and
gathering togethers of money, as that the mindes of men were not
set upon forreine warre, but vexed above measure howe to repell
private and domesticall injuries, and that therefore neyther pay for
the souldier, nor supplye for tharmie were, as neede required, put in
readines ; which mischiefes while the king gave no great regard
unto, neyther that Margarete his wife, who, notwithstanding she
had the government of the whole realme, was able to redresse ;
thereupon undoubtedly it came to psase that, after it was knowen
in what case the state of England stoode, both thenemy gathered
hart, and the Normanes and Aquitanes were so farre discouraged,
that, hopelesse of all ayde, they contended who might first revolt
to the Frenche. Therefore within fewe dayes after the bruit of so
great debilitie was blowen through Fraunce, the Frenche men
gained, almost with no busines at all, Constans, Gysors, Castle-

galiarde, Saint Lo, Fescant, Alanson, Newcastle, and in Gascoigny
Manlisson, with the castles thereof, being yeelded in thende by
thenglish men themselves, who, compelled by sodaine revoltinges
of the people, had retired thereinto. They tooke also by like
happ and successe the towne of Roane. This towne the duke of
Soommersett, and lorde Talbot, with other captaines of warfare,
defended for a while very valiantly and constantly, and would
without doubt have repulsed the present perill, if they had not
been more troubled to conserve the people in obedience then
to resist thenemy, who, notwithstanding seeking time incessantly to betray the towne, as soone as ever opportunitie served
to worke the feate, could be ruled by no meane, but receaved the
Frenche within the towne. Which thing once knowen, the captaines and garrison fledd into the castle. Here they helde themselves a fewe dayes, ever now and then annoying the towne with
shott: finally, both hope of ayde and victuall fayling, they were
forced to covenant with thenemy for safetie, and so departed to
Cane, which David Haule, the captaine thereof, a valliant and
pollitike warrier, kept with strong warde and watche. After these
thinges the Frenche men, pursuing the victorie, and imboldened
by fame of their atchieved enterprises, set forward to Hareflore,
and endeavoured to besiege it : Thomas Curson, a man of hault
courage, was captaine of the towne, who, notwithstanding he hearde
of the heavie event of Roane, was no whitt dismayed, but at the
firste assault destroyed many his enemies, which rashly assayed
with ladders to scale the walles. Afterwarde the Frenche man,
warned with his own losse, made trenches, planted his ordinance,
and battred the town continually. So the siege many dayes prolonged, when that Curson sawe no succours sent from his owne
nation, he lefte the towne to the Frenche. Not long after king
Charles arrived, and setting upon Hareflew, another towne by the
sea coast, on this side the river of Seyne, receaved it by compo-

sition. So farre from meane is fortune, who eyther favoureth or persecuteth too vehemently. While this stirre was otherwhere, Thomas Tirrell, having receaved anewe but very selender supplye of souldiers out of Englande, tooke on hande to besiege the towne of Liseaux, whereof he was master within a while, and, placing garrison therein, made haste towardes Cane, to joyne with Mathew Gough, who as we have before shewed, was taken at the siege of the castle of St. Selerine, and had a litle before redeemed himselfe, that they two togethers might somewhere encounter with thenemye, who was reported to be going to Cane, before he should come thither. But in that voyage himselfe, alone enterprising the very same day to joyne battaile with part of his enemies that he mett by chaunce, was, after much slaughter on both sides, put to flight: Thomas thother part of the French armie was alreadie arrived at Cane, which, his com-pany dis-comteted. because the discomfiture of Tirrel aforesaide had cutt off the citizens from all hope of reliefe, was within fewe dayes after yeelded upon composition that the duke of Soommersett, who was in the castle, with the residue of Englishmen, should have free libertie to depart. Uppon like condition also was yeelded the towne of Baieux, and Faloyse: but in the yeelding of Faloyse, over and besides the safetie graunted unto thenglishmen, the lorde Talbot, and all that were therein, were permitted to depart with armour, bagg and baggage: forasmuch as the Frenche men of an olde custome do boast and bragge, that their renowme and fame resteth not in golde and silver, but in dominion and conquest of the whole earth. By reason of mandie in which matters the remnant of Normans, all doubt sett aside, subjection yeelded, by ambassadours, into the obeysance of king Charles, so of France, that thonely castle of Chirrbrowhe, scituate upon the sea coast, except Chirr- remayned English. Thither lastly came the Frenche men, and after browghe, a fewe skirmishes thereabout they receaved the same also by com- also reco- position. The dukes of Soommersett and Yorke with the rest of vered by tharmie marched into Aquitaine, to helpe the decayed state thereof Frenche.

also. Thus lost king Henry all Normandie, thirtie yeres after his
father Henry the 5th had by armes recovered the same, which was
the yere of our salvation 1451, and the xxixth yere of his reigne.
About thende of the same yere departed this life Fraunces duke of
Brittaine, without yssue, by whose practises, as is even at this day
reported, his brother Gyles, a very noble man, was put to death.
Peter, another brother, succeeded him in possessions; but he
briefly bereft of life, Arthure his uncle was made duke; and he,
within two yere after, dyed of disease, without yssue, whereby
thinheritance descended to Fraunces the sonne of his brother
Richard.

After the conquest of Normandie, king Charles omitted no time
that fitt was for the warres, knowing very well that the fortune of
warre was often variable and subject to chaunge, and therefore
assoone as might be conducted his armie into Aquitaine, which he
reduced into his obeysaunce without much labour; for when the
fame of the towne of Roane lost came unto their eares, even then
mistrusting the forces of thenglish affaires, they seemed to foresee
that they should be compelled to come under subjection of the
Frenche. Although the dukes after their coming thither ceased
not to fortifie holdes, to supplye the decayed crewes of souldiers,
to exhort the people that they would remayne obedient and dutifull; also both by often letters and messengers to geve intelligence
unto king Henry concerning the hazarde of losing that province,
and to require ayde, yet none came out of Englande. Whereby it
fell out that the Aquitanes, seing afterwarde before their eyes
thenemy readie, as well to invade forceably as also to spoyle the
countrey, while that every man for himselfe regarded nothing els
but to defende his owne private fieldes, townes, and possessions at
home, were in that respect more negligent and fearfull to make
preparation for warre, least by resistance they might cause their
great losse. Yet thenglish nation, who of their owne naturall dis-

position are wont not to geve over, no not even at the very death,
endevoured with tooth and nayle to avert that adverse fortune ;
for seing that many of their people did revolt to the Frenche, and
that those of Cardeux beganne alreadie to be seditious, they encountered with thenemy by the way as he came and fought a
fielde not farre from the towne, which was mainteyned manfully,
but in the ende, oppressed with multitude, they were discomfited.
Many truely were killed, but some also taken ; yea, of the Frenche,
who were twise so many in number, were wanting tenn thousand,
who therfore lesse pursued thenemy, contenting themselves with
that victory though very blouddy, whereby finally they wanne all
Aquitaine ; for the forces and puissance of Englande were so
wasted with this overthrowe, that assoone as the cities adjoyning
hearde thereof, they sent forthwith to treate with the Frenche of
submission, and not longe after yeelded in very deede. After that
Bourdeaux was recovered, Baione, the last of all the cities in
Aquitane, came under the subjection of Fraunce. The Englishmen that were left alive, oppressed with so great calamities, made
repaire unto their shipps, under the conduct of the dukes of Soommersett and Yorke. Heare, when thenemy, who was glad of their
departure, did nothing urge nor hinder them, they prepared for
passage ; and so, after the redemption of captives, they tooke
shipping, lowsed forthwith, and with prosperous winde returned
into Englande. Thus was Aquitane lost, about 299 yeres after
that Henry the Second had receaved the possession thereof in the Aquitaine
name of dowrie of Aleonore his wife, as we have before mentioned loste to the
in the twelfth booke, which was the yeare of our Lorde 1153, and having
222 yeres after that king Henry the Thirde had recovered the same in
of Philip the Faire, king of Fraunce, being taken from John, his to England
father, a little before. This yere, wherein thenglish nation lost 299 yeares.
their dominion in Aquitane, was the yere of our Lord God 1452. 1452.
And as for these victories, so valiantly atchieved by king Charles,

they are (as is apparant) to be attributed not so muche to the
force as the falshood of the Frenche. For truely the force of Englande was not so farre spent at that time, but that it had been
puissant ynough to mainteyne warre; howbeit the dayly revolting
of people who were evill affected towardes that nation was suche
as no force could suffise; for surely there were, even from the beginning, who would say that one consideration was to be had of
citizens, another of the residue, and thereby concluded that none
was to be had of straungers; whereby it came to passe that the
common societie of mankinde was broken, and a certain naturall
hatred mutually bred of it selfe in both peoples. This venime,
therefore, hath already a good while since infected much people, so
as that (to be silent of others) it cannot be brought to passe by
any meane that a Frenche man borne will much love an Englishe
man, or, contrary, that an English will love a Frenche man; such
is the hatred that hath spronge of contention for honor and empire;
and that (as we have before declared) hath been these many yeres
increased by mutuall bloudshed and slaughter, wherefore this was
the very cause of thutter ruine that came to thenglish affaires beyonde the seas. But Charles, the lanterne light and mightie
emperor, was thonely man who by martiall prowesse restored
the corps of his common wealth, and by right of armes augmented
the same. When forreine warre was finished, intestine division
began to revive; for a great part of the nobilitie fretted and fumed
for the evill handling of matters in Fraunce: one sort laide the
fault upon another, and all generally detested and cursed above
measure William duke of Suffolke as thutter confusion and destruction of his countrey, that he had lavished out the common
treasure, that he had not geven paye to the souldier, that he had
not caused supplye to be sent to tharmye, that he had made the
court voyde of good councellours, whereby he might rule all as
himselfe list. By meane of these rumours it came to passe, that

The duke of
Suffolke
charged se-
verally, but
the death of
the duke of
e.

the commonaltie in great furye accused duke William and all his
fautours for the death of the duke of Glocester, and for robbing
of the common treasurie, and openly required that he might be
punished; which when the queene did see, fearing sedition, she
dealt with the king, that, for pacifying of the multitude, the duke
might be committed, which was done accordingly. But within
fewe dayes after, the queene, supposing that the common people
were satisfied with such kinde of ignominie as the duke was thus
put unto, commaunded him to be delivered out of warde, and
placed in as high favor with the king as ever he was before;
whereat the commonaltie in a rage begann to exclame more then
at the first, saying that it was a wickednes intollerable to suffer a
man convict of so many mischefes to remaine in the court, or to
be had in any reputation; which, after the king hearde, then
finally perceaving it was no boote further to dissemble the matter,
he first punished the fautours and adherentes to the saide duke;
then he commaunded the duke to goe in exile, upon such intent that The duke of
when the rage of the commonaltie should be appeased he might uffo
baneshed
call him home againe, because the queene could not well spare and killed
him out of her sight: but the ungratious man, that so well de- in his
jurney.
served death, could be saved by no meane; for when he tooke
shipping, and directed his course into Fraunce, he was sodenly
taken and killed of his enemies. And so this William (as meete is
to beleeve) receaved from God due deserved punishment, who,
besides many other fowle factes, was reported to have practised the
duke of Glocesters death, that by suche meane thinnocent bloud
of thone might at the last be revenged with slaughter of thother.
But when William duke of Suffolke was deade, peace could no
whitt the better be preserved, by reason of civill dissension, the
beginning whereof spronge through contention of factions, as
before is saide, which alway have been and ever will be more hurt-
full to common wealthes then forreine warre, then famine, or

sicknes; whereunto the Kentish people were most prone, as well
for that they can hardly beare injuries, as for that they are desirous

Jacke Cades of novelties; for whether it were by instigation of Richard duke
rebellyon. of Yorke, who, aspiring to the crowne, sought to make innovations,
-his pollicie tendyng to this ende, that by occasion of discorde
amongst the commons he might procure himselfe authoritie, and
become the head of some one faction, or els that they were desirous to revenge injuries done unto them, especially by the kinges
officers, so it was they tooke weapon in hande, made one John,
by surname Cade, their captaine, and gathering a great power togethers, marched towardes London, whither as soone as they
approched, they incamped themselves upon the next hill thereunto. Here, consulting deeply upon the matter, certaine were
chosen to present their supplication full of complaints unto the
king, and to declare, that there thassemble in this forceable
maner was for the libertie of their countrie, against certaine his
counsellours, who molested his people with intollerable exactions
of money; and if it might please him to cause them be dulye
punished, they were readie to laye weapon apart.   The king,
thinking it unmeete to geve audience to the messengers of this re-
bellious rowte, but rather with speede to represse the fury of their

Sr. Hom- inraged commotion, sent forthwith against them Humfrey Stafford,
ford sente knight, with a choyse bonde of men, upon whom they gave charge
rebelle ^{the} as he came, and at tne first encounter put him to flight.   After
Cade. which happy attempt they allured unto them on every side, in
hope of spoyle, an huge number, as well citizens as countrey people,
and so together in warlike maner marched towardes London,

Cade enters wherinto they entered at the first without any harme doing; but
London. afterwarde, moved by covetousnes, they spoyled the houses of certaine wealthie citizens; and yet, because they would not be reported to seeke after spoyle, they gave out, that the same was
done in revenge of wronges committed by the said citizens.   But

that dealing turned in the end to their owne damage; for many of
good calling, who were privily well pleased with that rebellion, in
hope of some reformation that might growe thereby, when they
saw the Kentish men fall to spoyle the towne, fearing what might
chaunce to themselves, they thought it not meete to expect any
longer the event of that furious enterprise. But all this while
that the Kentish commons raged with crueltie upon the citizens, John Saye
none went about to withstande them before that John Saye, lorde lorde trea-
treasurer of England, with sundry other gentlemen, were beheaded. England
Then Thomas Chalton, lorde maior of the citie, and the sheriffes, with otheres were be
Thomas Caninge and William Huline, determining by one meane hedded by
or other to make head against so great mischiefe, levied quickly Cade. Caningius.
a mightie force of souldiers, and because John, captaine of the Hulinus.
commons, kept his men beyonde Temmes, at the village of St.
George, in the suburbes, and thither repaired himselfe every night,
therfore, under the conduct of Mathew Gough, they set upon the
rebells about midnight, and tooke the bridge, killing the watch and
warde thereof. But they founde the Kentish men not unprovided,
for as soone as they, who for feare lay in armour both day and
night, understoode by clamor of their company that the citizens
were upon the bridge, by and by they russhed upon them, and the
fight was forthwith fierce and cruell. After that Mathew Gough
sawe the Kentish men make mightie resistance otherwise then he
would have weened, he anon advised his folkes no farther to proceede, but onely contended to keepe the place which he had taken
untill it were day, that the rest of the citie, hearing the noyse, L id n brid e fired
might certainly know to what place they should resort for relieving by the
of their felowes; but the commons so forceably preassed upon, re ucii Cade.
that the citizens were compelled first to geve a litle grounde, and
after, with great slaughter, to forsake the bridge. The Kentish
men anone supplied their places, and being masters of the bridge,
set fire on both sides in the houses builded thereupon. Then

might one beholde a lamentable sight, for some flying the fire,
ranne headlong upon the weapons of their enemies, to their owne
destruction ; other, alas, with horrible shrieks and cryes, were suf-
focate in the flame ; many, moreover, valiantly fighting, were killed

Mathewe in the conflict it selfe, and amongst them Mathew Gough, a man
of passing prowesse, very dutifull to his countrey, and of great renowme in martiall affaires, who had served beyond the seas with
great commendation more than twentie yeres; but finally, such
was the chaunce, that he who was invincible in so many conflictes
with forreyne enemies, was, in the ende, of his owne countrymen
rewarded with death. But when the king perceaved that the
Kentish people could not be subdued by force, thinking to pacifie

Pardon them by lenitie, he proclamed pardon to all them that were in that
ro ymed
to he rebellion, John Cade, their captaine, onely except, who being the
rebells ex- head of that heynous enterprise the fact of it selfe would by no
e
himselfe. meane suffer unpunished : whereupon the people, as having that
which they desired, hasted home immediately with the spoyle they
_had gotten, leaving their captaine, who was taken soone after, and
lost his life for his labour.

When this insurrection in Kent was pacified, soone after, another more perilous rose upon the sodaine, which much more sub-
verted the forces of the common wealth ; for as the body which
hath been recovered of infirmitie is more extreme sick when by
resydivation it falleth downe againe, so the common wealth, when
after the ende of warres beyond the seas, and of this Kentish commotion, the same fell againe into intestine division, was more ve-

Richard hemently afflicted. For Richard duke of Yorke, who aspired to
o
Yorke sett tne soveraintie, trusting to that title, whereby, as we have before
on foote his described in the life of king Richard the second, thinheritance of
ay
the crowne. tne kingdome was to descend unto the house of Yorke, after he
perceaved that the rebellion in Kent had with the rage thereof
nothing prevailed, then enterprising to attempt and practise

greater matters, begann to conferre his newe devises with Thomas
Courtney earle of Devonshire, and Edward Brooke, a man of a
sharpe witt, how he might, without note of treason, obtaine the-
same. And because Edward duke of Soommersett was thonely
man living at that day, who, by watchfulnes, care, and perills,
which he did often undertake, and also by good advise, supplied
the part of a good counceller, who also principally desired to have
the realme delivered from factions, the king safe, and all things
quiet; the duke of Yorke, therefore, not doubting but thother
would withstande his purpose and practises, determined to pushe
at him, that eyther he might be brought to utter confusion, or els
in hatred of the common people, and envie of the nobilitie. And
so he made haste with all diligence to gather an armie, to allure
unto him most lively youthes, promising to reward them with
great matters; and because he should not seeme to practise any
thing against the king, he published openly, under pretence of
revenging common injuries, that he woulde persecute with weapon
certaine of the kinges wicked councellers who afflicted dayly the
poore English people, where no neede was, with detrimentes innumerable, and spoyled the realme. Many mo thinges did he
sowe amongst the common sort, that his drifte might not appere
to his adversaryes. And so publishing that he toke this warre on
hande for thutilitie of the common wealth, he proceeded, conducting a right great armie into Kent, whither when as he came,
he choosed a place to encampe in tenne miles from London,-
where he had intelligence by certaine espials, every howre of the
day, what was done about the king. And to thend he might not
lack supplye of souldiers, in case he should joyne battaile, he commaunded Edward his sonne earle of Marche, a man both of great
courage and councell, to levye newe forces at home, and therewithall to folowe him; which thinges when king Henry understoode, he called the councell togethers, and explaned unto them

all such intelligence as was brought unto him of the duke of
Yorkes comming into Kent, and demaunded particularly of every
man what he thought of that commotion, and what remedie was
to be applyed to the same, being of so great importance. They
all thought it very meete to goe against the duke of Yorke
speedily, with an armie royall, to incampe the same in viewe of
the duke, and then to demaunde of him what the matter was, why
he should as an enemy to his countrey enterprise warre.

The duke
of Yorke in
mette by
the kingesThis councell was allowed, and the king conducted his armie
almost in a square battaile into the viewe of his enemies sooner
then they thought of : from thence he sent ambassadours to knowe
the cause of so great stirre, and to make an atonement, if so be
that they should understande the demaundes of the adversaryes
to be reasonable. When duke Richard had hearde the ambassadours, whether it were that he was afeard to daraigne battaile, or
that he was abashed of the kinges sodaine arrivall, or els upon
hope of better oportunitie afterwardes to proceede in the matter,
he aunswered that he would lay armor apart, and willingly come
to the king to aunswere that which his highnes would object
against him, so that first the duke of Soomersett might be by the
kinges commaundement committed to warde. When the king had
received this aunswere by thambassadours, considering that he
coulde not without mortal battaile reduce the duke to reason, nor
without great stirre appease civill dissension, if he should seeke
reconciliation by dint of sworde; he therefore upon good ad-
The duke
of Somer-
sete re-
strained.vise commaunded the duke of Somersett to withdrawe himselfe
into his house, whereupon the duke of Yorke dissolved his armie,
came to the king, and much complained upon the duke of Soom-
mersettes pride and avarice, and, by accusing him, seeketh onely
to winne favor of others. But the duke of Soommersett, thinking
it apperteyning as well to his dutie as to the profite of the
common wealth not to put up that open reproche, could not

refraine, but needes would come againe to the campe, and aunswere openly to thoffences wherewithall he was burdened ; he
appeached likewise the duke of York of treason, that he and his *The duke*
adherentes had conferred togethers howe to gett the kingdome. *o omer-*
et ap-
By meane of these speeches it came to passe that in the kinges *peached*
the duke of
returne the duke oɪ Yorke was brought as prisoner to London. *Yorke of*
Here while the king, having assembled togethers a councell of *treason.*
the nobilitie, sought to trye out the truth of the cause, the dukes
fell at great wordes betwixt themselves, thone objecting to thother
most high and heynous offences. But the duke of Soommersett,
who foresawe the thinges that soone after happened, was specially
earnest to have the duke of Yorke apprehended, and by torture
compelled to discover his secrete practises, to confesse his offence,
that upon his owne confession he might be attainted, and so by
losse of one noble man the flame of intestine warre extinguished.
Moreover that his sonnes might be proclamed enemies to their
countrey, and thereto he besought God that such an enemy might
not escape unpunished.

This did the duke of Soommersett, because he accompted it for
certaine that the duke of Yorke aspired to the kingdome, and had
determined the destruction both of him and also king Henry.
But the fatall desteny could not be avoyded by anye humane
pollicie, for many lettes there were why the duke of Soomersettes
sayinges tooke no place : first, the confidence and boldnes of the
duke comming to the king so simply without his army, which was
thought of many men to proceede of a cleere conscience, though
indeede it was plaine dissimulation ; secondly, a late rumor,
whereby it was bruted that Edward, sonne to the duke of Yorke
and heyre apparant, was marching speedily towardes London, accompanied with an huge hoste of lustie and brave souldiers :
thirdly, ambassadours were sent from Bordeaux who gave intelli- *Ambassa-*
gence to king Henry that their citizens, having conspired togethers, *from Bur-*

deulx to
offere their
submission
to H. 6.

were readie to turne into his obeysance if he would sende an
armie into Aquitaine, and that oportunitie served therefore very
well, insomucn that there was no force of Frenche souldiers with
them fit for the fielde, and that therefore nothing was to be preferred before this warre. For these very causes Richarde duke of
Yorke was permitted by the king to depart home, full of yre and
indignation, who even then resolved within himselfe to adventure
his very life, so that once at the last he might revenge thinjury of
his enemyes. But the duke of Soommersett by this contention,
when the duke of Yorke was in a sort exiled, gott greater authoritie, and with Margarete the queene ruled all thinges. That was
the yere of our salvation 1453, and since king Henry begann his
reigne the xxxist. when as of Margaret the queene was borne Edwarde, thonely sonne of the said king Henry. He even from his
infancie gave hope of most excellent disposition, and at the yeres
of discretion proceeded no lesse in vertue. In which yere also
dyed John Stafford, archbisshop of Caunterbury, in whose place
was surrogate John Kempe, bisshopp of Yorke, in order of bisshops
the lxii., wnom Nicholas the 5th bisshop of Rome made Cardinall.
Also William, both bishop of Coventre and Lichfield, was translated
unto the see of Yorke, who was in rewe of bishopps the 55.

The duke
of Yorke
arge .

1453.
Edward,

to H. 6,
borne.

ford, arch-
p of
Canter
bury.

Thambassage of the Burdeaux men being heard, it was thought
good that warre should be renewed; the fidelitie of the citizens
thereof was greatly commended, and the king promised to sende
the lord Talbot with an armie into Aquitane, and to make warre
upon the king of Fraunce by sea and lande. With this answere
(being according to their heartes desire) thambassadours privily
returned in like order as they came, and, reporting king Henryes
determination, confirmed their felowes in the purposed attempt.
But the lorde Talbot, after he knewe the kinges pleasure to be
that an armve should be levied, and assoone as it were readie be
transported with celeritie into Aquitane, tooke on hande tha

dores of

came into

for succore.

The lord
Talbo
ovnted to
prepare an
army for
Aquitane.

voyage with so much livelynes of minde as that he had not been seene more carefull touching any matter of warre at any time before; what shall we say to that he thought every hour longer than other while tharmye was prepared. Therefore he mustered out the best souldiers he could finde; he prepared weapon, horses, and other implements of warre; also victuall plentie; and finally all other furniture that is wont to be necessary for such warre as was to be kept in sundry sortes, and should have neede of many thinges. So having all thinges prepared to his owne satisfaction, and his navie furnished, he sayled into Aquitane, whither when he came with reasonable good winde, and had landed his armie, he scoured over all the countrey adjoyning upon Burdeux, he sent out certaine bandes of soldiers every way, who scaling farre abroade might put thinhabitauntes in terror. Thinhabitantes of Burdeaux, hearing of the lord Talbotes arrivall, sent secret messengers unto him, late in the night, that he would approche nigher the towne. In the meane time all others, except onely those who were privie to the conspiracie, were stricken in such sodaine feare, that all went out of order. But especially the Frenche souldiers who were lefte for defence of the towne, practising upon thapproche of the lord Talbot to flye away, fell into the handes of thenemies, who, neverthelesse, casting away their weapons, the lord Talbot preserved in safetie. When Burdeaux was recovered, Burdeulxe and fortified with garrison, the lorde Talbott, departing from by the receaved thence, receaved almost without any payne or trouble certaine Eng and diveres townes adjoyning, and their castles withall; for all people of those othere partes generally did willingly submitt themselves into the obedience townes and castles re- of thenglish nation, because they receaved often damage of the volted to Frenche men, and were brought nowe by reason of continuall Aqutaine. warre into great scarsitie of all thinges; wherfore, at the same time, came messengers to the lord Talbott, from cities afarre off, also, promising to doo with all their heartes whatsoever he would

commaunde. In the meane season king Charles, who laye about
Towres, after that he had receaved often intelligence of the lorde
Talbots doinges, and that he was also certified of the revolting of
Burdeaux and others, he gathered forthwith great forces, and
marched toward his enemies, sending before a great part of his
armye into the countrey of Perigneux, to besiege the towne of
Chastillon, which thenglish men had taken, and helde with garrison.
They proceeded on that voyage with great celeritie, they compassed
the towne with a siege, and erected fortifications for the purpose.
The lorde Talbot hearing hereof, marched to Chastillon with a
part of his armie; taking great journeys, he intercepted certaine
Frenche souldiers roving negligently abrode in the countrey as
he went; he incamped himselfe nigh unto the trenches of his enemies, and the day folowing, in good order of battaile, assaulted
them in their campe.   The battaile was blouddie in the very
trenche, and so doubtfull that hard was it a long time to discerne
whether side should gett the better. But when the Frenche men,
within a while, releived ever their weried and hurt souldiers with
fresh and new supplye, and so still renewed the fight, and that the
lorde Talbot fell sodenly from his horse, being hurt with the shott
of a peece, then finally the English souldiers, astonied by the
fall of their captaine, were put to flight.   Many yet were killed in
the place where they stoode.   The footmen ranne some one way
some another, who about sunne sett being assembled, came hardly
to their owne company: a thousand English men and moe were
wanting, and amongst them the lorde Talbot, and many other re-
nowmed men of very good calling. This was the ende of John
lorde Talbot earle of Shrewsbury, xxiiii. yeres and more after he
had warred in Fraunce with moste high renowme. Truely a very
noble and valiant man, whose puissant prowesse mad thenglish
name most terrible to the Frenche man. Of thenglish horsmen,
who fledd first, some repaired to such holdes adjoyning as were in

Chastillon
beseeged
b the
Frenche.

The battle
or Castilon
fought be-
tweene the
lo. Talbot
and the
French.

The lord
slayne and
the English
fited.

the handes of the English, some to Burdeaux ; but the Frenche
men, folowing the victory, pressed more earnestly then before the
Chastillions, whom they compelled soone after, dispairing of succours, to yeelde. When Chastillon was recovered, they gott soone Chastylon
loste to the
after from thenglish nation, partly by force, partly by composition, French.
all the residue of the townes. Burdeaux onely remayned, wherein
was all thenglish force. This tooke on hande king Charles to besiege, Burdevlx
recov rec.
and spending many dayes in vaine, did nothing annoye thenemy, by the
but rather himselfe dayly receaved damage, forasmuch as thenglish Frenche.
issued often out of certaine fortes which they had made upon the
shore : and on thother part, the citizens who were giltie of the
conspiracie, dispairing of pardon of the Frenche kinges hande,
valiantly defended themselves ; but at the last, both two, almost
sterved with hunger, were constrained by necessitie to receave
conditions, which king Charles had often before offred, for rendring
of the towne, which were as followeth, that the treason should be
imputed to no man, and that thenglish men should depart; who,
so dismissed, returned safely into Englande with armor and all
other substance.

This, finally, was the ende of forreyne warre, and likewise the
renewing of civill calamitie : for when the feare of outwarde enemy,
which as yet kept the kingdome in good exercise, was gone from The duke
of Yorke
the nobilitie, such was the contention amongst them for glorie and settes his
soveraintie, that even then the people were apparently devided into tytle on
foote again.
two factions, according as it fell out afterwarde, when those two,
that is to say, king Henry, who derived his pedigree from the house
of Lancaster, and Richard duke of Yorke, who conveied himselfe
by his mothers side from Lyonell, sonne to Edwarde the Thirde,
contended mutually for the kingdome. By meane whereof these
two factions grewe shortly so great through the whole realme that,
while thone sought by happ or nap to subdue thother, and raged
in revenge upon the subdued, many men were utterly destroyed,

and the whole realme brought to ruine and decay. But the source
of all this stirre rose (as we have before shewed) from Richard
duke of Yorke ; for he had conceaved an outrageous lust of prin-·
cipalitie, and never ceassed to devise with himselfe howe and by
what meanes he might compasse it ; thinking nothing better for his
purpose then to stirre up the hatred of noble men against the duke
of Sommersett, it greeved him very much that the realme was ruled
by his appoyntment. And therefore he dayly reported every where
to all the nobilitie, that the state of the common wealth was most
miserable ; the same he ceassed not to detest and bewaile ; and

The duke ascribed the cause of all that mischiefe to the duke of Sommersett
his descrip- onely, whom he termed, reviled, and dispraised, to be an unjust,
tion of -false, prowde, and cruell tyrant. He founde much fault also with
the duke of king Henry, saying that he was a man of softe and feeble spirite,
Somersete. of litle witt, and unmeete in all respectes for the right government
of a common wealth, and therefore that it touched nobilitie to
thinke of the matter, or rather to devise remedie. By complayning
of such thinges, the duke brought briefly to passe that well many
of the nobilitie did likewise mislike the present state of the realme
as it was nowe ruled, and withall studied to alter all thinges, as
men whom ambition and avarice had invaded a good while before,
and nowe vehemently oppressed. Then when as parties begann
by litle and litle to be diverslye affected, the duke of Yorke pro-

of Sales- cured chiefly to be of his faction two Richardes, Nevills, thone
Warwic earle of Salesbury, the other, his sonne, earle of Warwicke. This
take parte last had married Anne, sister to Henry duke of Warwicke, who
duke of
e died a few monthes before ; in the right of which yonge lady he was
Yorke. by the King created earle thereof. He was a yonge man, not onely
The dis- mervailously adorned with vertues in deede, but also had a speciall
gifte, as it were by art, even from his infancie, in the shewe and
of War- setting forth of the same ; for his witt was so ready, and his behaviour so courteous, that he was wonderfully beloved of the people.

He was also liberall to all men, which helped him much to thattayning thereof. Moreover, the haultines of his minde, with equal force of body, encreased the same popular good will. By reason of which matters the people were fully pursuaded that there was no matter of so great importance which the said Richarde was not able to undertake, wherefore he became within a while of such estimation, that whither as he inclined, thither also swayed the more part of the people. Thus much of the sonne. Thother Richard, the father, was equal to him in vertue, but not so well beloved. He had in marriage Alis, thonely daughter of Thomas Montacute, earle of Salesbury, who (as we have before written) was killed at the siege of Orleance, and succeeded to his inheritance. He begatt, of the said Alice, these children,—Richard, earl of Warwicke, John, and George. Nowe I returne to my purpose.

The mary-age and i ue of the earle of ;uesuurye.

After that the duke of Yorke founde the two Richardes, the father and the sonne, to be on his side, he prepared warre, and to that he applied wholly both witt and wisedome. Not longe after he begann his journey towardes London with an army well appoynted. The rumor of so great insurrection put the citie in passing terror, when every man did see beforehande, that eyther he must be in extreme daunger, or els runne in displeasure of some one or other noble man. When the king knewe of his adversaryes repaire, he levyed an armye, and determined with speed to goe against them, that he might joyne battaile with them in some place of Yorkshire, farre from London, because he held that citie suspected, for the inconstancie of the commonaltie, being desirous of novelties. But he was not past two dayes journey on his way, when he had intelligence that the duke of York, who had taken great journeys, was at hande; then, constrayned to encamp himselfe at St. Albones, he kept his men in armor, and sent in the meane time straite commaundement to his adversaryes that they should not come against him, nor, like enemies to their

The duke of Yorke the King' levies forces.

Att the bat- t. Albones was slaine

diveres
greate men
on the
Kings
party.

countrey, disturbe the people with sedition. While king Henry
-dealeth in this order, more desirous of peace then warre, Richard
earle of Warwick sounded the alarme, and first of all other gave
charge upon the kinges souldiers, because the company which he
ledd did exceede both in number, and in force of footmen. They
on thother side receaved also the charge willingly. They fought
fiercely upon both parties, from early in the morning till nine of?
the clock, with much slaughter, while at the last, by reason of the
dukes releeving his weried souldiers with fresh supplye, the
kinges armie was discomfited, and many souldiers killed, with their
captaines, of which number was Edmonde duke of Soommersett,
Henry second earle of Northumberlande, John Clifforde, and
many other valiant knightes : but king Henry conceaved great
and uncredible sorowe for the losse of the duke of Sommersett, because he had reposed all his hope in him, and for that such a
noble captaine, who had fought valiantly so many yeres against
the Frenche men, should nowe finally be killed of his owne countrymen, with whom yet the vertue of the man was of some ac-
_compt, insomuch that they caused his corps to be brought and

The duke
set buryed
at St. Al-
.

buryed in the abbey of St. Albones adjoyning. This Edmonde
lefte behinde him three sonnes, Henry, Edmunde, and John, who
also tooke part with king Henry. Moreover many were taken, in
the number whereof was king Henry himselfe. That was the yeere of

taken at
e   a
of St Al-
bones.

our salvation 1456, and since king Henry begann his reigne xxxiiii.
dishonoured with this domesticall discomfiture. In which yere
John Kempe, archbisshop of Canterbury, dyed, before he had sitt
in that see three yeres complete, whom Thomas Burscher
bisshopp of Ely folowed, the lxiii. in order of bisshopps of Caun-
terburye, who was within a while made cardinall of the title of

Osmond
bushope of

St. Cyriacus. About the same time Osmond, who sometime had
been bisshopp of Salsbury, was by Calistus bishop of Rome

canonized
for a St.

canonized for a saint, because he had been a perfect holy man.

His body is even at this day kept at Salesbury in the chiefe churche there, with great reverence, for that there are shewed many miracles. Also Charles king of Fraunce departed this life, who made his name famous universally, by reason of his often calamities ; for he exercised not his youth in pleasures, but in toyles and troubles, who had ynough to doo to recover his auncient inheritance of the kingdome. Hereof may we knowe, that calamitie bringeth oftentimes great renowme, which of the contrarie part pleasure doth never. Lewes the 11th succeeded his father.

Charles kinge of France diethe.

The duke of Yorke after the victory obteyned, calling to minde howe he had published at the beginning that his rising was for - reformation of the common wealth, armed himselfe with mildness, mercie, and liberalitie, and was so farre from laying violent hands upon king Henry, that also he brought him honourablye to London as conqueror of the fielde. Here consulting by and by with the two Richarde Nevilles, and divers other noble men, whom he thought meete to be called to that assemble, he procured himselfe to be made protector of the realme ; Richard Nevill, the father, lord chauncellor of Englande ; and Richard Nevell, the sonne, captaine of Calis ; whereby the government of the realme might rest in him, and Richard lord chancellor ; thother Richard might have charge of the warres ; and so Henry might be king in name and not in deede, whom they thought best to forbeare at that time, least otherwise they might stirre up the commonaltie against them, who loved, honoured, and obeyed him wonderfully for the holynes of his life. When matters were thus ordered, they three bare all the swaye, as well concerning civill as forreine affaires, who, to thende they might after their owne fantasies, without resistance, deprive king Henry eyther of kingdome or life at their pleasure, removed therefore from him by litle and litle his olde counsellors, put them from office and authoritie, and did substitute in their places new men of their owne faction ; like order they

The duke of Yorke the king ; ut himselfe his frendes in cheere place.

devised, decreed, and performed touching all offices within the
realme. But in the meane time Henry, who, not without the
kinges commaundement, succeeded his father Edmund in the
dukedome of Sommersett, and Humfrey duke of Buckingham,
with many other noblemen who helde and stoode with king
Henry, lamenting his adversitie, and not ignorant to what ende all
the duke of Yorke's craftie courtesie tended, thought as time
would serve to provide for the same. And therefore they went
secretly to queene Margarete, made her privie of their councell,
and declared that the duke of Yorke sought to deceave the king,
yea, in very deede to kill him unwares, and therefore required
that she would in time prevent the matter ; which she might very
well doo, if she would separate her husbande from those who lay
in waite to destroye him. The queene, much moved with this
admonition, who was afraide both for herselfe and her husbande,
tooke occasion within fewe dayes, upon the season of the yere, to
perswade him that he woulde, under colour of seeking for a more

H. 6 re- wholsome place, withdrawe unto Coventrie, and there provide for
moved to his affaires. Wherefore the king, seeing himselfe in daunger,
by direc- rode thither, and calling an assemble of his frendes, discharged
Queene,th to Richarde duke of Yorke of the protectorshipp, and therle of
avoid the Salesbury of his office, and sent by letters for them both to ap-
the duke of^g pere before him. But they, taking this new displeasure in evill
part, after they had deliberated betwixt themselves which way
of Yorke^e and nowe they would deale, at the last, with much indignation, de-
& his con- parted peaceably ; Richard unto Yorke, therle of Salsbury into his
seperate countrye, and the earle of Warwicke to Callis. Howbeit, what
themselves. their resolution was, or what was the cause of their departure, I
know not certainly what to write, except it were for that they were
--altogether unprovided for warres.

The Lon-   These seditions thus renewing, emboldened the commonaltie (of
donores London especially) to uprore, who, set aworke by meane of an

affray, ranne upon merchauntes straungers chiefly, as they are *ryse in rage*
commonly woont to doo, and both wounded and spoyled a great *the stran-*
number of them before they could be by the magistrates re- *gers.*
strained. But the brute of this busines being brought into
Fraunce, was cause of muche more harme : for the Frenche navie,
who at that time lay upon the coast of Normandie, for defence
thereof, hearing that all was in hurly burly in Englande, sent *The*
sodenly certaine shipps, upon the hope of spoyle, unto the Kentish *Frenche*
coast, where, landing their men, they burned divers villages, and *Kente*
gott great bootie. This civill discorde also allured James king of *James*
Scottes to make warre upon Englande. He at the first conceaved *King of*
mortall displeasure against William earle of Dowglasse, a noble *entres*
man of great partie, because he was fully perswaded in minde *England by force.*
that the earle affected the kingdome. The suspicion grew so *The earle*
great that hee being in the ende called by the king to conference, *of Dow-*
and upon confidence perchaunce of his innocencie, aunswering very *sodenly by*
boldly to the matter layde against him, was, by the kinges meanes, *Scots*
killed out of hande. With which injury Archbolde earle of Mur- *command.*
row, and Hewgh, thearles brothers, being much moved, determined to revenge the same with weapon upon the kinges owne
person, and made open warre against him, which helde king
James longe, and put him to much displeasure : but lastly he
subdued his adversaryes and set the realme in rest : which when
he had done, hearing that in Englande they were fighting amongst
themselves, he straitway sett forwarde to burne and spoyle the
boundes thereof, and when there was no army extant any where *Roxburghe*
to make head against him, he beseeged Roxbroughe, where, having *beseged by the kynge*
planted his ordinance, he framed to thassault. But as he was *of Scots,*
busied earnestly hereabout, beholde sodenly one of the brasen *was slayne*
peeces brake, whereof one peece hitt him, so that he fell downe *by the*
deade. Yet notwithstanding the kinges death, the Scottes would *of a peece*
not omitt the possibilitie which they had to atchieve that enter- *or orde- nance.*

prise, but, being very earnest thereupon, wonne it soone after.⌐
King James left three sonnes of his wife Mary; James, Alexander duke of Albany, and John.   James being but a childe for yeres, was created King, the thirde of that name, and committed to the teaching of James Chenneth, bisshopp of St. Andrewes, who longe time was the governor of the lande, because he was a very good man, and adorned exceedingly with all vertuous qualities.

In the meane while king Henry, advertised that the duke of Yorke did practise nothing as an enemy against him, returned to London, and calling togethers his counsell declared howe the Frenche men, knowing the great stirre of civill dissention within the realme, had of late enterprised to robbe and spoyle the sea coast in Kent ; and on thother side, the Scottes, moved for the selfe same cause, had wonne Roxbrowghe; and that it was very like that neyther of them would be quiet except they should understande some conclusion of argument to be made amongst the noblemen ; and to thintent that the same might once at the last be brought to passe, woulde himselfe seeke to reconcile the duke of Yorke, and to recover the good willes of all men, least otherwise by intestine division the libertie of the lande might be brought in hazarde.   Whose advise, when all men allowed, certaine grave personages were sent to the duke of Yorke, and other noble men of that faction, requiring them to repaire unto the king.   The duke of Yorke, and thearle of Salesbury, with other their confederates came to London garded with great force, because they would not be intrapped by any practise of their enemyes, whereunto they had speciall regarde.   The earle of Warwicke came thither also from Callis.   Here, after much mutuall rehearsall of olde injuries, and querulous repetition, as well of late as of almost forgotten faultes : finally, the feare of forreyne warre was of such weight, so yrke were all men of domesticall discorde, that the

noble men, omitting private hatred and offences, very carefull for
the wealth of the countrey, gave othe, every man particularly, to Mutuall
continue their olde accustomed amitie. The newes whereof made tn geven to the no-
all men so gladd, as that all sortes of men every where gave by bylletye for
mutuall congratulation apparent testimonie of rejoysing without ye.
measure. Wherefore, to geve God thankes, generall processions
were universally commaunded, and especially at London, to be
solemnized with much veneration, whereat the King and Queene
were present in person, and a great company of noble men withall.
This was the yere of mans salvation 1458, and since king Henry 1458.
beganne his reign the xxxvith.

But faithlesse and seditious folke forgat soone both concorde
and othe, according as it is commonly seene, that whoso de-
lighteth in dissension, bloud, and battaile passeth litle of possessions, lawe, nor league : for not many dayes after the king and his
nobilitie had been thus reconciled, a sodaine stirre there was,
whether by chaunce or of purpose it is not certaine. The matter An affraye
was thus : certaine of the queenes housholde made an affray upon made upo th . f
therle of Warwicke at Westminster, where after longe fight the Warwicke
earle could hardly by helpe of the multitude that came to part y some of the
get to the water, and from thence, by taking a whirrey, avoyde the Queenes nousnoiu.
daunger ; upon this ryot, the rage or warre did so fervently rise
as that all the realme was brought in uprore, and the hazarde of
armes did no man escape. The earle, after this displeasure to
him done, repaired to Yorke unto the duke, and his father thearle
of Salesbury : to them he made relation what injurye he had receaved of the kinges servauntes. After his saide complaint therein,
fearing least by his absence he might be thrust out of his office,
he transported to Calis, with intent there to tarrye from time to The E. of
time, while the duke might deliberately resolve upon the poynt of Warwi rei eth
the matter. The duke and thearle of Salesbury, much moved to Calis.
with this offence, spake openly betwixt themselves in bitter and
sharpe termes, that the matter was nothing els but the fraude and

fury of a woman, meaning the queene, who, thinking she might
do whatsoever she listed, sought nor minded any thing so much
as by womanish sleight to torment, consume, and utterly destroy
all the nobilitie of the lande.   But afterwardes they came to the
matter, and resolved betwixt them, that the earle of Salsbury

The E. of should, with an armie in good array of battaile, marche to Lon-
furnesheth don, tnere to complaine unto the king for this injurious breache
an army to of amitie and agrement; and that if he should perceave himselfe
ju   o aole to prevaile, not to omitt thoccasion of revenging his honor
wardes
London. against the queene and her counsellours, who so evill governed
the realme.   And upon this resolution the earle began to sett
forwarde.   In the meane time the queene, above all other, who
being assisted, ledd, and advised by the dukes of Soommersett and
Buckingham, was of herselfe, for diligence, circumspection, and
speedie execution of causes, comparable to a man, tooke it for
certaine that this late tumult had been stirred by thearle of Warwicke, purposely, to thende that upon such occasion he might set
forwarde his perpensed malitious enterprise, whereby the duke of
Yorke might once at the last attaine the soveraigntie.   Wherefore
this wise woman, supposing that it would be in vaine to treate
ever any more with her adversarye of attonement, after that she
understoode thearle of Salsbury to be in armes, called togethers
the councell to provide remedie for the disordered state of thinges.
Many thought it good to expect thearles approche, whereby it
might be certainly knowen whether he minded peace or warre.
Others gathered, by reason of the late seditious attempt, that
the matter would not be ended without fight, and therefore
that it was to be determined with all haste howe to goe against
him.   This opinion tooke place, and forthwith James Tuchete
lord Audley was sent with an armie to meete with thearle of
Salesbury by the way, and, if occasion so required, to fight with
him.   The saide James tooke great journeys, and so came into
the territory about Lichfielde, whither as his enemyes were al-

readie arrived, and pitched his tentes as neere as he could to The earle
theirs. The next day therle of Salesbury would not omitt the ~~or Sales~~
burye
possibilitie of fight offered, but early in the morning gave the joynes bat-
~~tell with~~
charge. The battaile continued divers houres, but in thende the Lo.
thearle wann the fielde, with great slaughter both of his enemyes Lichefeeld,
and of his owne men also. In which number was James Touchet; & over-
so that almost all the kinges armye, a few noble men only except the lord
who were taken, was destroyed.   Audley is
ther slayne.
After this battaile the duke of Yorke perceaving that his privie
practises and secret devises were discovered, manifested, and made
knowen to the king and queene, who endeavoured everywhere to
avoyde the mischiefe inevitable, thought even then that dissimulation could not take any longer place with them, and therefore,
as well for thobteyning of the kingdome, as for the safetie of his
owne life, determined with might and mayne to set forwarde that
cause. And so, togethers with Richard earle of Salesbury partaker The duke
of all his practises and further fortune, he gathereth a newe armie; and E. of
and soone after both togethers, having assembled an huge multi- Salesburye
~~gather a~~
tude of souldiers, encamped themselves in Yorkshire, meaning newe
eyther there to abide their enemies, or from thence to goe against ar nye.
them in their comming. The rumor whereof being brought to
London, greater then cause was, caused the king in all haste to
levye an armye from every hande ; wherewithall using great celeritie, as in matters of feare is often accustomed, he came into
Yorkshire, and encamped not farre from his enemyes, before ever
they were ascertained that he would come. But there was no
feate of warre done worthy memorye ; for the conspiratours diversly
departed upon the sodaine, the cause whereof was as followeth :
Richard earle of Warwick came to that warre from Calice with a The E. of
great bande of souldiers, and joyned with the duke, and with his Warwick
returned
father. Thaugmentation of which ayde so animated the duke, as from Callis
that he determined the next day after to joyne battaile with his forces to

the duke of
Yorke. enemy. But in the meane season, Andrew Trolop, a most faithfull man, and perfect warrier, who had longe served at Calis under
Andrewe
Trolope
and his
company
departed
from the
earle of
Warwick
to the
Kinge. king Henry, when he conceaved that they were to goe againste
the king, whose true subject and defender he tooke thearle of
Warwicke to have been, and no traitor or betrayer, without more
adoe, departed with his retinewe, in the night time, to king Henry,
of whom he was very courteously enterteyned as a faithfull olde
trained captaine, which thing as soone as the duke of Yorke
knewe, he begann wonderously to be abasshed and amased : for
being in doubt what best was to be done, it troubled him verye
much that the king (as he knew most certaine) did exceed him
in number of souldiers ; and it pinched him no lesse that Andrew
Trollop, a passing good captaine, was become his adversary, whose
prowesse and pollicie did nowe as much appall and dismay him as
The duke
of Yorke
and the
earles of it had before comforted and emboldened. So when after longe
consultation he could not resolve upon any poynt, because he
could devise nothing wherein seemed not some great daunger and
and War-
wicke de-
parted the
feelde with
out fyghte. difficultie, though finally he thought it damageable to depart the
field, yet presently as time required he deemed best to give place.
And therefore himselfe passed thoccean into Irelande, making
very fewe of his owne neerest frendes privie to his intent.
The duke
of Yorke
fleeth into
Ireland
and the
earles of
Salesbury
and War-
wicke flee
to Callis. Thearles of Salesbury and Warwicke, with Edwarde the dukes
sonne earle of Marche, got themselves to Callice. The residue of
tharmie were partly taken, and partly scattered. The king after
the flight of his enemyes marched great journeys into Wales, that
he might take the duke of Yorke as he fledd, of whom he had
intelligence geven that he should passe through that region unto
the sea coast, and premised certaine horsmen to besett all the
same beforehande. But the duke of Yorke had bought a shipp
for a great deale of money, wherein he passed the seas before ever
the horsmen approched the shore, whereof when the king was
advertised, he stayed at Ludlow. Here the while of his abode

he, by advise and councell of his lords, proclaymed all his adver- The duke of Yorke
saryes traitours to their countrie ; he pronounced their goodes to and E. of
be confiscate, which after that were solde, he commaunded their Sal proclaymed
wives and children to be safely kept. He also rewarded them who traytores.
had well deserved, and eyther caused execute the captives, or
punished them by the purse, or exiled them the lande. Here he
decided olde controversies, here he receaved into his protection
the people adjoyning, who following thither seemed to be gladd of The duke
his prosperous state and safetie. Here did he constitute and of Somer-
appoynt such noble men as were of approved loyaltie and goode sete made captayne of
minde towardes him, to governe and defende the counties of Calis.
Yorke and Durham : and here finally did he make Henry duke of
Soommersett captaine of Calice. But the olde proverbe is true : that
as soone sowing sometime deceaveth, so late sowing is alway naught.
Truely as touching this busines, long lingring hurt the king : for
if at the beginning he had bereft them of this refuge, without
doubt he had destroyed them utterly.

These thinges dispatched, the king returned to London, and,
trusting to the good will of the souldiers who were of his pay in
garrison at Calice, he sent with all diligence and speede possible
the duke of Soommersett unto his charge in the continent. The
duke went to Calice, and, shewing the king's commission, commaunded the towne to be delivered up to him, which thearle of
Warwicke denayed to doo, and, shutting the gates, kept him out
afarre of. The duke being much afearde, because he perceaved
that all the garrison consented thereunto, departed to Guynes, the
next towne of the kinges dominion there, and the same he receaved of the captaine, who obeyed his demaunde. Then indea-
vouring with greater care and courage to revenge thinjurye done
unto him, he begann daylye to skirmishe with thearles men. But
thearle of Warwicke, while his souldiers passed over the time in
skirmishing with the duke of Soommersett, gathered a great navie

and sent a good part of the souldiers which he had there with
him to Sandwiche haven in Kent, to spoyle the place, and to lett
thapproche of his adversaryes. They arrived sodenly in the
haven, where they assailed and tooke at unwares with litle
labour certaine shippes well furnished, and ready to transport,
which had been sent to ayde the duke of Soommersett, and were
nowe caried with much preay to Calice. Then thearle of Warwicke, seeing that there was no daunger to be doubted from his
enemyes, sayled speedily unto the duke of Yorke into Ireland;
with him he did conferre, deale, and deliberate howe to handle
their affaires, and that done returned forthwith to Calice, shewing
unto his father and unto Edwarde earle of Marche the dukes
opinion to be, that they should passe over with an armie into
England as soone as might be, and omitting no oportunitie for
the doing of any exployte to annoy the king by feates of armes,
untill he shoulde come unto them with a great supplye of souldiers. They, approving this councell, sayled with celeritie into
Englande, and marched towardes London; for that toune being
kept without watche, and nothing furnished like a toune of warre,
was of necessitie open to the first assailants. Here they put in
armes such of the rascall people, and others whosoever came
running to them. Here they made preparation of all thinges
necessary for the warre, and with an hoste gathered together of
all sortes marched towardes Northampton, where as the king was
arrived not longe before; which dealing knowen to the queene,
who was supported by the wealth and wisdome of the dukes of
Soommersett and Buckingham, who had more eye to such causes
then the king had, as in who monely all his care laye, she with
hawtie heart gathereth an armie, and sending for from every hande
the nobilitie of her faction, who also particularly repayred with a
choyse force of men, made up quickly an huge hoste. After the
king understoode that he had by thindustry and diligence of the

dukes and queene, an armie of no small accompt, he determined ^{The} to fight with his adversaryes, and incamped himselfe in the next medowes without the towne alonge by the river Nyne, and when he perceaved his enemyes at hande, encountering them by the way, he caused sounde the alarme. His enemyes deferred not the fight. The battaile begann very early in the morning, and a litle before noone the king was vanquished. There was killed almost tenn thousande, and amongst them Humfrey duke of Buckingham, John Talbot earle of Shrewsbury, a passing excellent yonge man, and most like his ancestours, Thomas lord Egromond, and many other. The number of prisoners was also very great, because manye of the horsmen had put their horses —from them, and, as their maner is, fought on foote; and principally above all other king Henry fell in the handes of his enemyes, a man borne to the miserie, calamitie, and adversities of this life. The residue of noble men who escaped the rage of this blouddy discomfiture, with the queene and prince Edwarde, fled into Yorkshire, and from thence into the bishopricke of Durham, eyther there to renew forces, or, if they should be destitute of the hope therein, to flee into Scotlande, and there to tary while the time might geve better possibilitie of fortunate successe. The earles being conquerours ledd king Henry captive to London, and calling a parliament labored earnestly to deprive him of all regall authoritie. At which time the duke of Yorke, being certified of the victory obtained, arrived straight out of Ireland, and, entering into the higher house, tooke firste that place which in the parliament is proper to the king. Then after, before all thassemble, he pronounced himselfe king, persuading that he did the same by good title and right. But at the last a reverence was had of the royall maiestie; for it was concluded by parliament that thinheritance of the kingdome should come to the house of Yorke after the death of king Henry; and in the mean time Richard duke of

The batlle of ampton, where the Ki was vanquesh- diveres lordes

K. H. 6 the battel'.

A parli. - moned.

The parlc:- mente res- tored H. , the duke of York pro- confyrmeu e dukes rizht to be afiere the ; of H. 6.

Yorke should be protector of the realme. Such was the pleasure
of God, that king Henry, a most holy man, should by so many
calamities, wherewithall he was continually afflicted, be deprived
of this earthly kingdome to enjoy forthwith the everlasting : for a
good man can never be but good, though he suffer a thousand
afflictions. But the common people beleeve that misfortune to
have been by signe prodigious before prognosticated, for as much
(as they say) that a litle before, when king Henry satt in parliament in his robes royall, the crowne fell from his head to the
grounde. The yere in which these thinges were done was of our

1460.   salvation 1460, and since king Henry begann his reigne xxxviii[th].

After these thinges the duke of Yorke, knowing for certaine that
the queene would not be content with the decree of this parliament, made speede into Yorkshire to pursue her, and pitched his
campe at a towne distant from Yorke upon the west about fifteen
The battell miles, of some strength, by reason of a castle adjoyning, which
f   ake-   towne is called Wakefielde ; and there he consulted with his frendes
feeld
wherein   as touching thassayling of his enemyes. Some there were who
York was   thought it not meete to joyne battaile before his sonne Edward
slayne, and should come with newe forces ; but the duke, trusting to his owne
others   knowledge in warfare, and the valiancie of his souldiers, yssued
taken by   out of his campe against his enemyes in good array. Likewise the
the queene.
queene, who was resolved in minde to demaunde her husbande
by dint of swoorde, and for that cause had alreadie assembled a
puissant armie, when she understoode that thenemie approached,
forthwith she made head against them and gave them the charge.
At the beginning the fight was mightily mainteyned mutually,
while that a great part of them who were in the front of the battaile being killed, the duke of Yorkes small number was environed
of the multitude. Then the queene encouraging her men, vanquished the residue of her enemyes in the moment of an houre:
There fell in that conflict Richard duke of Yorke, the head of that

faction, with Edmund his sonne, earle of Rutlande, Thomas Nevill, David Hall, John Parre, Walter Limbrike, John Gedding, Eustace Wentworth, Guy Harrinton, of thorder of knightes, and of courageous captaines James Fitzjames, Raphe Hastinges, John Baunne, and Roland Digbie. Richard earle of Salsbury, another head of The E. of Salesbury takene and behea ed with others. that faction, was amongst others taken, who were beheaded soone after, and their heades, put upon stakes, were carried to Yorke for a spectacle to the people, and a terror to the rest of thadversaryes. After that, the queene, with an armie well appoynted, made speede to London for delyverie of her husbande, and by the way, at St. Albones, mett the earle of Warwicke coming to ayde the duke of Th battele of St Albones, wnear e earle of Warwicke ucu. Yorke, and bringing as prisoner with him king Henry. Here the woman with no lesse courage then she had done before in Yorkshire, gave charge upon thenemy, put him to flight, and recovered her husbande. Surely this Margarete, wife unto the king, warred _much more happily by her owne conduct and authoritie then by the kinges. The earl of Warwicke, thonely man upon whom all the weight of the warre depended, being certified, after the discomfiture at St. Albons, that Edwarde earle of Marche, after that battaile at Wakefielde, wherein his father was killed, was gone into Wales, (and there prepared a newe armie, having put to flight Jasper earne of Pembroke put to flight, ba the earle of Marche. Jasper earle of Pembrowghe, who tooke part with king Henry, and made head against him,) went therefore unto the said earle of Marche, whom he founde by the way, comming with a great hoste of armed men, nigh unto the boundes of Oxfordshire. Here they _two, arguing upon the substance of the matter, concluded to goe to London, which they were sure helde on their side: and so, taking councell of their frendes, Edwarde was proclamed King, Edward ea f Marche proclaymed inge. and king Henry utterly deprived from all regall authoritie, because —he had not kept covenant, nor obeyed the decree of parliament, as though he had already woonn the fielde. But king Henry the meane while, who suspected the Londoners, and thought it not

best to goe thither, because he perceaved the remnant of his adversaries to be at hande, departed from St. Albons to Yorke, and
there encreased his forces, who thought himselfe nowe at an ende
of all travaile and daunger, seing the heades of the contrary faction
were destroyed, insomuch that in one other battaile finally he
hoped utterly to extirpe all that was lefte.   But the matter fell
out otherwise then he weened, when for two heades one yet remayned of passing valor and abilitie, which could not be sup-
pressed; for Edwarde was much desired of the Londoners, in
favor with the common people, in the mouth and speeche of every
man, of highest and lowest he had the good willes.   He was, for
his liberalitie, clemencie, integritie, and fortitude, praysed generally of all men above the skyes; wherefore there was concourse
to him of all ages and degrees of men, with wonderfull affection,
insomuch that some gave in their names to goe to the fielde with
him; others, in the behalfe of cities, promised their good willes,
and all that they might doo, and swore to be his true subjectes.
By which occasions this Edwarde, brought in hope of victory, prepared as great forces as he coulde possible, that in the conflict of
one day he might perfect all his travailes and victoryes.   Thus
being stronge, with these forces aforesaide he marched towardes
Yorke, and when he came about xi. miles from the same he
encamped himselfe at a village called Towton.   When king Henry
knewe that his enemies were at hande, he did not issue forthwith

The bat-
. " .
Towton on
Palmese
C........,
in which
the Kinge
is discom-
feted.

out of his tentes, because Palme Sunday (as they call it) being a
solemne feast was at hande, upon the which he was rather a minded
to have prayed then fought, that the next day after he might have
better successe in the fielde.   But it cam to passe by meane of the
    , who, as their maner is, like not upon lingring, that the
very self same day, by day breake in the morning, after he had
with many wordes exhorted every man to doo particularly his
devoire, he was forced to cause sounde thalarme.   His adversaries

were thereto as ready as he; tharchers begann the battaile; but
when their arrowes were spent the matter was dealt by hand
strokes with so great slaughter that the very deade carkasses
hindered them that fought. Thus did the fight continue more
than tenne howres in equall ballance, when at the last king Henry
espyed the forces of his foes increase, and his owne somewhat
yeelde, whom when by newe exhortation he had compelled to
presse on more earnestly, he with a fewe horsemen removing a
little out of that place, expected the event of the fight; but beholde,
sodenly his souldiers gave the backe, which when he sawe he fledd
also. There was wanting of both parties about twentie thousand
men. Amongst these was Henry the third earle of Northumber- The E. of
lande, and Andrew Trolop, and many other men of name. The berlande
number of prisoners and wounded persons, whereof some were and
cured and some dyed, were fullye tenn thousand. That battaile Trolop
weakned wonderfully the force of Englande, seing those who were slain.
killed had been able, both for number and force, to have enterprised any forreyne warre. Edward, that he might use well the
victory, after he had a litle refreshed his souldiers from so great
travaile and payne, sent out certaine light horsmen to apprehend
king Henry or the queene in the flight : but they journeyed all H. 6 and
that night continually, and all the next day without intermission, fled into
so that the second day they came safe into Scotland, and sent forth- Scotlande.
with lamentably unto king James, that for olde frendshipp and
familiaritie they might be receaved in his kingdome, and by
his might and puissance defended in so great calamitie. Divers
noble men had government of the lande there at that time
by reason of the kinges nonage, and chiefly James Chenneth,
archbisshopp of St. Andrewes, as we have before declared. King
James being but a childe, after he had heard who were sent,
was by advise of his saide nobilitie so far from neglecting the
request and fortune of king Henry, as that by and by he went

himselfe to meete him, and brought him into his palace, whom, after much consolation that he shoulde with a willing and patient minde beare thevent of this late discomfiture, he interteyned with all courtesie, and used both liberally and also honorably all the while he was in Scotlande. King Henry, being bounden by this great courtesie, to thintent he might also eyther binde unto him by some benefite the king, upon whose ayde he did presently much leane and trust, eyther els might diminish the force of his enemyes, delivered up to him, to have and holde for ever, the towne of Barwicke. Yet there is a saying that king Henry did not that willingly, but against his will constrained thereunto in this extreme miserye, that he might therefore remaine in Scotlande. But howsoever the matter was lapped up, it is apparent that king James, having receaved the towne, promised king Henry all the favor and furtheraunce that he could doo any maner of way, which he performed after with diligence. When this was done, queene Margarete, with Edward her sonne, passed the seas into Fraunce unto Rhenate, her father, duke of Angeow, there by her father's helpe to prepare a newe armie ; and king Henry, with certaine other noble men of his faction who folowed him, determined to tary in Scotlande, untill that by helpe of his frendes he might renewe warre againe, which he hoped would be shortly, and provide for himselfe and his owne affaires. Thus much of the variable and divers fortune of king Henry the Sixt, who reigned thirty eight yeres. But yet forasmuch as he recovered his kingdome againe tenn yeres after he had been expulsed the same, we shall more aptly in the next booke prosequute the residue both of his life and death.

H. 6 deli-
e   o
the kin e
of Scotes
Barwicke.

EDWARD THE FOURTH.

EDWARD, after that king Henry was dryven owt of the realme, being in mynde muche exaltyd, as well by reason of so great victory as of the generall revolt of the nobylytie and commons, returnyd to London lyke a tryumphant emperor, wher, having caulyd a great assemble at Westminster, he was created king the third calendes of July, and caulyd Edward the iiij[th]. of that name after Wylliam the first Norman king, which was the year of mans salvation M.CCCC.lxj. The very same yeare he held a parlyament, wherein first he establisshyd the state of the realme as it wer of new, muche for the benyfit of the commonwelth, being so long neglectyd by reason of cyvill warr. Secondly, all statutes enactyd in parlyamentes bypast during king Henryes raigne wer repealyd, abolisshed, and abrogated. Lastly, his two younger broothers, George and Richard, thone was made duke of Clarence, thother duke of Glocester; also John, broother to Richard earle of Warwick, was created marquyse Montacute, Henry Burcsher broother to Thomas archebysshopp of Canterbury earle of Essex, and William Fawconbrydge was made earle of Kent. To this Henry Burscher, being a very noble man, passing good, and by fame of martiall prowesse highly renowmyd, Richard duke of Yorke had geaven in mariage Elyzabeth his sister, that therby he might have him princypally his assuryd partaker alway in warres and other casualties whatsoever. The which self same thing was also the very cause why king Edward soone of Rychard dyd now create the same man earle of Essex as ys before declaryd, to thend that

Marginal notes: E. 4 came and crowned King ..... A parleament somoned. The staple by H. 6 repealed. E. 4 two brothers created Dukes. ... ther to the earle of ... ke ... M unta ue and dyvers created.

both the father and his soones also might ayd and support him;
for Henry had begotten of Elyzabeth his wyfe fowre soones,
William, Thomas, John, and Henry, and one onely dowghter
namyd Isabell, who lyvyd short whyle; all which soones wer poly-
tyke in ther practyses, peynfull in performing, in peryll of muche
fortitude, in forcast very provydent; but most of all those vertews
dyd abound in William, who was theldest.   This William had

Wm. Bur-
cher mary-
ed the E.
of St.
Paules
daughter.

maryed Anne a young lady of an approvyd vertew, and most
highe parentage, doughter to James of Lusembrowgh earle of St.
Paule, by whom he had yssue Henry, now erle of Essex (of whom
we will intreat more at large in the xxvjth. booke), Cecyly, and
Isabell; this dyed of disease before she was maryageable, thother
was maryed to Walter Ferryse; but let owr speache repar to
speake of that wherewithall yt began.

The duke
of Somer-
set ad-
heares to
E. 4.

The duke

ed from
E. 4.

H. 6 re-

with a
great pow-

-- - -is-
comfited at
the batle of
and flyeth

Whyle all things fell thus owt fortunately uppon king Edwards syd, Henry duke of Soommersett, despearing now in king
Henryes affayres, revoltyd to hym also, of whome he was very
curtesly entertayned; but the duke soone repentyd that he had so
doone, for king Henry had the mean while gatheryed in Scotland
an army not lyttle, wherewithall he made hast sodaynly into the
bishoppryk of Durham, which whan the duke of Summerset herd,
he pryvyly reparyd to him, and many that wer king Henryes
frindes folowyd after; yea an exceding great number of men, in
hope of spoyle, assemblyd quickly from every hand, so that for
force king Henry was thowght not muche inferyor to his enemy.
The fame wnereof was augmentyd for that every way as he went he
wastyd, burnt, and spoylyd towne and fielde.   Thus robbing and
destroying he came to a village caulyd Hexame, wher he met and
encounteryd with John marquyse Montacute, and after sharp fyght,
as had often happenyd before, was discomfyted, lossing the most
part of his army; himself with contynuall flight recoveryd Scotland, others otherwher by lyke meane savyd themselfs.   Ther

wer taken Henry duke of Summerset, Robert earle of Hunger- againe into
forth, and Thomas Rosse. The duke of Summerset. for altering or Prisoners
of his mynde, was beheadyd owt of hand ; thother wer browght to taken in
Newcastle and executyd not long after, wherby others might be e oa t of Hexam
owt of hope seing ther afflycted nobylytie bereft of this lyfe. But
king Edward, thowghe presently he thowght his affayres to be now
at the last, by reason of this late victory, suffycyently assuryd, yeat
was he very carefull that Margaret wyfe to kyng Henry showld by
no meane returne into England, to move the people ther unto
any further sedition ; wherfor he causyd lay all the costes with
garryson to stoppe thinvasion that might happen by sea, and
wrote to all thinhabytants of the south parts not to receave the
woman yf she showld coom, nor to ayd or releve hir any maner
of way, for if they showld, he wold accownt uppon them as uppon
his very adversaryes : he causyd lay watche also uppon all the
marches of England agaynst Scotland, least any should depart
owt of the realme unto king Henry.   But what danger so ever
might by possybilytie have procedyd from king Henry, the same
was taken away incontinent ; for himself, whether he wer past all
feare, or dryven depely to soome kynd of madnes, was not long
in secret, who enterprysing to enter England disguysed in appa- H. 6 as he
rell had scarce set foote therein when he was taken by the watche, m guised into
and browght to king Edward at London, was commyttyd to warde. England
When king Henry was apprehendyd the state of the realme Scotland,
became more quyet, for as muche as those of that faction thought and was taken and
from thenseforth yt was utterly unmete for them to practyse any brought to
innovations.   Wherfor king Edward, voyd almost from feare of London.
enemy, causyd a parlyament at Westmynster, and employed at A parlia-
his pleasure welnighe fowre whole yeres folowing for the setting ment somoned.
of thinges appertayning to the commonwealth and good government of the realme in order convenyent ; and first of all, because
(according to the owld proverb) thusbandman who toyleth owght

first to taste the fruyt of his travaylle, therfor by common assent, and authorytie of parlyament, he distrybutyd to his faythfull and well deserving servytors, the possessions of them who had holden with king Henry.   After that he provokyd the people generally to loove him by all kynde of lyberalytie, geaving to the nobylytie most large gyftes; and moreover, to gane unyversally the favor of all sortes, he usyd towardes every man of highe and low degree more than mete famylyarytie, which trade of lyfe he never changyd.

Also soome lawes wer reformyd, soome newly inactyd; besyde that he set abrode a coyne as well of gold as silver, which is usyd at this day, wherof the gold partly ys caulyd ryalls, partly nobles, and the sylver ys namyd grotes : fynally he causyd open proclamation to be made throwght the whole realme, that all his adversayres who wold lay arms apart, and submyt themselfes to his obeyssance, should be pardonyd; whoso wold not, should therfor suffer condigne punysshment.   How muche this clemency was for his profyt, and what good-will the people bare to him by reason therof, well appearyd evydent, whan for that only cause he semyd afterward to be unvyncyble.

But king Edward, not content with the favor of his owne onely subjectes, determynyd also to seke thamytie of forrane princes, and the same to confirm by affynytie, that ether they might help him, or at the least not hurt him when nede requyryd ; and therfor he dyd first place his syster Margaret to Charles soone to Phylip duke of Burgoygne; after that he sent Richerd earle of Warwicke ambassador into France, to demand in marriage a young lady cawlyd Bone, syster to Carlot queene of France, and dowghter of Lewys duke of Savoy.   But whyle the earle travalyed into France and delt with king Lewys touching this new affynytie, with whom this yowng lady Bone was attending uppon the queene, king Edwardes mynde alteryd uppon the soddayn, and he tooke to wyfe Elyzabeth, dowghter to Richerd earle Ryvers, wyfe soomtyme to

E. 4 geves
to his de-
servants

H. 6 his
followers.

E. 4

nobles,
and groats.

macon of
pardon to
all that
wold sub-
mit them-
selves of
H. 6 fac-
tion.

Margarete
sistere to
E. 4
maryed to
Charles
duke of
Burgyne.
The E. of
Warwick
sente into
France to
solyset
ladye of
Bona for

John Gray knight, by whom she had two soones, Thomas and
Richerd; which mariage because the woman was of meane caulyng
he kept secret, not onely from the nobylytie of his owne bloode
and kynred, but also from Rycherd hir father. Wherfor whan yt
was brutyd abrode throwgh the realme that the same was perfytyd,
all men incontynent woonderyd, that the nobylytie treuly chafyd,
and cast owt open speaches that the king had not doone according to his dignitie; they found muche fault with him in that
mariage, and imputyd the same to his dishonor, as the thing
wherunto he was led by blynde affection, and not by reule of reason. And surely hereuppon either first proceded the which
sprang up afterward betwixt king Edward and thearle of Warweke; ether els, as soom men think, an occasion was heareby
taken to utter ther malyce before conceavyd; for after that king
Edward had obtaynyd the kingdome by thearle of Warwekes
meane, as well was knowen to all men, he began to have thearles
estimation and authorytie, which himself had made very great, in
such iealousy that he thought yt mete to be abatyd, wherby he
myght now use all thinges as himself lyst without contradiction
both at home and abrode. So we fynde by experience that frindes
do very seldom aunswer lyke for lyke, yea rather unthankfull
myndes do requyte muche good with great evell. These practises
wer not unknowen to Rycherd earle of Warweke, whose hope
though yt was to have thankfully rewardyd, yeat he dyd esteme
yt best to dissemble the matter untyll such tyme as the
king might casually be dryven to soom distress wherein he
might be bold to upbraid unto him his benyfytes; and yt
caryeth soome colour of truthe, which commonly is reportyd,
that king Edward showld have assayed to do soome unhonest act
in the earles howse; for as muche as the king was a man who wold
readly cast an eye uppon yowng ladyes, and loove them inordi-
nately. But whatsoever the matter was for the which they fell

owt, whether for injury offeryd, or envye of authorytie, so yt came
to passe, that after thearle had intelligence from his frindes of the
kinges secrete maryage, and that his dealinge in the ambassage
with king Lewys, as touching the contractyng of this new affynytie,
fell owt in vane and to no purpose, he so highly began to be angry
thereat, that furthwith he adjudgyd king Edward as a man unwoorthy of the regall scepter, mete to be expellyd by all meanes
possible; yeat ther ys a common rumor at this day, that the
cause of ther variance showld have bene this, because the earle
had diswadyd the king not to place his syster Margaret in maryage
unto Charles soone to Phylip duke of Burgoygne, whom the earle
hatyd woorse than any man lyving, and for that king Edward
wold not heare his advise, therfor this grudge to have growen betwixt them; as who showld say that a matter of so smaule importance could or ought to have alyenatyd the earle from hys liege
lord; and this ys a mere fabell of the common people: but let
us returne to our purpose. The erle of Warweke beinge thus
vexid in mynde, moovyd, and angry, least otherwise he might
utterly overthrow him selfe and his devyse, determynyd therfor to
dissemble and covertly beare all these injuryes, while that time
might serve to bring his purpose to effect; who havyng receavyd
soone after the kinges letters of returne, excusyd king Edward
unto king Lewys as well as wold be for the alteration of his
mynde, assigning the same after a sort unto loove, wherin was
never any meane. And so returnyng into England, presentyd
himself before the king in manner accustomed, and mayde report
of his ambassage as well as he cowld, without any shew of greife
conceavyd. After that, within few days, he departyd the court, by
the kinges permission and leave, into his earldome, for the refresshing both of mynde and body, as he gave owt. That was the
yere of our salvation mcccclxvij, and the sixth since king Edward
began his raigne; in which yere also, George Nevyll, broother to

E. 4. the
E. of War-
wicke brake
into greate
termes of

The E. of
Warwick

out of
France.

1464.
[Sc. 1467.]

the earle, was placyd in the stede of William archebisshop of York, lately deade, in rew of bisshops the Lij^te. Also Phylip duke of Burgoygne dyed, whom Charles his soon succeedyd, a man both for haultynes of corage and martyall knowledge passing excellent.

When Rycherd was arryvyd in his earldome of Warwicke, as we have already shewyd, he sent for his broothers, George archebisshop of York, and John marquyse Montacute; with them, after a day or two, he commonyd of dyvers matters; and lastely, having gotten a fyt occasion to complayne uppon the king, he impartyd to them his intente, exoorting them with many woordes and reasons to joigne with him in taking king Henryes part, and to help that he might be restoryd unto his kingdome; sainge in this sort: ' Yt is no lightnes of mynde, from the which I am farre of, my well beloovyd broothers, that moveth me herein, but a settlyd jugement which I may now easily make of king Henry and Edward ; for he ys a most holy man, looving his fryndes intirely well, and thankfull for any benyfyt, who hath a soone, Edward by name, born to great renowme, bowntyfulnes, and lyberalytie, of whom every man may well looke for large recompense, whose care and travaile ys to releve his father in this calamytie. This on thother syde ys a man ready to offer injury, unthankfull, geaven wholly to folow sensualtie, and already shooning all honest exercyse ; who resolutely maketh more honorable accownt of new upstart gentlemen than of the ancyent howses of nobylytie ; wherfor ether must the nobylytie destroy him, or els he wyll destroy them. But we especyally who ar fyrst touchyd with displeasure must not put upp the matter; for I beleve yow ar not ignorant how that, after he was once settlyd in the royall seat, he began at the first secretely and than openly to envy thonor of owre howse, and, one way or other, dayly to dymynyshe the same, as thowgh he had exaltyd us unto that honor, and not we him to that royall powre and

George, the E. of Warwick made archebusshope of Yorke. The E. of Warwick related his gref to his 2 brotheres & re- advaunce H. 6.

authorytie; and therfor, as concerning our late ambassage in
France, we wer not accountyd uppon, to thintent that thonorable
renowme which we have gotten emongest all the nobylytie of this
land, partly by prowesse of owr parent, partly by owr owne tra-
vaill, might be utterly dymynsshyd, defasyd, and in no reputation.'

The arche- Tharchebisshop was with these perswations easly inducyd to be
o ad- of nis opynyon, but so was not tne marquyse, for he cowld never
hered to
the E. of be movyd from the begyning to alow uppon any practyse agaynst
but the ' kinge Edward; but in thende, whan therle of Warweke was pro-
marques mysed the ayd and assistance of many noble men. he was fynally
refused. drawen to joigne with the residew in that warre. After these
thinges, therle of Warweke, being a man of most sharpe wit and
George forecast, conceaving before hand that George duke of Clarence
Clarence was for soome secrete, I cannot tell what cause, alyenatyd in mynde
adheres to from his broother king Edward, made fyrst unto him soome mur-
Warwick. mur and complaynt of the king, therby to proove him how he
was affectyd; then after whan the duke dyd to him the lyke, explaning many injuryes receavyd at his broothers handes, he was
the more bold to enter into greater matters, and discoveryd to the
duke his intent and purpose, praying him to joigne therein. And
because ther showld no suspicion of lyghtness aryse, he gave demonstration evydent how warely, perfytely, and peynfully the same
had bene ponderyd and revolvyd in mynde, exhorting him also to
take care and consideration of so great a cause, wherby all thinges
might be throwghly provyded for, examynyd, and after a sort as-
George suryd; fynally, after many faire promyses, he affyancyd unto the
Clarence duke his doughter, which was then mareageable; by whose per-
maries the swation and request the duke was overcoome, and promysyd to do
Warwickes all thinges as he should think good. Thus therle of Warweke,
aug ter. having impartyd his practyse with the duke, determynyd to make
Warwick returne unto Calice, wherof as yeat he was captane, and ther
retyres to kept his wyfe and chyldren : but to thintent that this so huge

sedition, wherewith England was tossyd and tormoylyd many
yeres after, might once at the last have a begynning, he requyryd
his brothers, tharchebysshop of York and the marquyse, to procure soome uprore to be made in Yorkshyre, anone after his de- An uprore
parture, so that cyvill warre might be commencyd the while he & styre
sed in
was farre absent. These thinges thus determyned and his devyses Yorkeshire
approvyd, therle transportyd with the duke unto Calyce; and practys of
here, after the duke had sworne never to breake the promyse which the arche-
ousnope.
he had made, therle placyd unto him in maryage his eldest
doughter, Isabel, betrouthyd to the duke as is before sayd; which
busynes dispatchyd, they began both two to delyberate more
depely, and to conferre betwixt them selves of the maner and
meanes howe to deale in this warre. Whan in the meane time, as
had bene apoynted, an huge stere arose in Yorkshyre, begun
uppon a wickyd and ungodly cause. Ther was at York an aun-
cyent and welthy xenodochye, that ys to say, an hospytall dedi-
catyd to St. Leonard, wher powre and nedye people wer enter-
teynyd, and the sicke relevyd. To this holy howse all the whole
provynce dyd, for devotion sake, geave yerely certane quantitie of
wheat and first fruytes of all graynes, to serve thuse of the powre,
which quantyty of corne thusbandmen, by provokement and instigation of certane headesmen of therles faction, as the report
went, first denyed to geave, alledging that the thinge geaven was not
bestowyd uppon the powre but uppon the riche, and rewlers of the
place; aftirward, whan the proctors of the sayd hospytall dyd
urge the same earnestly at ther handes, they mayd an affray uppon
them; by which occasion secret assembles and conspyracyes further grew, so that within few days wer gatheryd togythers abowt An assem-
xv^ten thowsand men, who in battayle arraye marchyd spedely blye of
towardes York. Whan the frequent fame of so great commotion uou came
to the gates
came to the towne, all things wer replenysshed with a wonderus of York
feare, the cytecyns, casting in mynd carefully what best was to be comfyted.

doone, contynewyd as men mutually amasyd therwith, and uncertane whether yt should be better to yssew owt agaynst the rage
of this rural rowt, or to kepe the towne, and expulse ther forces
from the waules.   But the marquyse, lyuetenant of that countrye
for the king, delyveryd the cytie of that feere, who, taking a very
fyt way for avoyding of further danger, encownteryd with the
commons as they came at the very gates of the towne, wher, after
long fyght, he tooke ther captane Robert Hulderne, and furthwith
stroke of his heade, which when he had doone he causyd all his
army to retire from the battayle, very late in the night, and withdrew them into the towne.   But the people, no whyt appallyd,
but rather enragyd with the death of ther captane, passing bye
Yorke, whiche, withowt ordinance, and other engynes of warre
they could not assalt, marchyd towardes London, myndyng to set
all in uprore.   And as touching that the marquyse executed the
captane of the commons, whom his owne confederates in conspyracy had sturryd up, the cause semeth to have bene, for that
he might therby cloke and cover his intent, ether els because he
had already resolvyd in mynde to hold with king Edward, with
whom (as afterward appearyd) he joignyd in mutuall benevolence.
But the king, who now began evydently to espy and conceave the
secrete practyses of therle of Warweke, and of his brother the
duke of Clarence, according as he had before suspectyd, after
that he had intellygence, by often message and letters sent to him
with all spede possyble, how that mayne multitude marchyd with
banner displayed towardes London, he sent agaynst them furthwith William Harbert, whom two yere before he had created earle
of Pembrowghe, with a mightie hoste of Walshemen, geaving him
in charge, yf oportunyte should any wher serve, to fyght with them.
The earle, using great celerytie, found the Yorkshire men encampyd not farre from Northampton, wher he also pightchyd his
tents, and the next day after gave them battayll, wherin he was

The re-
marched
towardes
London.

quikly discomfytyd. The Yorkeshyremen, well satisfyed with this
fortunate fyght, waxed soodaynly more coole, and therefor procedyd no further forward, but loden with pray drew homeward,
mynding to stay whyle therle of Warweke should coome to them ;
who not long after, togyther with the duke of Clarence, his soon
in law. hearing of that commotion, had departyd from Calyce, and
was now arryvyd, muche commendıng the captanes of the commons, congratulatyng the victory to all the soldiers in generall,
and with all dyligence preparyd an army. The king, nothing
appallyd with therle of Pembrowghs late overthrow, sent him
agane with suche supply as for releyf of the present necessytie he
had in readynes to make head against the enemy ; himself with a
few foloweth after, who, that he might be preparyd at all assays,
contynewally, as he went, encreasyd his forces all that he might
with the people of his faction reparyng to him plentifully ; he pro-
fessyd openly that he went to extirp the rase of pernycious
parsons. But the earle of Warweke, whan he had intelligence of
thenemyes approche, sent with owt lingering unto the duke of
Clarence, who was hard by with an army, that he wold bring his
forces unto him, signyfying withall that the day of battayle was at
hand. Uppon this message the duke reparyd furthwith to the
earle, and so they both having joygnyd ther forces marchyd to a
village caulyd Banbery, wher they understoode ther enemyes to
be encampyd. Ther was a feyld fowghte. Therle of Pembrowghe
was taken, all his army slane and discomfytyd. Emongest this
number was killyd Rycherd earl Ryvers, father to Elyzabeth the
quene, and his soone John Vedevill. King Edward came after the
same day a lyttle before night with a smaule army, and, hearing of
the slaughter of his people, stayed about fyve myles from the
village. Therle of Warweke returnyd with his victoryus army
unto his owne towne, wher, within two days after, therle of Pembrowgh, with thother nobles taken in the conflict, was beheadyd.

The E. of
discom-
fyted by
the York-
shire men
in the
batle of
North-
ampton.

The Erle
of Cla-
rence and
Warwicke
aryved
from Callis.

The Erle of
Pembroke
sente
against the
E. of
Warw .

The batle
at Ban-
which the
broke was
taken.

Udevilla.

The E of
Pembroke
executed.

In the mean time they began to entreat of a pacyfycation, for the
concludinge wherof messengers passyd often to and fro, from
the king to therle, and from therle to the king; so that the king
was now browght in hope of attonement, and by reason therof
nether tooke convenyent hede to his owne affayre, nether fearyd
any owtward annoyance from thennemy, as thoughe all the matter
had been endyd.   Wheruppon therle of Warweke, conceaving by
espyalls what possybylyte he had to acheve soome fortunate ex-
plovt, approchyd the kinges camp as secretly as he could in the
night, and having kyllyd the watche and ward tooke the king at
unwares, whom he brought with him to Warweke, and from
thence, to deceave the kinges frindes, he sent him by secret journeys in the night season to bee kept at Myddleham Castle in
Yorkshire; but no place was so farre distant whyther as the fame
of the kinges apprehention dyd not reache, which made many
men tremble and quake for feare.   Howbeyt, when the king was
prysoner in the castle he began to speake fayre unto the constable
and keperes therof, to make request unto them, and to put them
in so great hope of rewards, that, corruptyd with his plentyfull
and large promyses, they let him go; yeat notwithstanding the
rumor was spred that the same was doone by therles assent, which
had bene credyble yf therle had afterward layd armor apart; but in
dede yt was the unfortunacy of king Henry, for surely hereby
might every man perceave perfytely that the fynale faule of his
howse was at hand, which cowld not be shoonnyd nether by pollycy
nor powre humane; suche perchance was the will of God; for
therle of Warweke and his frindes, for the speciall ayd, defence,
and preservation of king Henry alone, objected ther parsons to
perill, consumyd ther substance, as men assuryd so long as king
Edward lyvyd that nether they nor king Henry could beare the
sway, and yeat, being in ther handes, they sufferyd him to escape.
Thus may we see that whan our causes ar utterly to decay,

E. 4 taken
and sent to
Mydlham
Yorksh.

E. 4 es-
of prisone.

soometyme feare, soometyme folyshe hardynes, soomtime madnes, soomtyme melancholy, bereaveth us of all wyt, sense, and
understanding.

But king Edward, being thus delyveryd from thand of his enemyes, got himself incontynent to York, wher he was plausybly
receavyd of the cytecynes, and stayed two days in the towne to
levy and arme soome force of soldiers; but whan he was not hable
to make up ther a mete army, and that he was resolvyd to passe
to London throwgh the myddest of his enemyes, he went from
thence to Lancaster, wher William Hastinges, his lord chamberlane,
than lay. Heare by thayde of this William his powr was augmentyd, wherwithall being furnyshed he cam safe to London; and
not to omyt any carefulnes, travale, nor cownsell, that mete was
for his availle in this troublesom time, he regardyd nothing more
than to wyn agane the frendship of suche noble men as wer now
alyenatyd from him, to confyrme the goodwyll of them who wer
hovering and unconstant, and to reduce the mynde of the multytude, being browght by these innovations into a murmooring and
dowbtfulnes what to do, unto ther late obedyence, affection, and
goodwill towardes him. But whan therle of Warweke and the duke
understood that king Edward was escapyd by trechery of ther
owne folkes, and that all ther former practyses wer in a moment
commyd to nought, they ragyd, fretyd, and fumyd extremely, and
by and by assemblyng togytheres ther noblemen, they enteryd into
conference agane, searchyng owt the pollycy and dryft of ther
enemys, that they myght enterpryse ther warres of new, which
when the king was taken they thowght to have bene fynysshed.
These princes wer muche encoragyd because very many who
lyked better of discord than of peace offeryd to serve frely in
this new warre. The king also made preparation for the lyke
with no lesse diligence than his enemyes, ether to bring home into
unytie and obedyence or utterly to destroy his adversaryes, that

all men might once at the last lyve as for them in tranquyllyty
and peace.

Thus was the state of the realme, by reason of intestyne hatryd
and dyvysyon emongst the nobles, most myserable, for churches
and houses wer every wher spoylyd, swoord and fyre ragyd all
over, the realme was wholy replenyssed with harnesse and weapon,
and slaughter, bloode, and lamentation ; the feildes wer wastyd,
towne and cytie stervyd for hunger, and many other mischiefes
happenyd, which procede commonly from the rage of warres ; for
which causes many of the nobylytie pytyed the ruyne of the commonwelth, and therefore delte diligently as well with the king as
with therle of Warweke and the duke for reconciliation, per-
swading soomtymes thone, soomtymes thother, rather to revolve
with themselfes thankfully the benyfytes receavyd than wrothfully
to revenge the late injuryes and to caule to remembrance that
seeing yt ys an heynous offence not to releve owr parentes, muche
more is yt detestable to subvert and by contentyon to ruynate
our countre, the common parent of all, seking, by these meanes,
to take owt of the way and fynally once abolishe this intestine
deadly dyvision.   Both thauthorytie and also intreatie of the
nobylytie so movyd the mynde of the king and earle, that, uppon
mutuall promise of assurance made, the earle himself and the duke
of Clarence came to London, gardyd with a sclender crew of soldyers in respect of so great danger, and had at Westmynster long
talke with the king concerning composytion ; but both parties
wer so replenysnyd witn ire, tnat in thend nothing touching peace
could be concludyd ; and so the king went to Canterbury to vysyte
the snryne of Saint Thomas, for performance of his vow.   The
earle and duke departyd to Warweke, and in Lincolnshyre preparyd a new armv, wherof he made captane Robert Welles knight,
soone of Richerd Wells, an expert and valyant man of warre.   The
newys hereof wer caryed spedely to London, wherwithall the king

'h
of Clarence
and E. of
came to
L   o
treate with
the king of
)ut
nothing
done.
rte
Welles.
captene of
1 e
and E.
armye.

was vehemently moovyd, whose hope was his enemyes wold
rather condiscend to soome maner conditions of peace than any
more to make warre; but the more the rumore therof encreasyd,
contrary to his expectation, the more spedyly dyd he muster owt
and levy an armye, and incontynent sent sundry and often messages
for Rycherd Welles to repare unto him. Wherunto Richard first Richard
excusyd himself by reason of debylytie, want of helth, and other Welles and
busynesses; afterward, when his excuse wold not be admyttyd, he Dymock
rode to London, and browght with him Thomas Dymmok, knight, London.
who had maryed his sister; but having intelligence ther by his
frindes that the king was highly offendyd with him, he fled in hast
as a man in great feare with the sayd Thomas into the saintuary
at Westmynster, meaning ther to tary untill the kinges ire should
be asswagyd. Kyng Edward, who hopyd to suppresse this uprore
without force of armes, gave his fayth and promyse for ther safe-
tyes, and caulyd them unto him owt of sayntuary. They uppon
the kings promyse cam; than the king commandyd Rychard to
will his soone Robert to leave of the warre, and, in the meane time
having his forces in readyness, marched on agaynst his enemyes,
leading with him the sayd Rycherd and Thomas; and whan he
cam within two days journey of the towne of Stamfoorth, wher
the camp of his enemyes lay, he understood that Robert, nothing
moovyd with his father's letters, contynewyd styll in armes;
whereat, taking great indignation, he caused as well the sayd
Richerd as Thomas, contrary to fayth and promyse geaven, and to Ricnerd
the woorst example that might be, to have ther heades stryke of Wells and
from ther showlders. But whan Robert perceavyd the king ap- mocke
proche, and understoode that his father, with Thomas aforesayd, behedded.
wer executyd, he withdrew himself to the next village caulyd
Edgecote; ther he stoode a whyle in dowt whether he showld fyght
or no, because yt was a matter of great hazard to fight with so
great forces before therle of Warwekes arryvall; but at the last,

The batle uppon confydence of youthly corage, he arrayed his host furthwith
and came into the fielde. The fyght was mayntaynyd certane
the kinge howres with great devoyr, many being killyd on both sydes; in
feeld and th thend, while that Robert travaleth with earnest affection to kepe
tooke   his men in order, beinge came at the poynte to fly, he was envy-
Welles and ronyd of his enemyes and taken, togethers with Thomas de la
land, knight, and many others; after whose apprehensyon all
and shortly tharmy was dryven bak and dyscomfytyd. Whan the king had
er   :t
off their gotten this victory, he put to death by and by the said Robert and
heades.   Thomas, and dyvers others. The report ys that abowt x^M. men
Delalante. were kylled in that conflict.

The earle of Warweke who was than at hys owne towne aboutward to come very shortly unto the camp, after he had intellygence that battayle was joignyd sooner than he wold have wenyd,
and that his partie had the overthrow, nowtwithstanding he had
smaule confydence in his affayres, yeat thówght he yt necessary to
dissemble the matter, for that often times in the warres dissimulation serveth the turne better than plane dealing; wherfor to
thintent he might mynyster occasion of comforth to his company,
being in utter despere, and eaven at the poynt of flight, not by
woord only, but also by soome matter in deede, he began therfor
busyly to prepare new supply, and laboryd withall to induce, by
Thomas   many fayre promyses, Thomas lord Stanley to be of his faction ;
lord Stan-
ley refused which when he could not compasse, seeing that Thomas flatly de-
to joyne   nayed to beare armes agaynst king Edward, than fynally seinge yt
earle of   was to no purpose to wast any more tyme, and despearying that
Warwick.   he should be hable to cownter the force of his enemyes, he, with
the duke of Clarence, his soone in law, departyd to Excester, and,
The duke   whyle he stayed ther a few days, having no store of suche thinges
& tne earie
of War-   as wer mete for the warre, ne resolvyd to go unto Lewys the
wick flye Frenche king, as soone as might bee, whose frendship he had
into
France.   gotten a few yeres before, the whyle he lay with him as ambassa-

dor, uppon hope ether to get ayd of him, or els incense him agaynst king Edward ; and in the meane time he hyryd for that voyage shippes on every syde wher he could get them, causing them to be brought into the haven caulyd Dertmouth, which shippes not long after he furnysshyd with artillery and other thinges necessary, and therin they two, with ther wyfes and great number of ther retynew, saylyd with the first fayre wynde into Normandy, wher the lyvetenant of that regyon entertaynyd them honorably, and anon advyrtysd king Lewys of therle of Warwekes arryval. King Lewys had already the earle of Warwyke in so great admyration for the fame of his noble actes, as that he wisshid nothing more than to gratify the man ; wherfor, understanding that he was landyd in France, he sent with great rejoysing certane noble men to mete him, and commandyd them to say unto the earle, that he had long wisshyd occasion wherby to helpe him, and the same now offeryd he wold not omyt, requyring therfor him, with the duke his soone, to take the paine to coome unto him at Amboyse (that is a maner of the kinges, sytuate uppon the ryver of Loire), for the matter showld so faule owt as they should never repent them of that travaille. This flight of therle of Warweke happenyd in the ix[th] yeere of king Edwardes raigne, and of man's salvation M.cccclxx[tie]. King Edwardes care was much aug- 1470. mentyd by reason of the flight of his adversaryes, for that thabsence of therle causyd all men to long dayly more and more to se him agane, as men who thowght themselfes bereft of the soone in this world; so famous was the name of this man amongest the commonaltie as that they had nothing in more reputatyon, extollyd nothinge with more highe commendation. What shall we say to that, the common people had none other song in ther mouths whan so ever they wer disposyd publykly to make disport and be mery. Wherby yt came to passe that therles faction was within few days augmentyd woonderfully. Wherfor the king was

vexid two maner of ways, for he fearyd his enemy both abrode
and at home ; but princypally he thowght yt mete to beware of

Messen-
gers sent to therles returne.   And therfor, with all spede possyble, he sent
messengers to Charles duke of Burgoigne, who (as we have before
duke of shewyed) had maryed his sister Margaret, requyring him, for that
urg
toperswade he was in league witn tne Frenche, to advyse king Lewys not to
the king of ayde, nether with inen nor money, therle of Warwycke and duke
c
[not] to of Clarence, enemyes to king Edward his felow in amytie, and by
ayde them. most sure bond of affynytie his allye.   Duke Charles dyd not
onely accomplishe the same request owt of hand, but also threat-
enyd king Lewys if he showld assist them.   But the Frenche
king thowght those woordes so lyttle to be regardyd, as indeed he
dyd contemne them, awnswering therunto, that he both might,
without breache of league, and wold also ayd his frindes, and especyally those who wer famouse for ther noble factes, of which company the earle of Warwicke was one, the doing wherof should be
nether cost nor charge to the duke.   When the newys hereof
was browght into England, they mayd kinge Edward very sadde,
and browght him muche more cause of care, in so muche that by
examynation and torture of them who wer in warde he sought owt
dylygently who wer frindes to his adversaryes ; by occasion wherof
Divers no- yt came to passe that right many, fearing the woorst, partly fled
for feare of into sayntuary, partly submyttyd themselves to the king ; of this
the king, number was John marquise Montacute, who yealdyd agane, and
sanctuary. gave himself upp wholy to the frendship and partie of king Edward, whome he receavyd with muche curtesy and in the fayrest
maner, to thintent he might therby allure the hartes and amytie
of others.

In this meane whyle therle of Warwicke and the duke rode to
Amboyse, for the seing of whom all the way as he went people resortyd in great number, so muche frequentyd was the fame of this
nobleman, yea emongest the Frenche men.   Whan he cam thyther

he was curtesly and sumptuously receavyd of king Lewys, unto whom he, by long discours, discoveryd the cause of his cooming. King Lewys, no lesse enamoryd and delighted with the presence of his frind than before with his renownyd fame, promysyd that he showld want nothing wherwithall he was hable to help him.

Not long after arryvyd ther also Margarete, wyfe to king Henry, with Edward hir soone, prince of Wales, Jaspar earle of Pembrowghe, and John earle of Oxfoord, who a lytle before had passyd over to quene Margarete. Heare, after they had conferryd of many matters touching ther owne safty, they grew finally, by meane of king Lewys, to the maner of making a league. Fyrst of all, Anne dowghter to therle of Warwick, whom he had browght over with him, was affyancyd to prince Edward; after that, the earle and duke promysyd by othe not to surcease the warres before the kingdom of England showld be restoryd to kinge Henry or Edward his soone; fynally, the quene and prince swore to make therle and duke protectors of the commonwelth, so long to contynew that office till the prince showld be mete and fytt by himself to undertake that charge; and all these thinges they promysyd in most religyouse and devout maner to kepe inviolate. Many moe condytions wer entreatyd uppon emongest them, which both the reason and weyght of the cause requyryd. This league thus concludyd, king Lewys grantyd to thearle of Warwick armor, men, and navy, wherwithall being furnisshed he might the safelyer repare into England. Also Rhenate, quene Margaretes father, helpyd the same what he myght. Now was ther musteryd and apoyntyd an army of no smaule account; the navy lay ready at anchore in the mouth of Seyne, when as the earle receavyd letters from his frindes in England, signyfying that the people unyversally throwghout the realme dyd so muche looke, hope, and long for his returne into England that they wer already every wher in armes, awayting his

Queene Margarete & the prince, with Jaspar E. of Penbroke, & J. E. f Oxford arrive in France.

Upon a lea agreed Anne, da. of Warwick, affiance prince Edward.

arryvall, willing him therfor to make haste, yea thowghe yt wer
withowt any army, for as soone as he showld set foote a land
many thowsands of men wold repare to hym thyther furthwith,
(as afterward happenyd in dede) to folow his direction in all
poyntes, and that the comons wer wholy thus affectyd ; yea moreover that many noble men also wer right ready to mynyster
money, munytion and mayntenance of vyctwall to that warre, and
with hand and hart to help the same. Whan the erle had receavyd
those letters he was woonderus glad, and, determynyng not to
omyt so great possybylytie of well dooing, when quene Margarete
with her soon could not be as yeat ready for that voyage, he and
the duke with the erles of Oxfoord and Pembrough determynyd
with part of the host and navy to go before and geave the first
adventure, which yf yt should well succede, than the quene with
the prince might follow after. Therle of Warwicke therfor, thinking the matter was to be delt in withowt delay and put in execution furthwith, after that he had extollyd as muche as he could
with most humble thankes the benyfyte of king Lewys towardes
king Henry and himself, and was permyttyd by the king to depart,
came, togyther with the duke and other his assocyates, unto his
navy, and shipping his men directyd his course into England.
During this season Charles duke of Burgoigne, grevyd in mynde
that thearle, having receavyd ayd of the Frenche king, should
The E of conduct an army against king Edward, dyd dispose alongest the
Warwick coste of Normandy a great navy of ships to intercept him by the
companye way; but therle, without any damage receavyd by the dukes navy,
arrived out arryvyd with his company safe in the haven of Dertmouth, from
whence six months before he had transportyd into France. Whan
his people wer set on land, he causyd proclamatyon to be made in
the name of king Henry the sixt, that all men, who might for age,
showld arme themselves agaynst Edward duke of York, who
presently contrary to right and law usurpyd the kyngdom : wher-

uppon yt ys uncredible to speake how quickly the brute of therles arryvall was spred throwght all partes of the land, and at the fyrst newys therof, what thowsands of armyd men came to him at once. Whan therle was furnysshed with so great forces, he marchyd towardes London. But when king Edward knew of therles ap- Kinge E. proche he was presently past all hope of habylytie to defend him- his brother selfe; and, therfor, supposing yt best to reserve thuttermost of hys fled into devoyr untill soome better time to coome, he myndyd not the Flaunaeres. levying of an army wherwith to withstand his adversaryes, but, carefull for his owne safty, went with Richerd his broother duke of Glocester unto Lynne, a toune uppon the sea coaste, and, ther fynding a ship ready to make sayle and passe the seas, he saylyd into Flanders to duke Charles with a rowghe and tempestuouse gale of wynde, and for that not without great danger of lyfe. Elyzabeth his wyfe, great with chylde at the same time, fled Elyzabethe into Westminster and ther tooke sayntuary, wher she brought wy to E. 4. fled to forth a soone whom she cawlyd Edward. When the flying of king the sanc-Edward was knowen abrode, therle made more haste, and without tuarye. all resystance came to London, and set the cyty in peace, trubblyd as than with a commotion of the Kentishemen, who abowt the tyme of kinge Edwardes departure had spoylyd the suburbs; for which benyfyt he was more welcome to all men. From thence he went to the towr, and delyveryd king Henry owt of pryson, whom H. 6 sette he browght in his royall apparell throwghe the middest of the at lybertye f cytye, accompanyed first with Richard Lee, lord mayre of the towre. towne, and the two shyryfles, Robert Draper and Richard Gardener, than with the whole cowncell of the cytie, unto the chirche of St. Paule, the people on the right and left hand rejoysing with clapping of hands, and crying, God save king Henry. And then for thys good successe, which happenyd according to his hartes desyre, therle gave thankes to God. This yere wherin king Henry was restoryd to his kingdom was of our salvation M.CCCC.lxxi.

Thus king Henry, so often before conqueryd, begann agane to raigne, and after these doinges abowt the 6th calendes of December held a parlyament at Westmynster; wherin first of all king Edward was proclaymd traytor to his countre, because he had usurpyd the crowne, and all his possessions wer confyscate; lyke sentence was geaven uppon all them who tooke his parte, and also yt was enacted that all such captyves as wer of his faction should suffer condigne punysshement. Moreover, all thinges decreyd, enactyd, and doone by king Edward were abrogatyd. Lastely, therle of Warwicke, as one who had well deservyd of his country, was mayd protector of the realme, with whom was joynyd in commission the duke of Clarence. Thus was the state of the commonwelth alteryd and becoome new. John marquyse Montacute came to that parlyament, who, purgying his fawlt by long discours that his late inclyning to king Edwardes syde was for feare of lyfe onely, obtayned pardon that as he dyd the same unwillingly, so he should never afterward do his frinds good, for yf he had stand fast with king Edward lesse harme undoutydly showld he have doone being an open enemy than a faynyd frynd, seing that the thynges we beeware of very seldome or not muche annoy. But quene Margaret every day, after that day wherin therle of Warwicke departyd into England, trublyd in mynde with incertane expectation of thevent, ceassyd not to preay humbly unto God for victory; wherof fynally, after intellygence had by letters from hir husband, she anon after with Edward hir soone tooke shipping, and assayd to sayle into England. But because the wynter was sharp and stormy, she was by force of tempest dryven bak agane unto the land, and constreynyd to differre hir voyage unto an other time. During the same season Jaspar earle of Pembrowghe returnyd into Wales to his earledome, wher he fownd Henry, soone to his brother Edmund earle of Richemond, not fully x. yeres owld, kept as prysoner, but honorably browght up with the wyfe of William Harbert, who (as we have before remembryd) had bene by king Edward created earle of Pembrowghe, and after taken in battaylle was by commandment of therle of Warwicke beheadyd. This chylde dyd his mother Margaret, thonely dowghter of John first duke of Soomerset, bring foorth whan she was scarse xiiij^{ten} yeres owld, who thowghe afterward she maryed to Henry soone to Humfrey duke of Buckingham, and thirdly to Thomas earle of Darby, yeat never had any mo chyldren, as one thinking yt sufficient for hir to have browght into this world one onely, and suche a soone. And so Jaspar tooke the boy Henry from the wyfe of the lord Harbert, and browght him with himself a lyttle after whan he cam to London unto king Henry. Whan the king saw the chylde, beholding within himself without speache a prety space the haultie disposition therof, he ys reportyd to have sayd to the noble men ther present, ' This trewly, this is he unto whom both we and our adversaryes must yeald and geave over the domynion.'

H. 6 pro nosticate the succe of H. 7.

Thus the holy man shewyd yt woold coome to passe that Henry showld in time enjoy the kingdom.

In this very yeare (that I may remember in dew place the thing which above in my ixth. booke I sayd that I would not omyt) Sixtus the iiijth. bysshopp of Rome, advertysyd from James the iii^{d}. king of Scotland that the bysshops therof had no prymate whom they might consult concerning religion, by reason of the cyvill warres in England, and being requyryd to provyde as mete was for the same, did creat the bisshop of saint Andrewys prymate of all Scotland, that, by reason of tumultes both intestyne and forreyn which often arose betwene both nations, the bisshops themselfes should not be sayd to want an head; althowgh Richerd Nevell archbysshop of York made muche labor to the contrary. And to the sayd prymate he made subject the bysshopps of Glasco, Rosse, Brechen, Donkell, Doumblane, Aberdeyn, Cathanes, Galloway, Thyles,

Candidæ casæ, Li morensei o or n.

Moray, Orchaney, and Sodorne. This bysshops see was placyd in thile of Man, which ys thowght to be of the diocesse of York.

Whyle these thinges were doing otherwher, king Edward, thowgh he wer owt of his country, yeat dyd he not despeare but to have shortly a very fyt and convenyent time for recovery agane of the kingdome ; for partly the duke of Burgoigne promysyd him great ayd, partly he was laboryd dayly to returne by letters and messengers from those of his faction ; and contynually right many, ether for feare of lawys, or for envye of the present state, and desyrus of lybertye to lyve as them lyst, fled to him owt of England, urging him more and more to that journey. With these fayre promyses king Edward was so insensyd that he thowght yt shame to tary one day longer, and covetyd nothinge more than to fly over in all hast; wherfor whan he had gatheryd togythers scarce two thowsand men, and preparyd a few shipps, at the beginning of the spring

E. 4 arived
again in
E1

ne transportyd into England, and arryvyd uppon the coaste of Yorkeshyre at an haven caulyd Ravensporne. Heare, setting his men on land, he consultyd with his captanes whyther he might first go, for, consydering his smaule number of soldiers, he cowld not conceave which way to passe in saftie sufficient. After long consultation they thowght yt best to send owt certane light horsemen abrode into the cowntrye adjoyning, to try the good will of the rurall people, whether they wold ryse with king Edward or no. These men rode furth and dyd ther dewtie with great diligence. Trewly yt ys not lyke that king Edward, being a wyse man, wold have enterprysyd to enter England with so smaule forces except he had knowen to receave great help owt of hand ; by which reason, yt ys not to be dowtyd but the duke of Clarence

Clarence

was even than secretly reconcylyd unto him, and that the mar-

marques
Montague

quyse also Montacute was becoome his partaker, wherof afterward the shew was evydent. But the scurryers, who wer sent to fele

E. 4.

as far as might bee how the people wer affectyd, returnyd the next day folowing unto king Edward, and made report that all the cowntrye ther held firmly with king Henry, and that yt should be but in vane to labor them any further, for thowghe they had bene earnestly in hand with many to joigne with him, yeat not one man durst enter in any talk therof for feare of therle of Warwick. Which whan king Edward knew he alteryd hys purpose of necessytie, and wher at the first he made report that he demandyd the crowne, now he causyd yt to be blowen abrode that he sowght onely for his dukedom of Yorke, to thintent that by this reasonable and rightewouse request he might get more favor at all handes. And yt ys incredible to be spoken how great effect that feygnyd matter was of, suche ys the force of righteuousnes generally among all men; for whan they herd that king Edward myndyd nothing lesse than to require the kingdom, and sowght simply for his inherytance, they began to be movyd ether for pyty to favor him, or at the leest not to hinder him at all from thattayning of that dukedome. Thus, having fownd owt the meane how to mollyfye or gather unto him the good will of the people, king Edward purposyd to go to York, and went first to Beverley. Whan therle of Warwycke, who at those very days lay at Warwycke, had intelligence that king Edward was returnyd into England, and marchyd towardes Yorke, he sent letters by post streight way to his broother Montacute, who had wynteryd at Powntfrayt with no smaule army of soldiers, certyfying him how great the danger was if thenemy showld attayne York, and commandyng him ether to mete and fyght with him by the way, or to stay his passage unto suche time as he himselfe showld shortly coome with more forces, which he was gatheryng with all dylygence. And because he was not sure by which part of Yorkshyre his enemyes wold journey, therfor first he sent perfyte woord by post, and commandment in the kings name to every particuler towne of Yorkshire, and than to Yorke ytself, that all men should be in armes, and to shutt the gates agaynst king Edward.

In tne meane season king Edward approchid York withowt resistance, which whan the cytecyns knew, they, by and by, taking weapon in hand came to defend the gates, and sent two chyefe men of the cytye to mete and requyre him in all ther names not to coome any nearer, nor to object himself to hazard, for they wer amyndyd to repulse him all maner of ways by force of armes. Whan king Edward had herd the messengers he was no lyttle trubblyd in mynde, and these thinges molestyd him most of all, least, yf he should retyre, the country people would pursew him for desyre of spoyle; again, yf he should procede, that the cytecynes sallying owt wold coompasse him rownd abowt; wherfor supposing yt best not to deale by vyolence, but in most curtes maner, he most hartely besechyd the messengers to say unto the cytecynnes in his name that he came not to demand the crowne of England, but his awncyent inherytance of the dukedome of York, and therfor requyryd them to assyst ther duke, who, yf he might by ther good help recover the same, he wold never ferget the benyfyt theŗof; and so with fayre speaches he dismyssyd them home, and wythall drew nere to the gates in good order of battaill. The cytecynes wer soomwhat softenyd with king Edwardes aunswer, for that he semyd, as he sayd, to purpose no practyse agaynst king Henry; and therfor they commounyd with him from the waule, requyring him to depart, which yf he wold do withowt delay they affirmyd he showld receave no damage; yf he wold not, they tould him he was in danger of his lyfe. But he gave curtesse speaches to every of tholder men and rewlers by name, cawling them worshippfull and grave magistrates, he made them many fayre promyses, and besowght them to suffer him to be safe in his owne towne. Thus the whole day almost was spent in this

parley; at the last the cytecynes, uppon hope of benyfyt so bounty-
fully promysed, came to composytion, that yf king Edward wold
geave his othe to entertayne the cytecynes curtesly, and from
thencefoorth to be obedient and faythfull to king Henry, they wold
both receave him into the towne and helpe him to ther powre.
With these condytions king Edward was joyfully contentyd, so
that the next day very early in the morning, *whyle a pryest sayd* Facta per
masse at the gate wherby he was to enter the towne, he *emong* *sacerdotem*
re divina
the holy mysteryes promysyd by othe, devoutly and reverently, *inter sacra.*
to observe both two, and so he was receavyd into the towne; who,
notwithstanding, was so farre from having any minde to observe
thone (according as furthwith after appearyd evydent) that he
resolvyd to regard eaven nothing more than to persecute king
Henry, and to thrust him from the possession of his kingdom.
Thus oftentimes as well men of highe as of low cawling blyndyd E. 4 tooke
with covetousnes, and forgetting all religyon and honesty, ar an oathe
woont to make promyse in swearing by thimmortal God, which mente to
promyse neverthelesse they ar already determynyd to breake breake.
before they make yt.   Of this matter yt shall not yrk me to
make mentyon in the lyfe of king Richerd the third in place
convenyent, wher perchaunce yt may be well conceavyd that
thissew of king Edward did partycypate also the fault of this perjury. The stere of the people thus pacyfyed, king Edward enteryd
into York, and, all memory of his othe put apart, he fortyfyed the
towne with garryson, least any innovation might grow therin; he
also augmentyd his forces, and whan they wer ready, hearing that
his adversaryes wer slow in ther dealings, he supposyd yt so
muche the more necessary for him to make hast, wherfor he set
forward towardes London, and, omytting of purpose the right
way that ledeth to Pountfreyt, wher we have before sayd that the
lord Montacute with an host lay, he turnyd owt towardes the
right hand scarce fowre myles from the camp of his enemyes,

which whan he had passyd without any head mayd agaynst him
by thenemy, he returnyd into the right way agane, a lyttle beyond
the place of ther camp, and marchyd furth to Notingham.   But this
heynous fact of king Edward muche moved the cytecyns of York
to anguyshe and sorow, for they wer ashamyd to have bene deceavyd so pretyly, I will not say unhonestly.

But whan yt was brutyd abrode that king Edward was coomyd
to Notingham without any domage receavyd, than the chief and
headesmen every wher began to revolt to him, as they who thowght
that ether the marquyse wold not set uppon his enemyes because
he held with them, ether els that he durst not marche out of his
camp because he was inferyor to them in force, and therfor they
demyd yt more safe to joigne with king Edward, being now furnished with a mayne army, than with danger to defend the quarell
of king Henry.   King Edward also encoragyd with this successe
removyd his camp quickly to Leycester, wher he had intelligence
that therle was at Warweke, and that John earle of Oxforth was
coomyd thyther to him with a large company of soldyers, both two
to make head agynst him ; who, thinking to prevent that matter,
determynyd to depart thyther with his whole hoste, hoping ether
to encounter with them in the field, ether els to joigne with his
broother duke of Clarence, whom he thought to mete soomwher, as
he was alreadie on his way marching with an army from London,
before he showld coome unto his late confederates, least otherwyse
he might be brought from the mynde he was now in, because he
knew the duke was not very constant.   The erle of Warweke
trewly was in the meane tyme heavy in hert, and much trubblyd,
that wheras he had polytykly provydyd for all thinges, yeat the
marquise had not onely not reparyd thyther wher his enemyes
began first to raise forces, according as he had bene advisyd, but
also had sufferyd them with so smaule powre to passe by him
unfowghten withall.   Wherfor that he might in time convenient

joigne battaille with thenemy, who as a ryver augmentyd his forces
in going, he gathereth powr for every hand, and causeth the duke
of Clarence to be sent for in all hast, who was levying an army at
London. But whan he perceavyd the duke to linger, and do all
things negligently as a man dowtfull whether it wer warre or peace,
eaven than suspectyng that he was corruptyd by his broothers; he
marchyd forward with his forces furthwith unto Coventry, to
thintent he might encounter thenmy as he came. Emong these
matters king Edward came to Warwicke, and took yt, being voyd
of garrison; from thence he marchyd agaynst the erle, and encampyd himself nigh unto him, and the next day after his arryvall
ther he browght furth his men in battaille array, and offeryd therle
the feylde, who, suspecting himself to be betrayed by the duke, as
we have before sayd, kept within the waules; and in this meane
whyle woord was browght that the duke himself was at hand with
an huge army; which when king Edward understoode, he raisyd
his camp and went to mete the duke. Howbeyt, because yt showld
not seme soome suttle practyse concludyd betwixt them two, he
marchid in good order of battaylle, as one that myndyd to fight.
The duke dyd the lyke. But whan they came within view thone
of thother, Richerd duke of Glocestre, as thowghe he had bene
apoyntyd arbyter of all controversy, first conferryd secretly with
the duke; than he returnyd to king Edward, and dyd the very
same with him. Fynally, not warre but peace was in every mans
mouth; than, armor and weapon layd apart uppon both sydes, the
broothers gladly embracyd one an other.

After this king Edward commandyd proclamation to be made in
the same place, that the duke and his adherents should be frely
pardonyd for ever. They thought good also to move the earle of
Warwick to revolt, unto whom the duke had sent of his fryndes
certane noble men, first to excuse his fact, than to exhort him that
he would, whyle he might, make soome composytion with king

E. 4 sur-
prises the
Warwicke.

George ¹
duke of
Clarence
meete and
joyne
togither.

E. 4 at the
same time
published
by procla-
mation the
same
agreem¹.

Edward. Whan therle had herd the duke's message, first he accursyd and cryed owt uppon him, that, contrary to his faith and promise geaven, he had in suche shamefull maner fled unto king Edward. Than, as touching his message, he gave none other awnswer but that he had rather be lyke himself than a false duke, and that therfor he wold not surcease the warre tyll ether he had lost his lyfe or wer revengyd uppon his ennemyes. From thence king Edward, having his forces thus mightyly encreasyd, set forward with assuryd confydence towards London, whyther whan the newys came that the duke of Clarence was reconcylyd to his broothers, and they altogyther wer a coomming to the cytie, suche trembling feare moovyd the cytecynes as that they knew not which way to turne them; but within a while the very same causyd them inclyne to king Edwardes syde. Abowt the same time came letters from therle to king Henry, to Edmund duke of Soommerset, to tharch-bisshop of York, and others of the kinges cownsell, that they wold have regard to kepe the cytie in obedience two or thre days after the coomming of thadversaryes, for he wold in the meane time be ther with a mayne army to releve them. But John Stokton, knight, lord mayre of the towne, with John Crosby, and an other John, Warde by surname, cauling togythers at that very instant into the yeald haule the cownsayll of the towne, began to dely-berate emongst themselves whether partie they had best take. In thend, whan they consyderyd that king Henry was suche a man as by himself cowld not very well governe the commonwelth, agane, that king Edward was wont to rewle the realme not after others but after his owne direction, and was suche a parsonage as cowld defend both himself and his from injury, they all agreyd to hold with him; which whan yt was knowen, the common sort, desirous of noveltie, as soone as they herd of king Edwardes approche, cowld not be holden bak, but they wold goe lustly to mete him, and to salute him in the way by the name of king. The duke of

Summerset and others of that faction, every man shyftyd for himself; but king Henry was, as a sacryfyce to be offeryd, left alone
in the bysshops howse besides Powles, and ther, ignorant what
way to take, as a man amazyd and utterly dullyd with trubbles and
adversitie, was taken by king Edward and commyttyd agane to
ward. King Edward entryd London the iij^d. ides of Aprill, syx
monthes after that he had transportyd into Flanders, and assembling the people togythers did first greatly commend the loyaltie
of the cytecynes, and gave specyall thankes to the magistrates that
they had conteynyd the people in obedience; he dyd also vehemently rebuke with many woordes dyvers others, whether they
wer cytecynes or merchant strangers, whom he knew to have
geaven money to king Henry for levying of an army, and greatly
complanyd of ther offences; fynally, he willyd every man to be
withowt feare, and pronouncyd free pardon of ther infirmyties, by
which mylde dealyng he muche bound to him the myndes of the
multytude.

Therle in the meane time, seing thevent of the whole battaille to
consyst in celerytie, marchyd great journeys after his enemyes, to
thintent that, yf they wer hinderyd throwgh any occasion by the
way (as he hopyd they should be), than he might fyght with them
before they should coome to London, which to do he thowght was
of great importance ; for he was not ignorant how that towne,
being nether sufficyently vyttaylyd nor entrenchyd with any forty-
fycation, was not hable to abide a siege, and therfor woont for the
most part to yeald to the conqueror. And thus when he was
already well forward in his journey, he herd that king Edward had
enteryd London, and had cast king Henry agane in pryson; wherfor
conceaving than the whole matter to be browght of necessytie
unto this ende, that all thinges must fynally be committyd to
thevent of one feilde, he stayd at Saint Albones, partly to refreshe
the soldiers, partly to delyberate more depely uppon the cause.

H. 6 takene
by E. 4 in

Ther was in the army John duke of Excester, an other John earle
of Oxfoorth, Edmund duke of Soommerset, and the third John
marquise Montacute, brother to therle, whom therle himself perceavyd well now to serve in this warre agaynst his owne mynde,
and therfor knew not how muche he might trust unto him, but
the brootherlie loove tooke away almost all suspycion ; howbeyt,
whatsoever he conceavyd of him or others, himself alone above
the rest without all feare determynyd to go agaynst his ennemyes,
and so departing from Saint Albones came unto a village in the
myd way betwixt Saint Albones and the cytie of London, and

'h
at Barnete
x^{ne} myles from tne cytie ytself, which they caule Barnet. This
village ys sytuate uppon an hill, in the top wherof ys a place fyt
for daraignyng of battayll. Heare the erle encampyd himself and
abode his enemyes. Whan the rumor of therles approche was
browght to London, king Edward musteryd owt incontynent a
new army of most hable yowthes adjoyning the same to thoste
which he had browght with him a little before unto the cytie ; also
he sowght for new supply from every hand ; he preparyd afreshe
for armor, weapon, and all other furnyture of warre ; to be short,
he applyed this matter with hart and hand to thuttermost of his
powre, as the thing which he hopyd should make an end of all his
travales and tormoyles. Thus furnished with an huge hoste he
set forward agaynst his enemyes, and to thintent that, yf nede
requyryd, he might be readyer to fyght whersoever he showld
fynde them, he marchyd on in square battayle : he had with him
also king Henry as captyve, for that purpose peradventure that
his enemyes seing in the fight ther king prysoner showld be more
throwghly afeard, or els, if the battaille showld go against him,
that by king Henryes meane he might be safe. He came in this
order after the myddest of the day uppon the hill at Barnet, and
ther encampyd himself not farre from his enemyes, wher, because
he wold not be constraynyd to joigne battaille that night, he sod-

danely entrenchid himself with new fortyfycations; for to prolonge
the time was for his advantage, seing that muche ayd came to him
from every hand; the same was on thother syde hurt to his enemyes, for they being farr from ther fryndes had no hope in new
supplyes; yeat both the hostes contynewed all the night in harnes,
for, by reason of the nighnes of ther tentes, the noyse and nighing
of man and horse was so great that nether army durst geave yt
self to rest. But whan the day began to breake, therle of Warweke
thus arayed hys armye: he placyd the marquyse his brother
and therle of Oxfoorth with part of thorsemen in the lyft wyng;
himselfe with the duke of Excester held the right; in the myddest,
betwixt both two, wer the archers, wherof the duke of Soommerset
had the government. Whan his soldyers wer in this order, he
than with many woordes exhortyd them to fyght manfully, to be
of valyant and prompt corage, and to remember that they wer to
fyght for lyberty of ther country agaynst a tyrant who had
wickydly invadyd the royall seat. King Edward dyd the same,
who also, after that he had orderyd all his owne forces, seing yeat
an huge company of soldiers remane (for as muche as noble men
assemblyd continually to gratifye him), gatheryd moreover all that
multitude togythers, to make supply as nede should requyre, who,
being arrayed in order of battayll, he encoragyd with many perswations, rehersing that he had browght them to fyght agaynst
seditious parsons, who sowght nothing els but dissension emong
all men, the bloode and slawghter of ther countrymen, and thutter
ruyne of ther country. So after yt began to be light day, thalarm
being sowndyd on ether partie, the battaile was begun: first they
fought with arrow afur of, and aftirward with swoordes hand to
hand. King Edward, trusting to the multitude, wherin he farre
excedyd thother partie, pressyd on earnestly. Therle, remembryng
his renowmyd vertew and prowesse, resystyd valyantly. Thus the
fyght was myghtyly mayntayned on both sydes; many wer slane

every wher, whose rowmes freshe men dyd ever of new supply. In this tyme, whylest all men, myndyng busyly the fyght, expectyd the event, therle, after long conflict, perceavyng his partie to be oppressyd with multytude, relyved them who fowght in the first front with a troup of light horsemen, and causyd thenemy soomwhat to geave ground; which whan king Edward saw, he sent furthwith others to succor them. Than was the fyght renewyd with greater slawghter than any time before. Now had the battayll dowtfully contynewyd from early in the morning till almost noone, whan king Edward, whom yt yrkyd that the conflict should last any longer, commandyd the forces which he had hovering owt of the mayne battaille, to geave charge uppon thennemy. But therle of Warwicke, seing the supply of his enemyes enter into the battayll, was therwith no whyt dismayd, but, in great confydence and hope of victory, most earnestly exhortyd, vehemently encoragyd, and hartyly desyryd hys soldiers, thowghe very weary, yet now to abyde this last brunt with valyant corage, crying now and than emong that the battayll was at an end: howbeyt, when they, overtoylyd with long labor, wer nothing almost styrryd up with these woordes, he, with invincible corage, made way emongest the myddest of his enemyes, wher, whyle he entryd unadvysydly, beating down and killing thennemy, farre from his owne forces, The E. of Warwicke ques Montague slayne. nim also was thrust throughe and slane, manfully fyghting, together with the marquise his broother, who folowyd him, having almost the victory in his hand. After therles death the resydew wer put to nygnt and killed universally. This end had Richerd erle of Warweke, which, after so many sundry chances, happenyd unto him throwgh haultines of corage long before his tyme by course of yeres. Ther was killyd on both sydes abowt x^M. men, and the nomber of captyves so great as by no meane was hable to be rekenyd. Edmund duke of Soomersett, with John erle of Oxfoorth, flying incessantly towardes Scotland, alteryd his purpose

for the length of the way, and got him into Wales to therle of
Pembrowghe. Every man shyftyd for himselfe, soome one way,
soome another. The duke of Excester also hardly escapyd into
the saintuary at Westmynster, and ther kept himself secrete.
King Edward, althowgh he got a bloody victory, yeat, lyft up in
mynde excedingly with the joy thereof, returnyd to London with
captyve king Henry, in most triumphant maner. The dead corses
of therle and marquise wer afterward conveyghyd to the same, and
sufferyd to ly in coffyns the space of two days in the churche of
saint Paule before they wer buryed, that all men might se they
wer dead, least the people might be stirryd afterward to new
garboyles by any pretensed name of Warweke. But men
say that king Edward was not so glad for therle of Warwickes
death, but that withall he was right sory for the destructyon
of the marquyse, whome, as we have shewyd, he accowntyd his
frind.

In the meane time Margaret the quene being advertysyd that, Q. Marga-
by reason of king Edwardes returning into England, all thinges were againe in
agane in trubble, made owt furthwith of choyse soldiers no smaule England.
army, and, together with her soone Edward, contendyd with all
spede possible to returne into England ; but, Godes will being to
the contrary, the wynd and wether wer so agaynst hir as that she
arryvyd at an haven caulyd Waymouth later than the matter requyryd. Here, whan she came a land, she understood that king
Edward was lord and master ot all, that king Henry hir husband
was forsaken and taken, that therle of Warwicke and his broother
wer killyd, and that his forces wer partly destroyed, partly scat-
tryd ; and, fynally, that a scourge was receavyd most sharp and
bitter, as well in respect of the conflict yt self, as of the tyme.
Whan she herd these things the myserable woman swownyd for
feare ; she was distrawght, dismayd, and tormentyd with sorow ;
she lamentyd the calamyty of the time, the adversity of fortune,

hir owne toyle and mysery; she bewaylyd the unhappy end of
king Henry, which now she accowntyd assurydly to be at hand;
and, to be short, she so afflictyd hir self as one more desyrus to dy
than lyve, foreseing perchance inwardly in mynde woorse matters
immynent and hanging over hir head. Than might quene Margaret have caulyd to mynde that these maner myschiefes had
chancyd princypally for the death of Humfrey duke of Glocester, of which practise, thowgh percase she wer no partaker,
yeat not giltles, because she myght have preservyd that good nobleman; for surely yf that one man had lyvyd and rewlyd the
realme, king Henry had never comyd in so many hazards of hys
lyfe. Wold to God many wold well weygh the causes of suche
eventes, who measure equytee and right according to ther power

Queene
& hir ^{are}
soone
sanctuary.

and will: but I will returne to the matter. Quene Margaret perceaving yt was in vane to provyde for warres, and now almost
despearing of hir owne saftye and hir soons, departyd to the next
abbay, of the cystertyan order, which ys at a village caulyd Beaw-
lyew, and there tooke sayntuary. The report in the meane time of

nobles^s
that ad-
Q ^{ea} Marga-
ret.

hir coomming being brutyd abrode, Edmund duke of Soommerset,
with John his broother, Thomas Cortney erle of Devonshire (who
before had alway been of thother party), Jasper erle of Pembrowgh, John lord Wenlocke, and John Longstroth[r] chief captane
of the knightes of Rhodes, met together quikly at Beaulyeu, and
went to the quene. The dolefull wooman, seing the noblemen
who wer hir frindes, was soomwhat refreshyd in mynde, and, layng
feare soomwhat apart, to thintent they showld not think she had
doone any thing unadvysdly, she talkyd with them of many matters, and declaryd the cawse why she could not be present in
tyme, and what reason movyd her to fly unto that saintwary; beseeching them particularly, fyrst before all other thinges, to provyde for the safetie of hir soon; and, despeyryng utterly to pre-
vayle at this present by force of armes, she thowght yt best to

sayle againe into France, yf the tyme of yeare, and malice of
the meny wold so permyt, and ther to abyde till God should geave
better opportunytie to use armes. The duke with thothers, after he
had comfortyd the quene with many perswations, began to make a
long discourse of the state and condition of warre; and first he
thowght that no delay was to be made, least therby themselves
showld be weaker, and king Edward becoome stronger, who now
had no army in readynes, seing that in the late conflict almost all
the yowthly force of that factyon was broken and abatyd; and that
he who in the late battayle against therle of Warwicke had had so
good successe, might by good reason have the contrary in the war
to come, consydering the chance of warre was woont right often
to be varyable, eaven at an instant; secondly, he affirmyd that a
good part of the nobylytie stoode with king Henry, and that soldyers wold willingly coome to ayde hyr, yf so be that she wold, as
she had often, becoome captane agaynst thennemy, and hereunto
himself offeryd large forces, and more ample dyd promise in the
name of both therles; lastely, after that he had shewyd many reasons why the victory was lyke to be thers, he besowght all men to
be of good chere, and, because the matter requyryd haste, to treat
no more of the state and condytion therof, but of thenterprising
presently the warre yt self. To this the quene, whose care was
most not for hir owne but for hir soones safety, and for that tooke
great care and thowght, whose owne most provydent mynde gave
her that no good wold coome hereof, made awnswer, that she could
lyke well of his opynion yf nothing wer to be hazardyd more dere
than her owne lyfe; but she suspectyd least, whyle they sowght to
succore the decayd case of the commonwelth, the lyfe of prince
Edward should be in danger, in whom the whole hope of that
howse consystyd, and therfor wisshyd that ether the warre might
be put of unto an other time, or that hir soone might be sent into
France, ther to be kept safe and secrete, whyle thevent of the first
conflict showd fawle out. Treuly the mother had good cause

dylygently to provyde for the lyfe of hir soonc, seing that next
unto hir husband, whom she accowntyd lost, ther was not unto
hir any thing better belovyd, dearer, nor more to hir comfoorth.
Thus this most prudent quene requyryd that these princes, polytyk
in martiall affayres, would well weygh all these thinges before
hand, because, yf afterward they showld think yt mete to com-
mence warre, she wold not deny to be of ther mynde. But yt
was no boote to argew longer uppon the matter, the duke affirming
that they wer all determynyd whyle lyfe dyd last to mayntaine
warre agaynst ther enemyes, and therfor the thing that was with
most mature delyberation concludyd was also with lyke firm consent to be performyd. And so all everiche one being encoragyd
to make warre, every man for his part gatheryd forces. The duke
through all hys domynyon musteryd with dylygence, likewyse did
therle of Devonshire: therle of Pembrowgh also departyd to his
earledom for the same cause. The Quene at the last, browght into
the lyke hope of well doing, sayd, I pray God spede us well,
and furthwith procedyd to Bath, as the duke had advysyd hir, ther
to tary while hir confederates returnyd ; but wher a way so ever
she mynded to go, few knew thereof, to thend that hir intent
showld not be discoveryd to hir adversaryes before she arryvyd
in the place wherunto she travayld.

E. 4 levied   Also king Edward, whan he understoode that quene Margaret
foarces &   was coomyd into England, and that the duke of Soommerset and
Marl-   his allyes dyd gather an army, sent incontinent certane light horse
ridge .   men abrode every way to espye how great the forces of thenemyes
wer, and whyther they tooke the course. They rode foorth
spedyly, as they had bene commandyd, and having scurryed all the
west part of the regyon, made relation what they had perceavyd
and knowen. By whose travayle, whan the king could not be
sure what way his ennemyes tooke, he determynyd to encounter
with them soomewher before they showld approche London, and
so he marchyd with that force which he had levyed at London

into Oxfoorthshire, and seking a place fyt for pightching his tentes, he chose the same at Abyngton, commanding that all powr to be gatheryd otherwher showld thyther resort. Here, when he had assemblyd all his hoste togethers, and understoode that his adversaryes wer coome to Bathe, tarrying ther to augment the number of ther soldiers by confluence of people who from every hand resortyd to them, he departed from thence to Marlebridge, which village is distant from Bath about xv^{ten}. myles, and thyther he made hast, to thintent that by geaving his enemyes a possybylytie of fyght he might joigne battaill with them before they went into Wales, whyther he suspectyd (as ther meaning was indede) that they wold go to joigne themselves with therle of Pembrowghe, who preparyd huge forces in those partes. But whan the Quene understoode that king Edward was before hir, she departyd from Bath and went to Bristow, sending certane horsemen from thence before to searche whether she might have safe and open passage throwgh Glocestershire into Wales, whose intent was first to go thyther for increasing of hir army, and than incontinent without delay to marche with baner displayed against thenemy whersoever he showld abyde; her scurryers cam quykly agane, declaring that the towne of Glocester was firme and fast to duke Richerd, king Edwardes brother; and thowgh they had first assayed them with fayre promyses, and than after with threatenings, to revolt, yeat they wer no whyt moved therwithall. That being knowen, the quene departyd from Bristow, and marchyd to a towne sytuate uppon the ryver Severne which is caulyd Tewkesbury, passing by Glocester, because she wold wast no time in beseiging the towne. Here, whan they had pightchyd ther tentes, the duke of Soomersett, having intellygence that king Edward, who folowyd them foote by foote, was not fur of, drew his men foorth into battaile aray, muche against thadvise of thother captaines, who thought best to tarry til therle of Pembrowghe showld coome. King Edward also was

The battle wx. bury.

at hand not long after with his army well orderyd ; and, thalarme sowndyd on both sydes, they joignyd battayll. After long and sharp fight, Edmund the duke, perceaving his smaule number to be overlayd with the multitude of his ennemyes, drew furthwith his men bak to thir standerdes, that, being close togythers, they might more easely resyst. The same also soomwhat refresshyd the corage of the soldiers, so that they began more fiercely to lay on : but whan the quene had not freshe soldiers to supply the places of wearyd and woundyd, she was overmatchyd of the multitude, and in thend vanquisshed ; hir company being killyd and taken almost every one. Ther dyed in that battaill of noble men, Thomas earle of Devonshire, John lord Wenlock, lord John, broother to the duke of Summerset, with many other. Ther wer taken, Margaret the quene, Edward the prince, Edmund duke of Soomerset, John lord of Saint Johns, and xx^{te}. moe knightes. All those, except quene Margaret and the prince, wer within two days after beheadyd in the same towne. Edward the prince and excellent yowth, being browght a lyttle after to the speache of king Edward, and demaundyd how he durst be so bowld as to enter and make warre in his realme, made awnswer, with bold mynde, that he came to recover his awncyent inherytance ; hereunto king Edward gave no awnswer, onely thrusting the young man from him with his hand, whom furthwith, those that wer present wer George duke of Clarence, Richerd duke of Glocester, and William lord Hastinges, crewelly murderyd ; his corse, with the resydew of them that wer slane, was interryd in the next abbay of monkes of thorder of St. Benedict. But quene Margaret was convayd captyve to London, and, not long after being ransomyd, was of thenemy sufferyd to depart, who saylyd into France, lyvyd in perpetuall moorning, and yeat not that so muche for hirself or hir husband, who wer now well agyd, as for the losse of hir soone Edward, whom she, whom Henry his father, thowght to leave in

Edward
the prince
slaine in
the kings
ice.

Q. Marga-
ret ran-
     &
sente
overe.

saftie, after the losse of ther owne lyves and dignyties, by reason wherof ther could not have happenyd to them in all this world a matter of more grefe. But king Edward, rejoysing immortally for the victory, which endyd intestine dyvysion, after he had viewyd circumspectly all that part of the realme wherin his adversaryes had assemblyd, returnyd to London, wher was woonderfull rejoysing of all sortes, with contynuall prayer, the space of thre days. This was thend and conclusion of king Edwardes martiall exploytes, which was the yere of our salvation M.CCCC.lxxi., and the xi^th of king Edwardes raigne.

About the time of king Edwardes returne, Thomas Faucon- Bastard bridge, base begotten soone to William Fauconbridge erle of Faucon- Kent, a man of much audacytie, and factious withall, whom evell the Kent- lyfe especyally stirryd upp to disturb the commonwelth, made a yshe men, came to great garboyle : for he had somtime bene made admyrall by the surprise erle of Warweke to kepe the passage betwixt Calice and Dover, that London. none of king Edwardes syd might frely pass ; after that, being become nedy and offensyve, as well to frend as foe, he began openly to play the pyrate, wherby yt came to passe that within short space, being furnished with good store of shippes, he robbyd and spoylyd all abowt the coaste. At the last, arryving in Kent, he cam a land, and, having gatheryd no smaule powr of Kentishe people, he marchid foorth right to London, and at his very first cooming made great spoyle, all his men showting and crying that they wer coome to delyver Henry ther king. But whan yt was knowen that quene Margaret was vanquisshed in battaille, than William Edwardes, lord mayor for that yere, with John Aleyn and an other John, Chelley, shyryffes, assemblyd a good number of soldiers, and geaving charge uppon Fawconbridge reskewyd the spoyle and put him to flight, kylling and taking many of the Kentish folk in the chace.

This stere, lyttle thowgh yt wer, yeat yf yt had bene rasyd a

lyttle befor, no dowt but yt had browght King Edwardes affayres
in great hazard.   But trewly king Edward was in these last warres
the happyest man in the world, in that his adversaryes assayled
him at severall times.   Surely, yf at the same time that therle of
Warwycke hastenyd to London with his most forward and well
furnisshyd forces, quene Margaret had of an other syde enteryd
England, as she thryse had earnestly assayed, wherby she behinde
and he before had urgyd thenemy at one instant; or yf Edmund
duke of Soomerset had not at Teuchesbury daraignyd battaill before Jaspar erle of Pembrowgh had with his supply arryvyd; or yf
Fawconbridge had assaultyd the cyty withall at the same time,
thone or thother of these thynges nedes must have folowyd; that
ether king Edward of fyne force must have fled. or bene compellyd fowly to yeald.   Thus may we se that, as in all other
thinges so in warre especyally, according to the common proverb,
the good fortune of a man ys all.   Yeat yt may be peradventure
that this came to passe by reason of thinfortunacy of the howse of
Lancaster, which wyse men thowght eaven than was to be ad-
scrybyd to the rightewousnes of God ; because the soveraignty
extortyd forceably by Henry the Fourth, grandfather to king
Henry the Sixt, cowld not therby be long enjoyed of that famyly,
and so the grandfathers offence redowndyd unto the nephews.
But now agane to the matter.

Bastarde
Faucon-
bridg
beheded.

The Fawconbridge sped him spedyly unto his ships, but soone
after arryving unadvysydly at Southampton he was taken and
beheadyd.   Howbeyt, Jaspar erle of Pembrowgh, whan he understoode that the Quene was vanquysshed in a fowghten feilde at
Tewkesbury, and that matters wer past all hope of recovery, retyryd with his retynew, which he was conductyng to his confederates, bak agane to Chepstow.   Whyle he heare taryed lamenting
that headynesse, which alway ys blynde and improvident, had
utterly overthrowne the universall powr of king Henry, and dely-

beratyng with his frends what course was best to take, behold one
Roger Vaughan, a very valyant man, sent thyther by king Edward
for that purpose, went about by a trayn to take him; wherof
therle being advertysyd tooke the sayd Roger within the towne Rogere
and cut of his head; and so he sufferyd death at therles apoynt- loste his
ment which himself assayd by guyle to have brought therle unto. heade,
Hereof may we gather that a man ought to feare a plague to
hinge over his owne head who seketh an others destruction.
Therle departyd from thence to Pembrowghe, whom incontinent The earle
Morgan Thomas, sent by king Edward, besegyd, and kept in with broke is
diche and trenche that he might not escape; but the viijth day beseegede.
folowing he was delyveryd from that distres by Davyd, broother
to the sayd Morgan, hys assuryd faythfull frind, and departyd
furthwith to a towne by the sea syde caulyd Tynby, wher having
a barke preparyd owt of hand he saylyd into France with his Jasper E.
broothers soon Henry erle of Richemond, and certane other his of l'en-
broke and
frindes and servantes, whose chaunce being to arryve in Brytayne Henry E.
he presentyd himself humbly to Francisse duke ther, and, report- Rich.
mond sayl
ing the cause of his cooming, submyttyd himself and his nephew to Fraunce
to his protection. The duke receavyd them willingly, and with
suche honor, curtesy, and favor intertaynyd them as thowgh they
had bene his broothers, promysing them uppon his honor that
within his domynyon they showld bee from thencefurth far from
injury, and passe at ther pleasure to and fro withowt danger.

King Edward, whan his realme was thus pacyfyed, to thintent
ther showld be no new insurrections, travalyd not long after
throwgh Kent, wholy because the last tumult under the conduct
of the Fawconbridge had procedyd from thence, and he punyshed
severely those who had made the sedytion; which busynes being
dispatchyd, to thintent every man might conceave a perfyte peace
to be attainyd, and that all feare of enemyes might be abolisshyd, H. 6 mur-
Henry the Sixt, being not long before depryvyd of hys dyademe, the Towre.

was put to death in the tour of London. The contynuall report
is, that Richerd duke of Glocester killyd him with a swoord,
whereby his brother might be delyveryd from all feare of hosty-
lytie. But who so ever wer the killer of that holy man, yt is
apparant ynoughe, that as well the murtherer as the procurers
therof sufferyd punysshement for ther offences, who, whan as
afterward they had none enemyes uppon whom to satisfy and
satyate ther crueltie, exercysyd the same uppon themselves, as
hereafter in place convenyent shalbe declaryd, and embrewyd ther
handes in ther own bloode. Afterward the corse of king Henry
was without any honor browght from the towre to Saint Paules
churche, wher yt lay uppon the beere all one day, and the day
folowing was caryed unto an abbay of moonkes of Saint Benedicts

H. 6 buried Order, in a towne caulyd Chertsey, distant xv^{ten} myles from London,
twise.   and ther was buryed; but not long after yt was transferryd from
that place to the castle of Wyndsore, and ther layd in a new tombe
The foun- in Saint George his chaple. The sayd abbay was buyldyd of old
at   time at Chertsey by St. Erkenwald bishop of London, abowt the
Chertsey
Abbey.   vere of our Lord six hundreth seventie nyne, as we have shewyd in
H. 6 dis- the fourth booke. King Henry raignyd xxxviij^{te} yeres, and, after he
cribed.   receavyd the kingdome agane, vj. monthes ; he lyvyd lii. yeres. He
begot of quene Margaret Edward his onely soone, prince of Wales.
He was taule of stature, sclender of body, wherunto all his mem-
bers wer proportionably correspondent ; he was of coomly vysage,
wherin did glister contynually that bowntefulnes of disposition
wherwith he was abundantly endewyd. He dyd of his owne
naturall inclynation abhorre all vices both of body and mynde, by
reason wherof he was of honest conversation eaven from a chylde,
pure and clene, partaken of none evell, ready to conceave all that
was good, a contemner of all those thinges whiche commonly corrupt the myndes of men, so patient also in suffering of injuryes,
receavyd now and then, as that he covetyd in his hart no revenge,

but for the very same gave God Almighty most humble thankes,
because therby he thowght his sinnes to be wasshyd away; yea,
what shalle we say, that this good, gratious, holy, sober, and wyse
man, wold affirme all these myseryes to have happenyd unto him
both for his owne and his ancestors manyfold offences; wherfor
he dyd not muche account what dignitie, what honor, what state
of lyfe, what soone, what frinds he had lost, nor made muche dole
for the same; but yf in any thing he had offendyd God, that had
he regard of, that dyd he morne for, that was he sorry for. These
and suche lyke actions and offices of parfyte holynes, made, that
for his cause God shewyd many myracles in his lyfe time. By
reason wherof king Henry the vii[th], not without desert, began a few
yeres past to procure at the hande of Julius byshop of Rome
that he might be canonyzyd for a Saynt, but being preventid by
hasty death he could not perform that honorable fact. Moreover, *id officiu.*
this Henry was of lyberall mynde; he had good learning in great
reverence, and loovyd them who wer indewyd therwithall, wherfor
he helpyd his owne people that they might be instructyd; for he
foundyd a sumpteuous schoole at Eton, a towne next unto Wynde-
sore, in whiche he placyd a colledge of priestes, and children in
great number, ther to be browght upp and taught ther grammer
frely and without coste. The same man was also fownder of the
Kinges colledge at Cambrydge, which so floryssheth at this day
with thornaments of learning that yt may well bee cawlyd the
prince of all colledges. But now I will returne to the matter.

Thus king Edward, being delyveryd from a great part of his
cares and causes of feare, to thintent ther showld not remane any
trace or tracke of the faction adverse, determynyd utterly to
destroy the remnaunt of his enemyes whersoever they wer; and
therfor he sent George archebisshop of York, therle of Warwickes
broother, to pyne away in pryson at Guyons, wher he contynewyd
long in ward, but being afterward set at lybertie, he dyed by and

by for sorow; unto whom succedyd Laurence Both, and to that
Laurence, dying three yere after, Thomas Rotheram bisshop of
Lincolne, who was by orderly succession the liiij[th] bishop.   Also
the king found meane to coom by John erle of Oxford, who not
long after the discomfyture receavyd at the towne of Barnet fled
into Cornewall, and both tooke and kept Saint Mychaels Mount,
and sent him to a castle beyond the sea caulyd Hammes, wher he
was kept prysoner more than xij. yeres after.   Many moreover wer
uppon lyttle suspytion taken in many places, and other commyttyd
to ward or grevously fynyd.   Besydes these thinges, to thintent that
his foes might fynde no succor in the countries adjoyning, he tooke
treuce with James king of Scottes for xx. yeres.   But yeat because
he might have soomwhat to think uppon, and that he showld not
lyve altogethers in perfyte securytie, he had intelligence at the
same time that therles of Pembrowgh and Richemond were transportyd into Bryteyn, and of the duke ther curtesly receavyd and
intertaynd; which matter indede he tooke very grevously, and
thowgh hys mynd gave him that soome evell wold coome therby,
which to prevent he sent in all hast secret messengers to the duke,
promysing to geave great rewardes so that he wold make delyvery
of both therles.   The duke herd willingly king Edwardes ambassage, and whan he understoode that therles were so riche a pray
he determynyd not to let them go, but to kepe them more warely
than befoor, making awnswer to thambassadors that he might not
delyver them to the king, bye reason of his promyse and fydelyte
geaven to the contrary; but he wold for his cause kepe them so
sure as ther should be none occasion for him to suspect that they
should ever procure his harme any maner of way.   Whan thambassadors could not obtaine the thing they requyryd they receavyd
that for awnswer, and returned to the kinge, who than wrote
agane to the duke, requiring that for his honour, good fame, and
constancy, he wold performe the thing which of his owne accord

John E. of
for
sent t ri
soner to
s
Castle.

he had offeryd, and he promysyd both money, ayd, and huge
gyfts, and payd the same plentyfully every yeare afterward. The
duke than seing that the remanyng of those two erles with him
redowndyd to his advantage, least peradventure they might depart
soome other wher, devydyd them in sundre, and, removing from
them thinglishe servyteures which they brought with them, placyd
men of his owne country to wayt uppon and gard them. In the A parlea-
meane time the king caulyd a parlyament at Westminster the ment
iij^d ides of October and xijth yere of his raigne, which was of mans
salvation M.CCCC.lxxiij.; wherein first wer revyved all suche his con-
stitutions and lawys, which had bene repealyd and abrogatyd a
lyttle before by king Henry the vith, and statutes made for the for-
fature and sale of all his adversaryes possessions, and the cawlyng
home again from exile of them who a few monthes before had bene
attaintyd of treason by his enemyes; secondly, a taske was imposyd for money, wherof the kinges coffers were very bare; thirdly,
as well publyk as pryvate quarrells rysen emongest the nobylytie,
wherof the number was few, the better part of them being consumyd with domesticall dissention, was pacyfyed, appeasyd, and
taken upp. The king himself helpyd this matter as muche as in
him lay; who to move other men by his good example to forget
injuryes and lay hatryd apart, grauntyd fre pardon for all treason
and breache of law to all men that presently wer within the realme
and had bene hytherto of thother faction. Not long also after
that he receavyd to his grace and favor the German marchantes The Ger-
who wer borne uppon the sea coast of Almany, whom he had mane ar
chantes
before cast in pryson, confyscatyng ther goodes, because certane restored.
ships of Lin had bene interceptyd by the Danes for a murder
wherof thinglishe men wer accowntyd guyltie, of which sayd fact
the Germane merchantes wer reportyd to bee pryncypall procurers. But whan tryall of treuth endyd the controversy, king
Edward made unto the merchantes full restitution, who being

afterward by reason hereof made more circumspect, have with
great diligence conservyd ther pryveledges receavyd both of king
Richerd the iij^{rd} and of king Henry the Seventh.

E. 4 joyned
in warre
with the
duke of
against the
K. of
Fraunce.

Whyle that king Edward gave himself wholy to the setting in
order nis causes at home, behold he was cawlyd by the duke of
Burgoyne to thenterprysing of forreyn warre agaynst Lewys the
Frenche king, that so soomwhat myght alway remane to the dis-
turbing of cyvyll tranquyllvtie. The kinge cowld not choise but
joigne in that warre for many causes, wherof chiefly wer two;
thone because king Lewys was his enemy, as he who had armyd
therle of Warwicke in Fraunce agaynst him, thother for that,
besydes thaffynytie which he had with the duke of Burgoigne, he
was also singulerly beholden unto him for hys manyfold benyfyttes
bestowyd uppon him whan he was dryven owt of England : wherfor, after conference had with his nobles of so weightie warres, he
awnsweryd the duke of Burgoigne that he wold joigne with him
therein agaynst the Frenche king. Trewly at that time the rage of
warre was great betwixt duke Charles and king Lewys, and because king Lewys being an hard and froward man of nature was
injuryous and spytefull both to frind and foe, therfor many noble
men of France, abhorring his unreasonable dealing, conspyryd
ether openly or secretely with the duke of Burgoygne : in the
number of whom was Lewys of Lucembrough, constable of France,
who conferryd with the Burgoignyon and right many of the
nobylytie to bring the king in suche distress, as that ether he
might reforme his lyfe, or els be in jeopardy, insomuche that the
commonwelth of France showld be urgyd both with forrein and
intestyne warre all at once. The duke discoveryd all his secretes
to king Edward, the rather therby to allure him to take armes,
which matters indede, as assuryd signes of victorye, drew fynally
the king into that warre, who with all spede possyble preparyd
both hoste and navy ; and because muche money was necessary to

be had for diffraying the charges of that army, and that the money
gatheryd a lyttle before by meane of taske was disbursyd and
spent already in his domesticall affayres, a devyse cam in his
heade, wherby he might pollytykly procure his more wealthy
frindes to geave money, in so muche that they who wold not part
withall might be cawlyd unkynd.   And therfor he causyd certane
his officers of receit and commissioners to caule before them all
riche men generally, and to explane to them particularly, the
cause he had to make warre, themptynes of his coffers, and for the
trew hart, goodwill, and favor which they bore his maieste, to
require ther help of soome money, to support the charge of this
warre: but to be short, his practyse so prevalyd, that soome remembring the benyfytes receavyd, soome for shamefastnes, soome
other for very feare, every man professing to shew his goodwill,
according to his habylytie, aydyd the king with money, and he,
to shew his thankfull accepting of this benyfyt, and for the perpetuall memory therof, caulyd the trybute thus frely geaven a
benevolence, though perchance very many gave that benevolence
with evell will.   Thus king Edward, furnisshyd perfytely with all
thinges appertanyng to the warres, and having assemblyd an army
of 20,000 men, passyd the seas to Calyce the fourth nones of
July, to whom duke Charles reparyd furthwith, and, putting him
in comfoorth of victory, earnestly exhortyd him to apply this
warre with all devoyr, wherby he might and should recover his
right from the Frenche.

But whan king Lewys understoode that king Edward was E. 4 sent
already arryvyd with an army, in the contynent he augmentyd his an army
int   ance
forces, and the more danger that he saw hung over his head from in aid of
the duke of
so many most mightie enemyes togythers, with so muche more Burgundy.
celerytie determynyd to make head agaynst them; wherfor he sent
before, with suche force as he had hastely gatheryd, Robert Stote-
vylle, his lyvetenant, to the bounds of Artoyse, who might

receave the first brunt of thinglishe approche ; himselfe the meane
whyle stayd at Senles, ymagening by what meane he might bring
the matter to a treaty ; for, seing he was forsaken of his subjectes,
whom himself had rejectyd, he dyd inwardly forsee, that yf bloode
wer once drawen the warre wold be longer and more perillus,
wherfor he was desyrus of nothing so muche as of peace.   Suche
matters as these wer in king Lewys head, whan king Edward
removyd from Calice and entryd Artoyse, unto whom the French

Ambassa-
te
from the
Frenche
o
treate of
peace,
which was
concludyd. king sent furthwith ambassadors for peace.   The king of England
gave tnem audience, and having herd ther ambassage, began to
grow coole, and not muche to mislyke of peace: for thowghe he
wer a valyant man, and by fame of his nobles factes encoragyd
rather to desyre warre than peace with the Frenche. thancyent
enemy of thinglishe name, yeat whan he revolvyd with himself,
how that the forces of England were so consumyd with cyvyll
contentyon as yf nede should require a new supply of soldyers
yt was almost vnpossyble to levy the same convenyently of his
owne subjectes, and whan also he was not ignorant of emptie
coffers, so that he should not be hable to make pay any long
time to the soldier, he thowght that of very necessytie he must
yealde and refrane from warre in the end, which he myght now
fynish with honorable conditions, having especyally just cause to
complane that the Burgoygnyon and he of Lucembroughe dyd
not performe that which they promysyd at the begynning.   Therfor, to thambassadors requestyng that he wold coome to a parle
with the king, he aunsweryd at the last, that he wold so do, and
so, having apoyntyd tyme and place, suffryd them to depart. Whan
they made relation that thaunswer was geaven according as was
desyryd, king Lewys, being fortyfyed both with men and money,
came first with hart and goodwill to Pinquigny, which is a towne
in the terrytory of Amyens, wher the meting of the two kinges
was appoyntyd ; whyther also came not long after king Edward,

gardyd with great force of soldiers. Here the two kinges meting
uppon the brydge which is over the ryver Some, had long talk
togythers, and fynally concludyd a treuce for many yeres, uppon
these condityons : that king Lewys showld pay presently unto king
Edward for his expenses in the preparation of this warre lv^{M.}
crownes, and yerely afterward l^{M.}

After these thinges, to confirme, strengthen, and tye fast thys Elizabeth
new frendship with soome knot of allyance, Elzzabeth, king Ed- maryed to
wards dowghter, was covenantyd in mariage to Charles, king Charles
prince of
Lewys his soone. In that warre no man miscaryed but John Friunce.
duke of Excester ; he had bene in sayntuary, as I have shewyd John duke
before, and, serving king Edward in this voyage, was afterward, con- slaine.
trary to promyse, taken sooddenly owt of the way : that was the year
of mans salvation M.CCCC.lxxv^{to}. King Lewys from thencefurth
payd the trybute trewly to the king of England unto the begyning
of that yere wherin he dyed, than (as I suppose) he denyed to pay
the same as a man knowyng his fate approche ; wheruppon we
may gather argument that the kings concludyd at the beginning
a league, and not a trewce, which was for both ther advantages.
But whan the Burgoygnyon, and he of Lusembrough knew that The duke
king Edward had concludyd peace with king Lewys, they chafyd o urgun
dye dis-
at the matter woonderously ; they sentt to him byting, threatening, pleaz'd
with the
and envyouse letters, laing uppon him the blame why they wer peace we
not revengyd uppon king Lewys, which he was so farre from made with
geaving regard unto (as one who, after so long troubles in warres,
sowght now onely how to acquite and lowse himself at the last
from all martiall affayres,) as that he set not a rushe therby. But
Lewys of Lucembrowghe was specyally damnyfyed by thys alye-
nation of king Edward, by whom the secret practyses of the conspyrators wer discoveryed, who within few days was apprehendyd,
and beheadyd at Paris, the last constable, as they caule him,
emongest the Frenche nation.

E. 4 sent
of Britany
to have
H----- F.
of Rich-
)n
delvvered
King Edward having by this meane pacyfyed as well martiall
as cyvill causes, althowght by victory of so many battaylles he wer
accowntyd the happyest man of that age, who might now passe
the rest of his lyfe in most perfyte peace and securytie, yeat for
as mucne as yowng Henry erle of Richemond (thonely ympe now
left of king Henry the 6ths bloode) was yeat on lyve he adjudgyd
this onely thing to disturb all his felycytie, so that he lyvyd, as yt
wer, in perpetuall feare; wherfor he determynyd yeat once agane
to solycyte Francisse duke of Bryteyne, with gyfte, promise, and
prayer, to betray that young erle into his handes, who he thought
wold the rather satisfye his desire, because all king Henrye the vj^tes
faction was by him in effect extynguished; and therfor he sent
ambassadors in all haste to the duke, loden with great substance
of gold, and that his demaunde might seme more honest, he commandyd them to tell the duke that he desyryd erle Henry because
he might make soome matche with him in mariage, by affynytie,
wherof the rootes of thadverse faction myght be utterly pullyd

upp. Thowghe in dede he had no meaning to bring the same to
passe by affynytie, as afterward ensewyd (so that yt may be
thowght the kyng dyd prophecy), but eaven by the very death of
erle Henry. The duke herd thambassadors curtesly, and first
began to denay, and make many excuses why he might not lawfully do yt. At the last, weryed with prayer and vanquisshed with
prvce, ne delyveryd therle to thambassadors, commending him by
his letters to king Edward, not supposing that he had commyttyd
the sheepe to the woolffe, but the soone to the father, as one who
thowght that king Edward ment simply to mary with Henry
Elizabeth hys eldest dawghter. Thambassadors having obtaynyd
the pray they desyryd, departyd with great joy to St. Maloes, a
towne uppon the sea coste, ther to have take shipping, and so to
have saylyd into England. But erle Henry, knowing that he was
caryed to his death, throughe agony of mynde fell by the way

into a fever. In which mean time John Chenlet, a man of suche
reputation emong the nobles of Bretayne as that regyon had few
lyke, and whom the duke acceptyd specyally well above all other,
was in the country; but after he knew of the matter, being percyd
with the shamefulnes thereof, he spedely reparyd to the court,
and, as he was wont, presentyd himself famylyarly unto the duke,
standing a prety whyle very sad and heavy without speaking, so
that the duke, marvaling to se him in suche dumppes, demandid
what the matter was that made him so pensyffe as his cowntenance pretendyd. Whereunto John awnsweryd: 'Most noble duke,
this palenes of countenance ys unto me a messenger of death,
which yf before this day had happenyd showld trewly muche lesse
have grevyd, for I showld not have bene reservyd to so great sorow
as your late fact hath depely pryntyd within my brest, which surely
will cause the losse of my lyfe, or alteration of my condition and
state, or at the leaste from hencefoorth perpetually to lyve most
myserable; for yow, O duke, have by most honorable dealinges
gotten a renownyd and vertewous report, whom all men with one
assent extolle above the skyes, yeat this, alas, of most highe and
huge accownt (by your favor and leave be yt sayd) your self seme
to have leest regard unto of all other thinges, who lately, forgetting
your promyse and faith geaven, have delyveryd Henry earle of
Richemond, that most innocent ympe, to be torn in peces by
bloody butchers, to be myserably tormentyd, and fynally to be
slane; wherfor all that loove yow, whereof I of many am one,
can not choose but be grevyd when we se yowr most famous
renowne to be stanyd for ever with the note of falshoode and
trechery.' To these woordes the duke replyed immediately:
' Peace, my trustie and welbeloovyd John, I pray the; ther will no
suche thing happen to erle Henry, for king Edward is desirous to
make him his soone in lawe.' Than John sayd moreover: 'Beleve
me (most noble duke) Henry ys almost lost alreadie, whom yf yow

shalle once permyt to step one foote owt of your jurisdiction, all
the world shalle not after that be hable to save his lyfe.' The
duke was movyd with these woords of John Chenelet, who
before that time ether had not suspectyd that king Edward
sowght by suche meane to deceave erle Henry, ether els was
being seducyd by mony from honestie, fayth, and good dealing,
had not consyderyd what stoode with his honor, and sent incontynent Peter Landofe, his treasurer, to stay therle. Peter usyng
great celerytie came anon after thinglishe ambassadors unto St.
Maloes, and counterfatyng soome busynes, while that by long
talk devysyd of purpose he hinderyd them of ther intendyd voyage, he causyd erle Henry, almost dead, to be browght polytykly
into a most sure sayntuary within the sayd towne, and not long
after reducyd him agane to the duke, delyveryd from feare of
death, and by that occasion pretyly well amendyd. Hereof may
we know that Greke adage to be most trew—Man, to man, God;
for Henry, a young noble man betrayed to death without his owne
desert, was preservyd sooddenely, by thelp of John Chenelet, a
passing good prince. God grant that suche as have soveraigntie
over others may receave instructyon by this example, that suche
as lack good cownsayllers may once at the least learne both to
receave into ther famyly, into ther pryvy cownsaille, them that
know how and when to geave admonytion, and also to folow ther
wholsome advise. But as to thinglishe ambassadors, being thus
spoylyd both of money and marchandyse, and for the same grevously complayning, because they should not returne home altogether voyd, Peter promysed to do his indevor that Henry showld
ether be kept in sayntuary, wherunto he had got himself by ther
neglygence (as he sayd), or els showld be commyttyd to ward agane
with the duke, so as ther should be no cause to feare hym. And
thus derely dyd the king of England bye the custody of his enemy
for thre days.

King Edward, who in the meane time desyryd to know of his ambassadors proceedinges with the duke, and therfor thowght the tyme very long till he might heare therof, when he understoode that they had bene so nighe the very poynt of conveyghing erle Henry prysoner to him into England as nothing could be more nere and escape, was very sory that the matter had not succedyd. But hearing that therle showld be safely kept his mynde was easyd, and from thencefoorth thowght best to have more regard how to encrease his owne welth, which was very sclender, than of any thing els; and so for a while gave himself to seke busyly his owne profyt; whereby when he had fyllyd his coffers with gold and silver suffycyently, remembring then what appertanyd to honor, he shewyd himself furthwith a lyberall, bowntyfull, and profytable prince to the commonwelth: but eaven loe sudaynly he fell into a fact most horryble, commandyng rashly and uppon the suddane his brother George duke of Clarence to be George apprehendyd and put to death, who was drowned (as they say) in duke of Clarence a butte of malmesey; the woorst example that ever man cowld committed remember. And as touching the cause of his death, thowgh I Tower. have enqueryd of many, who wer not of leest authorytie emongest The maner the kinges cownsaylle at that time, yeat have I no certaintie of therof to leave in memory. A report was eaven then spred rences emongest the common people, that the king was afeard, by reason of a soothsayers prophecy, and so became incensyd agaynst his broother George, which prophecy was, that, after king Edward, showld raigne soome one the first letter of whose name should be G. And because the devels ar wont in that sort to envegle the mynds of them who conceave pleasures in suche illusions, with ther crafty conceytes and subtylties, menn sayd afterwardes that the same prophecy tooke effect, whan after Edward the duke of Glocester usurpyd the kingdom. Others lay an other cause of his death, which ys in this sort. That abowt the same time thold hatryd renewing betwixt the two brothers, then the which nothing ys more vehement, the duke, being a wydower, requyryd, by meane of his sister Margaret, to have in maryage Mary, thonely dowghter of Charles duke of Burgoigne, and that king Edward, envying his brothers prosperytie, hinderyd that affynytie. Theruppon pryvy grudge further growing, a certane servant of the dukes was the very same time also convict of sorcery and execentyd, against which dede whan the duke could not hold him content, but vehemently speake and cry owt, the king muche movyd with this exclamation commyttyd the duke to warde, and not long after, being condemnyd, by right or wrong, put him to death. But yt ys very lykly that king Edward right soone repentyd that dede; for (as men say) whan so ever any sewyd for saving a mans lyfe, he was woont to cry owt in a rage, " O infortunate broother, for whose lyfe no man in this world wold once make request ·" affirming in that manvfestly, that he was cast away by envy of the nobylytie. The duke left behind him two chyldren, Margaret, who after maryed to Rycherd Pole, and Edward, whom the king made erle of Warwicke. These thinges were doone that yere which was of mans salvation M.CCCC.lxxx^{tie}, and the xix^{ten} yere of king Edwardes raigne. And thus being delyveryd from all care of warres and cyvill seditions, which before that time might have happenyd, the king began to marke more severely thoffences of noblemen, and to be more covetous in gathering of money, by reason wherof many were perswadyd in ther opynyons that he wold from thencefurth proove an hard and severe prince; for after the death of his brother, as he perceavyd that every man fearyd him, so now he fearyd nobody. But that matter was preventyd by brevytie of his lyfe. And thus may we se that as well prosperytie ys soometyme cause of evell unto them who enjoy yt, as adversytie profytable to them who ar patient.

Abowt the sayd tyme, James king of Scotts delt, by ambassa-

dors, with king Edward, that he wold bestow Cecyly his dowghter
upon his soone James, whom he dyd handfast to that young
prince. This Cecyly was yownger than Elyzabeth, whom I have
before mentyonyd to have bene bethrouththyd, a prety while ago,
to Charles, soon to Lewys king of France. But nether thone
affynytie nor thother tooke effect; for the better part of high
estates ar woont oftentimes rather in thend to folow that serveth
for ther present profyt, then that which ys honest and honorable;
for after that king Lewys was delyveryd from hostyle feare, he
than dyd not onely contemne thaffynytie confirmyed already by
fayth and fidelytie with king Edward, but began almost openly to
deny payment of the money which he had promysyd; and so by
wrangling and shifting, had alreadie defraudyd the king of England of one yeres trybute, which the king determynyd to revenge
by dint of swoord. And the Scottishe king also, an assuryd and
contynewall confederat of the Frenche, after he herd that the
Frenche king wold not perform his woord, supposing that he
might do what him lyst, brake treuce with England, and molestyd
the borders therof with suddaine incursions; wherfor king Edward,
with great indignation, determynyd to make warre uppon Scotland; yeat afterward, whan king James excusyd the fact as
doone by the arrogancy of soome his subjectes without his pry-
vytie, the matter might have bene easyly appeasyd, yf in thend
king Edward had not bene laboryd by king James owne broother
to enterpryse the same warre : for king James, being a man of
sharp wytt, and trusting more than mete was to his owne head
and opynyon, gave lyttle care to good advyse; and because he
wold not be fownd fawlt withall, he therfor tooke to be his cown-
cellers men of meane cauling, and becam so offensyve to the
nobylytie by appeaching soome dayly of haynous crymes, and
punishing others by the purse, that he causyd them ether to go
willingly in exyle, or, fayning soome busynes, to fly soome other

A motyon s mauc by K. James of Scotland for the lady Cecely to be maryed to his sunne.

wher. Of which number was his brother, Alexander duke of Albany, who, as he travalyd into France, tarying with king Edward, ceassyd not to incense him to revenge his honor, and augment his desire that way. Therfor whan kinge Edward had in mynde, as sayd ys, to revenge the late injurye, and was also eggyd on to armes by the duke, who promysyd great ayd, he fynally determynyd with good will so to do, both because king James, besydes the late breache of treuce, had relevyd king Henry the vjth and those of his faction with all thinges necessary, and also for that he had good hope the duke wold be faythfull unto him, yf, his brother being expulsyd, he might enjoy the crowne : and therfor he addressyd furthwith agaynst the Scottes, Richerd his brother, duke of Glocester, Henry the fourth erle of Northumberland, Thomas Stanley, and the said duke of Albany, with an army royall. King James the meane whyle advertysyd of thinglishe mens approche, furnisshyd furthwith in readynes suche forces as he presently could levy, and going agaynst his enemyes, cam unto Berwicke for defence of hys borders ; but whan he understoode that the Englishe men excedid him both in force and number, and perceavyd also that his owne soldiers was scarce well to be trustyd, removing therfor abowt midnight, he retyryd to Edenbrowgh, ther to abyde thennemy. The duke of Glocester, entring Scotland, wastyd and burnyd all over the countrie, and, marchyng further into the land, encampyd himself not farre from his enemyes ; whan as, perceaving that not one man of all the Scottishe nation resortyd to the duke of Albany, he suspected treason, not without cause ; wherfor he tooke treuce with king James, and returnyd the right way to Berwicke, which in the meane time Thomas lord Stanley had woone, without losse of many his men. And king James, whose subjectes bare him no good will, was forcyd by nesitie, after treuce taken, to disgest that displeasure of winning the towne. The duke of Albany, repenting afterward that he had bene the author of that war, wherby both his country and himself was annoyed, and seing himselfe in no reputation emongest thinglishe men, departyd into France, wner not long after he was killyd in runnyng at tylt. He left behind him a soone cawlyd John.

Thys exployt fortunately fynysshed, king Edward, mynding to take on hand, as soone as time wold serve, thother war that was immynent, caulyd an assemble toguythers, and, supposing all thinjuryes before receavyd of the Frenche was to be of no account in comparyson of this present now commyttyd, made relation to his noble men that the league was lately broken by them, the trybute denayd, the maryage of his dowghter forsaken ; and therfor exhortyd that they wold, as time showld serve, defend thonor of ther realme. With which matters all being equally incensyd, made awnswer, that they knew well, every man wold be desyrous to fyght with the Frenche men, whom they had so often vanquisshyd, and that for thonor of ther country they ought to refuse no travale, and therfor they wer ready at his commandment to prosecute so great injury with swoord and fyre. Whan he knew the mynde of his temporall lordes, a subsydye was assessyd also uppon the clergy perticulerly, for the mayntenance of that warre, because yt was not lawfull for them to beare armes. But behold, while king Edward taketh care and thowght for these matters, he fell sicke of E. 4 re. an unknowen disease ; wherfor, perceavyng himself caulyd to thend sicke, of this lyfe, fyrst, lyke a good Chrystian man, he reconcylyd him died. to God, whom he thowght he had, by sinning oftentimes, offendyd, that whan the body wer dead, the sowle, throwghe Godes mercy, myght returne unto him ; than he made his Will, wherin he constitutyd his soones his heyres, whom he commyttyd to the tuytion of Rycherd his brother, duke of Glocester, and bestowyd muche goodes devoutly. And so, within few days after, he departyd this lyfe the vth ides of Aprill, at Westmynster, whar thassembley was made, being abowt fifty yeres old, which was of his raigne the xxiijrd, and of mans salvation м.cccc.lxxxiij. His corse being caryed with

all pomp and solemnytie to Wyndsore, was ther enterryd in Saint
Georges churche. He begot of Elyzabeth his wyfe ten children,
wherof seven he left alyve ; two men chyldren, Edward prince of
Wales, and Richerd duke of Yorke, and the third, base gotten,
caulyd Arthure, of very verteuous and lovely disposytion ; five
women, Elyzabeth, Cyeyly, Anne, Catheryne, and Bryget, wherof
all wer maryed save Bryget, who was made a nonne. King Edward was very taule of parsonage, excedinge the stature almost of
all others, of coomly vysage, pleasant looke, brode brestyd, the
resydew even to his fete proportionably correspondant, of sharp
witt, hault corage, of passing retentyve memory towching those
thinges which he had once conceavyd, dylygent in doing his affayres, ready in perylls, earnest and horryble to thenemy, bowntyfull to his frinds and aquayntance, most fortunate in his warres,
geaven to bodyly lust, wherunto he was of his owne disposition
inclyned ; by reason wherof, and of humanytie which was bred in
him aboundantly, he wold use himself more famylyarly emong
pryvate parsons than the honor of his maiestie requyryd, wherfor
ther was a great rumor that he was poysonyd. A lytle before
thend of his lyfe, we have sayd, that he began to slyde by lyttle
and lyttle into avarice, who before had usyd towards all men
hyghe lyberalytie : but after all intestine dyvision appeasyd, he
left a most welthy realme abownding in all thinges, which by
reason of cyvill warres he had receavyd almost utterly voyd as
well of hable men as money. He had alway regard to bestow
rowmes of honor, especyally appertaning to the clergy, upon every
of them that wer most trew nobylytee, and suche chiefly dyd he
caule to his cownsill ; others of the meaner sort, whom he dyd
specyally favor, them did he adorne with welth, not with dygnytie,
which many princes, having no regard of honor, do not ; by which
vertues he had so bound to him the peoples good will as that
they mournyd for him long after his death.

RICHARD THE THIRD.

RICHARD duke of Glocester, at the self same time that his brother king Edward departyd this lyfe, was in Yorkeshire, unto whom William Hastings his chamberlaine sent from London trusty messengers in post to certify him of his brothers death, and from himself to signify, that the king at his death had commyted to him onely, wyfe, chyldren, goodes, and all that ever he had, and therfor to exhort him, that he would with all convenient spede repare unto prince Edward into Wales, and coom with him to London to undertake the governement. Whan Richard had intelligence hereof, he began to be kyndlyd with an ardent desyre of soveraigntie; but for that ther was no cause at all whereby he might bring the same to passe that cowld cary any colour of honestie, so much as in owtward shew and apparance, he differryd the devise thereof presently unto an other time, and the meane while sent most looving letters to Elyzabeth the quene, comforting hir with many woords, and promysing on his behalf (as the proverbe is) seas and mountanes, and, to increase the credit of his carefulnes and naturall affection towards his brothers children, cawling togythers unto York thonorable and worshipfull of the countrie therabowt, he comandyd all men to sweare obedience unto prince Edward; hymself was the fyrst that tooke the othe, which soone after hee was the fyrst to vyolate. So all the resydew planely pronowncyd and sware the same. These thinges doone, having gathcryd no smaule force of armyd men, he preparyd to

E. 4 by
is w
ordayne1
his brother
p........
over his
children
and the
realme.

Richard
swore obe-
dience unto
Edwarde.

set forward when time showld serve. Prince Edward, being but a
child in yeares not hable to rewle hymself, lay the same time
within his princypalytie at Ludlow, under the tuytion of his uncle
Anthony earle Ryvers, Thomas Vaughan chief of his chamber, and
Richard Gray, knights. Elyzabeth the quene, and Thomas marquyse Dorset, hir soonn by John Gray hir former husband, who
was at London, advysyd these men by often messages to conduct
the prince furthwith to London, that after the funeralls of his
father solemnyzed, he might, after the maner of his auncesters, be
crownyd king. They according to the quenes and marquyses
commandment tooke there journey not long after towardes London. Richard also hastenyd thyther, whom Henry duke of Buckingham met at Northampton, with whom the duke of Glocester
had long conference, in so muche that as is commonly beleeved
he eaven then discoveryd to Henry his intent of usurpyng the
kingdom, and especyally for because the duke folowyng afterwards
his humor, whether yt were for feare or for obedience, held ever
with him. And so Richerd from thencefurth determynyd to assay
his purposyd spytefull practyse by subtyltie and sleight, which yf
by that meane showld not faule owt so fortunately as he hopyd,
than lastelye, with malice apert, to attempt the same; not myndyng, myserable man, that he could offend therin withowt extreme
detryment of the commonwelth, and thutter subvertion of his
howse. Surely so yt happeneth to graceles people, that who
seketh to overthrow an other, his owne frawd, wicked and mis-
chevous intent, his owne desperate boldenes, maketh him frantyke
and mad.

And thus whan they had taken cownsell Rycherd made haste
unto the prince, who journayd on before with a smawle trayne,
Richard took and was now coomyd to Stony Stratfoorth (so ys the towne
possession caulyd) whan he, togyther with Henry the duke gardyd with a
of the prince. bande of soldiers, overtooke the prince and receavyd him into his

rewle and goverment; but he apprehendyd Anthony and Thomas Anthony
Vawghan, and dyvers other, whom after he had taken, supposyng Tho. ‾‾‾‾'
that they wold not assent to his intent and purpose, he sent bak Vaughan
and others
to be kept in ward at Pounfrayt castle. sent pri-

But whan the fame of so owtrageous and horryble fact cam to Pomfrette
London, all men wer woonderously amasyd, and in great feare, castell.
but especyally Elyzabeth the quene was much dismayed, and
determynyd furthwith to fly; for, suspecting eaven than that ther
was no plane dealing, to thintent she might delyver her other
children from the present danger, she convayed hirself with them
and the marquyse into the sayntuary at Westmynster. The very Q. Eliza-
same dyd other noble men who wer of hir mynde for the safegard her othere
of hir chyldren. But the lord Hastinges who bare pryvy hatryd to childrene
and the
the marquis and others of the quenes syde, who for that cause marques
had exhortyd Richerd to take upon him the government of the D ‾‾‾ te
tooke
prince, whan he saw all in uprore and that matters fell owt sanktuary.
otherwyse than he had wenyd, repenting therfor that whiche he
had doone, caulyd together unto Powles churche suche frindes
as he knew to be right carefull for the lyfe, dygnytye, and estate of
prince Edward, and conferryd with tham what best was to be
doone. Here divers of them who wer most offendyd with thys
late fact of Richerd duke of Glocester, adjudgyd yt mete with all
spede to procure the lybertie of prince Edward, whom they accowntyd as utterly oppressyd and wrongyd by force and violence,
that so the fyre, which was kyndling, myght be put owt before yt
showld sprede further abrode; affirming that from thencefurth no
devyse wold be voyd of danger except the wicked enterpryse,
which gave good testymony that duke Richard had inwardly no
good meaning, wer with present force avoydyd. All the resydew
thowght that ther was no nede to use war or weapon at all, as men
who little suspectyd that the matter wold have any horryble and
cruell end. Wherfore they concludyd to tary whyle duke Richard

should coom and declare what the matter was, why he had cast them who had the prince in government into prison. And this resolution fynally lyked them all, because in apparance yt stood with the profyt of the commonwelth that every of the nobylity, as much as might be, showld avoyd varyance and contention. Not long after arryvyd the duke Richard and Henry with the prince, and lodgyd at the bishopp of Londons howse besydes Powles, wher ther will was the prince showld remane tyll other matters myght be put in readynes. Than dyd duke Rycherd assume the governement wholy; but yt grevyd him spytefully that he might not receave into his tuition, without some great stere, his brothers other soon Richerd duke of York, whom his mother kept in sayntuarye ; for, except he might get them both togethers into his powr and custody, he utterly desperyd to compasse that which he longyd for. Conceaving therfor soome hope therein, he bent all the forces of his wyt how to wrest and bereve him from his mothers lap. And so, as he had purposyd, he laboryd to bring abowt by sleyght which by force he could not, who cawling to him a good number of the nobylytie, sayd : ' I pray God that I never lyve yf I be not carefull for the commodytie of my nephews, whose calamytie I know well must nede redownd lyke-wyse to the commonwelth and myself also. Therfor, seing that my broother Edward owr king dyd uppon his death-bed consty-tute and appoint me Protector of the Realme, I had more regard of nothing than to repare hyther and bring with me prince Ed-ward his eldest soon, that in time convenyent all thinges might be doone by thadvise of cownsaile ; for I am determynyd to do nothing withowt your authoryties, whom I am willing to have myne assocyates, ayders, and partakers in all dealinges, that you thereby may well beare wytnes what soever I shall from hence-furth do as touching the government of the realme, the same wholy to be employed, feythfully, and without fraud, for thutylytie

The prince

Richerd D
of Gloster
~~lodged at~~
the bus-
hope of
~~~~~~~~
house.

of the commonwealth, and the commodytie of prince Edward, the
charge and government of whom I suppose you know suflycyently
that his father commyttyd to me for that onely cause. But Antony Rivers attemptyd of late to hinder me, that I showld not
accordeyng to my dewty take on hand that charge, whom therfor
we have bene compellyd to commyt with others who also made
resystance therein, that by ther examples other men might learne
not to have owr commandments in contempt. But what shall we
say of the evell cownsayle which they who most maligne and hate
me have geaven to quene Elizabeth? who, withowt any just
cause, cownterfayting feare so folyshly, hath enterprysyd to cary
in all haste the kings children as wicked, wretched, and desperate
nawghtie parsons into saynctuary, thonly refuge in earth of
povertie, det, and lewd behavyor, as thoughe we went abowt to
destroy them, and that all owr doinges tendyd to violence. Which
thyng, thowghe yt be exceding great dishonor to us and the
whole realme, yet the sex ys to be borne withall, from the which
suche rages readyly procede. But we are to provyde remedy be-
times for this womanishe disease creping into owr commonwelthe,
to the woorst example trewly that may be. What a sight I pray
you shalle yt be to se the day wherin the king shalbe crownyd, yf,
whyle that the solemnytie of tryumphant pomp is in doynge, his
mother, brother, and sisters shalbe remane in sayntuary? What
manner of concurse of people shalle ther be, by whose authoryty
he is to be creatyd king? What signe of rejoicing shalle that
assemble geave unto the soveraigne, the same being more full of
hevynes than exultation? Surely ther is not one amongest all
the people who may not justly be in feare of himself, and think
that all majestie of lawis is already violated, yf the Quene and hir
chyldren shalle remaine any longer in sayntuary! May yt lyke
yow therfor that soom of yow go to the quene hirself, and procure
the reducyng of hir and hir children as soone as may be into the

A resone
she ve
whie the
earle of
rivers an
others wel
comytted.

palace, whom, yf peradventure yow shalbe hable by no meane to withdraw from hir opynyon, as seducyd by them who loove mee not, who study to stirre up envy against mee, to lay some fault uppon me, yeat at the least to deale that she may uppon generall assurance yealde Richerd thother soon into your handes, so that he may be present with other noble men at his brothers coro-

Persones sente to ~~~~~~ ~~~~ the Q. in sanctuary.
nation. Yow have already my mynde, do now what yow think best in the behalf of the commonwelth; for at my hand yow both may and owght to expect all that is good and honorable.' Whan he nad spoken these woordes all men who suspectyd no subtyltie thowght duke Richardes advyse both mete and honest. And so yt was agreyd that Thomas archebisshop of Canterbury, Henry duke of Buchyngame, John lord Howard, and sundry other grave men should deale in that cause, who reparing unto the sayntuary began to perswade the quene with many fayre wordes and perswations that she wold returne with hir children into the palace, unto whom they gave both pryvate and publyke assurance; but the woman, forseing in a sort within hir self the thing that folowyd furthwith after, could not be movid with any perswations to com-

Richard, yonger ·t delivered oute of sanc- tuarye.
myt nir self to tne credyt of duke Rycherd, which whan they understoode, fynally they demandyd to be delyveryd to them hir soon Richard onely, which they obtaynyd hardly after many fayre promises. And so was thinnocent chyld pullyd owt of his mothers armes.

The prince and his brother removed to e.
Richard having by this meane obtaynyd almost his hartes desire, convaighed his nephewys from the bysshop of Londons howse unto the Towr; and yeat all this causyd no suspytion, for that thusage ys at the kings coronation for the whole assembly to coom out from thence solemly, and so procede to Westmynster. This doone, Richerd, whose mynde partly was enflamyd with desire of usurping the kyngdom, partly was trubblyd by guyltynes of intent to commyt so haynous wickednes (for a guiltie con-

science causeth thoffendor to have dew punishment alway in ima-
gination before his eyes), thowght aftirward nothing better than to
mollyfy the multitude with largesse and lyberalytie, than to wyn
the hartes of his adversaryes with gyftes, rewardes, and promyses,
than in the Towr, wher himself and his nephews remayned, to
consult, conferre, and delyberate of new with the noble men dayly
in most craftie and subtyle maner for the dealing and disposing
of suche thinges as wer furthwith to be doone. And this was his
dryft, that, whyle stayng and tarying made the people desyrus of
this solemne sight, he, by consultinge from poynt to poynt, might
sound and serche out how the nobylytie was affected, saying alway
that he did not seke the soveraigntie, but referryd all his dooings
to the profyt of the realme. Thus covering and cloking certane
days his desire, under the colour and pretence of common welthe,
he so enveglyd the myndes of the nobilitye, that they all, few only
exceptyd who wer not ignorant from the beginning what marke
he shot at, dyd by no meane espy the cause of his lingering, or to
what ende his practyses wold faule owt, so many matters dyd he
so often propone and so few explane, according as a guyltie conscyence ys wont to be of many myndes. But in the mean time
perceaving that William lord Hastings was most vehement and
earnest to have prince Edward once crowned king, who chiefly
amongst all the nobylytie was, for his bountifulnes and lybe- Wm. lo.
ralytie, much beloved of the common people, bearing great sway Hastings
by practys
emong all sortes of men and parsons of best reputation, whe- slain in the
ther yt wer that he fearyd his powr, or despearyd yt possible Tower.
to draw him to his syde and opynyon, he determynyd to ryd
the man owt of the way before his purpose showld be discoveryd to the resydew, whom he did not yeat fully trust. Wherfor,
burning with rage incredible to bring to effect the thing which in
mynd was resolvyd, he drew a plot for the lord Hastinges as
foloweth : he placyd pryvyly in a chamber adjoyning to that with

himself and other lords sat usually in cownsayll a sort right ready
to do a mischiefe, geaving them in charge that when he showld
geave a signe they showld suddaynly rushe owt, and, compassing
about them who should syt with him, to lay handes specyally
uppon William lord Hastinges, and kill him forthwith. This
trayne thus layd, abowt the day before the ides of June he commanded to be sent for specyally by name Thomas Rotheram
archebisshop of York, John Morton bysshop of Ely, Henry duke
of Buchingham, Thomas lord Stanley, William lord Hastinges,
John lord Haward, and many others whom he trustyed to fynde
faythful ether for feare or benefyt. The resydew of the nobylytie,
togethers with John Russell bishop of Lincoln, lord chancelor of
England, whom his will was not to have present at suche an owtrageous and fowle spectacle, he commanded to be the same day at
Westminster haule, with other magistrates, to proclame the day
of prince Edward's coronation. But the nobles who wer cawled
came well early all into the Towr as to delyberate of the whole
matter. Here, whan the doores was shutt, whyle they thus alone
without testimony of any other than onely God, had goodwill to
consult of the most weyghtie affayres, Richard duke of Glocestre,
who thowght of nothing but tyranny and crueltie, spak unto them
in this sort: 'My lords, I have procuryd you all to be caulyd
hyther this day for that onely cause that I might shew unto you
in what great danger of death I stand; for by the space of a few
days by past nether nyght nor day can I rest, drynk, nor eat,
wherfor my blood by lyttle and lyttle decreaseth, my force fayleth,
my breath shorteneth, and all the partes of my body do above
measure, as you se (and with that he shewyd them his arme), faule
away; which mischief veryly procedeth in me from that sorceres
Elyzabeth the quene, who with hir witchcraft hath so enchantyd
me that by thanoyance thereof I am, dissolvyd.' To these sainges
whan no man gave answer, as making lyttle to the purpose, William

lord Hastings, who hatyd not duke Richerd, and was woont to speke all thinges with him very frely, awnsweryd, that the quene deservyd well both to be put to open shame, and to be dewly punysshyd, yf yt might appeare that by use of witchecraft she had doone him any harme. To these Rycherd replyed: 'I am undone (I say) by that very woomans sorcery.' Whereunto William made the same awnswer that befor. Than Rycherd, to geve a sygne for them who wer withowt layd pryvyly for the nonce, spak with more shirle voyce: 'What than, William, yf by thine owne practises I be brought to destruction?' He had scarce utteryd these woordes whan as they to whom charge was commyttyd in that behalf yssewyd, and with open assault apprehendyd all at once William lord Hastinges, both the bysshops of York and Ely, and also the lord Stanley. These thre last wer cast ther into severall prisons; but William lord Hastinges had scarce leysure to make his con= fession before his head was stryk from his shoulders. So the lord Hastinges learnyd, by his owne losse at the last, that the law of nature wherof the gospell speaketh (what soever you will that men do unto yow, do you so also unto them) can not be broken with-out punishment. He was one of the smyters of prince Edward, king Henry the vj^{ths}. soon, who was fynally quyt with like maner of death. Would God suche kind of examples might once be a learning for them who think yt lawfull to do whatsoever lyketh them. Now I returne to the matter. As soone as this dede was doone they cryed treason, treason throwght the whole towre; which noyse whan it sprede abrode throwght the cytie the citecyns and all other people, takyng the fyrst rumor to be trew, and ignorant of that which was doone within, began to cry owt lykewyse; but after that they understoode, by terryble speache brutyd abrode, the truthe of the matter doon within, then began every man on his owne behalf to feare the hurt of inward enemyes, and to look for nothing els but cruell slawghter or myscrable flight; and all

The bis 's of York and Ely and t Lord Stan-ley were to severall prisons.

men generally lamentyd the death of that man, in whom both they
and the nobles who favoryd kinge Edwardes children had reposyd
their whole hope and confydence.   Now perceavyd they well that
duke Richerd wold spare no man so that he might obtayn the
kingdom, and that he would convert the regall authoritye into

Lord Stan-
ley re-
leased.
tyranny.   But the duke after this, being satisfyed with the death
of William lord Hastinges, delyveryd Thomas lord Stanley safe
and sownd, fearing, perchance, least yf he showld have doone him
any wrong George lord Strange his soon showld have stirred upp
the people to armes soomwher agaynst him.   As for John Morton
bysshop of Ely, who dyd farre excede them all in wysdome and
gravytie, him he commyttyd to the duke of Buckingham, whom
the duke sent furthwith into Wales to his castle at the towne of
Brechnoch.   But Thomas Rotheram archebishop of York he committed to the custody of sir James Tirrell, knight.   His meaning
was to make those bisshops sure whom he thought wold not alow
uppon his purposyd intent, until that, having gotten the soveraigntie, he showld nede to feare no man.

Whan these thinges wer doone, Richard, knowinge then for
certane that ther was no cause why he showld any further dis-

Order
to
behead
Anthony
Richard
Graye, and
Vaughan.
semble the matter, sent his letters of warrant to the keper of
Pontfreyt castle to behead in hast Anthony lord Ryvers, Richerd
Gray, and Thomas Vaghan, which was doone soone after.   In the
meane whyle, himself at London, fearing now all thinges, garded
first his parson with a company of armed men, then after sowght
with all dylygence to wyn unto hym the chief of the nobylytie
by large gyftes and fayre promyses, a good part wherof he drew
unto his amytie, seducyd rather for feare than for hope of benefyt ;
by the suportation of whose puyssance and authorytie he determynyd to attempt soone after an other devyse.   For surely he was
owt of all hope to be hable so to bynde the comonaltie to him by
rewardes, as that they wold willingly away with his government,

who he knew well wold, for defence of lyberty and conservation
of the royall right, be readyly stirryd to take weapon in hand,
wherfor he feared them. Theruppon, revolvinge many matters in
his mynde, at last he bethowght him of a devyse wherby the
people, being seducyd by a certain honest pretence, should the
lesse grudge at his doinges. And so the man, being blinde with
covetousnes of raigning, whom no fowle fact cowld now hold bak,
after that he had resolvyd not to spare the bloode of his owne
howse, supposing also all regard of honor was to be rejectyd, devysyd and bethowght himselfe of suche a sleyght as foloweth :
He had secret conference with one Raphe Sha, a divyne of great Richards
reputation as than among the people, to whom he utteryd, that practise
with Rafe
his fathers inherytance ought to descend to him by right, as the Sha, a
eldest of all the soones which Richard his father duke of York preacner,
to publish
had begotten of Cecyly his wyfe ; for as much as yt was manyfest in a ser-
ynowghe, and that by apparent argument, that Edward, who had Poules
before raignyd, was a bastard, that ys, not begotten of a right and Crosse his
lawfull wyfe ; praying the said Sha to instruct the people therof in
a sermon at Powles Crosse, wherby they might once in the ende
acknowledge ther trew liege lord. And sayd that he greatly requyred the same, because he estemyd yt more mete to neglect his
mothers honor and honestie than to suffer so noble a realme to be
pollutyd with suche a race of kinges. This Raphe, whether dasyd
with feare, or bereft his wyts, promysed to folow, and obey his
commandment. But whan the day came, duke Richard, who,
under the colour of serving another tourne, had made himself
mightie, came in royal maner, with a great gard of men armyd,
unto the churche of St. Paule, and ther was attentyvely present
at the sermon, in whose hearing Raphe Sha, a learnyd man, taking
occasion of set purpose to treat not of divyne but tragicall discours, began to instruct the people, by many reasons, how that
the late king Edward was not begotten by Richard duke of York,

but by soome other, who pryvyly and by stelth had had knowledge
of his mother ; and that the same did manyfestly appeare by sure
demonstrations, because king Edward was nether in physnomy
nor shape of body lyke unto Richard the father ; for he was highe
of stature, thother very little ; he of large face, thother short and
rownd. Howbeyt, yf suche matters were well consyderyd, no man
could dowt but Richard, now in place, was the dukes trew soone,
who by right owght to inheryt the realme dew to his father ; and
therfor he exhortyd the nobylytie, seing they presently wantyd a
king, to make ther king Richard duke of Glocester, the trew yssue
of the royall bloode, and to forsake all others basely begot. Whan
the people herd these woordes, they wer woonderus vehemently
trublyd in mind therwith, as men who, abasshyd with the shamefulnes of the matter, all to be cursyd and detestyd as well the rash-
nes, foolehardynes, and doltishnes of the preacher as the madnes
of Richard the duks wycked mynde, who wold not se how great
shame yt was to his owne howse and to the whole realme, how
great dishonour and blot, to condemne, in open audience, his mother of adultery, a woman of most pure and honorable life ; to im-
prynt upon his excellent and good brother the note of perpetuall
infamy ; to lay upon his most innocent nephews an everlasting
reproche. Wherfor at the very instant yow might have sene
soome, astonyed with the noveltie and strangenes of the thing,
stand as mad men in a mase ; others, all agast with thowtrageous
crueltie of thorrible fact, to be in great feare of themselves because they war frindes to the kinges children ; others, fynally, to
bewayle the misfortune of the chyldren, whom they adjudgyd now
utterly undoone. But ther ys a common report that king Edwards chyldren wer in that sermon caulyd basterdes, and not king
Edward, which is voyd of all truthe ; for Cecyly king Edwards
mother, as ys before sayd, being falsely accusyd of adultery, complanyd afterward in sundry places to right many noble men, wherof

soome yeat lyve, of that great injury which hir soon Richard had doon hir. But Richard, whan his mother was thus openly defamyd as an adultress, and a slander publysshyd upon Edward his brother, was no whit ashamyd, as he owght to have bene, but, rejoysing that a matter was boltyd owt in the face of the world wherby he sought to make aparent to all men that he had good right to the realme, returnyd into the toure with a royal trane, as thowe he had bene of the magistrates proclamyd king. But Raphe Sha, the publisher of thabhomynablenes of so weightie a cause, (who not long after acknowledgyd his error, throwgh the grevous rebukes of his fryndes that wer ashamyd of his infamy,) so sore repentyd the doing therof that, dying shortly for very sorow, he-suffered worthie punishement for his lewdnes.

Sha th reacher at his death hiⁿ errore.

Now by these meanes was yt thowght that duke Richard had attaynyd the soveraygntie, and the same was every wher so reported, thowgh more for aw than good will; whan, for feare of perilles hanging every way over his head, he resolvyd that of necessitie yt was mete to stay a whyle, notwithstanding many of his frindes urgyd him to utter himself planely, and to dispatche at once that which remayned, yeat, least his doinges might easyly be myslykyd, his desire was that the people might be earnestly delt withall, and the whole matter referryed to the determynation of others as judges in that behalf.   And so, abowt the xiijth calends of June, he commandyd the judges and magistrates of the cytie, Robert Bylles, lord mayr, Thomas Norland and William Maryn, shyrifles, with thaldermen, to assemble in the yeald hawle, and to them he sent the duke of Buckingham, with dyvers other noblemen that wer of his counsayll, to deale in his cause, and in his name to requyre that they, hearing the reasons concerning the dispatche of so weyghtie affayer, wold decre that which stoode with the welthe of the whole realme and of thinhabytantes therof. The duke of Buckingham delyveryd, in long proces, duke Ry-

The duke ingham and other lords sent to publishe Riard title in t e yeld halle London.

chards mynd, and in his behalf declaryd that ther was not to
enforce the cause any other thing but right, loyaltie, constancy,
honesty, and equytie, seing he demaundyd the kingdom from the
which he had bene defraudyd before by his broother Edward, and
therfor prayed that by ther authorytie they wold deale and deter-
myn of so weyghtie a matter, wherbie he might, with good will of
the commonaltie, who wold be rewlyd by ther judgement, enjoy
once at the last his royall right, which wold be for the profyt of
the common welth ; for as muche as duke Richard was of that
wysdom and modestie that all men might well hope for, at his
hand, both right and reason.   This was the dukes demand and
determynation also, agaynst which, because wher force ys right
beareth no rewle, no man durst gaynsay.   But Richard duke of
Glocester, as thowgh the terryfyed judges had decreyd of his syde,
rode the next day after from the Towr throwgh the myddest of

Richard
o
Westmin
ster and
bli ed
his ur
poses.

tne cytie unto Westmynster, in robes royall, and gardyd with
fyrme force of armyd men, syttinge in the royall seat.   He then
fyrst of all tooke uppon him as king ; for some matters he determynyd, others he promysyd he would heare ; to the magystrats
he gave in commandment that from thencefurth they showld do
all things in his name ; also he apoynted a day for all the people
and nobylytie to mete, and be ready to sweare him homage.   Whan
the fame of these doinges wer spread abrode throwgh all partes of
the realme, they wer dyversly taken : for who so wer of king Edwards and the howse of Yorke part detestyd the presumptuous
boldnes of duke Richard as a very pestylence that fynally wold
consume and utterly ruynat that howse.   Agane, who so held in
hart with king Henry the Sixt thowght that all those thinges
wold be for ther advantage, because within short time yt wold
fawl owt that the rigor of Rychardes government wold be intollerable to every man, and that the nobylytie, for the exterping
utterly therof before yt showld take any depe roote, wold, withowt

dowt, yeald ther allegeance unto Henry earle of Richemond, king
Henryes brothers soon, and send for him to be king. Richard, in
the meane time, according as his force and tyranny well requyred,
was afeard least that many should becoome the quenes frynds,
and procure the commonaltie to commotyon, whan they should see
the crowne bereft from prince Edward; therfor he commandyd
furthwith five thousand soldiers which wer levyed in Yorkshyre
(for to them he most trustyd) to be sent unto him, under the conduct of Rychard Ratclyf, and gave to him in charge to dispatche
dyvers thinges by the way. Hee, gardyd with that companye,
stayed at Poyntfrayt, and commandyd the keper of the castle to
Anthony
Rivers
put to death Anthony Lord Ryvers, Rychard Gray, and Thomas Richard
Vaughan, as the Glocestryan had commandyd (according as I Tho
ye,
have before wrytten), that by reason of his presence such an Vaughan
horryble fact might be executyd without uprore, which doone he
e) ccutcu.
conducted his company to London. Richard, thus garded with
that number of faythfull and trusty soldiers, attemptyd confy-
dently to execute all other things. And so, having assemblyd
togyther a company of the nobylytie, he was creatyd king at West- R. 3
mynster the day before the nones of July, and adornyd with the crowned at
regall diademe, togethyr with Anne his wyfe, the people rather not ster.
repyning for feare than allowing therof, and was cawlyd Rychard
the iij^rd. That was the yere of mans salvation M.cccc.lxxxiiij.

Thus Richerd, without assent of the commonaltie, by might and
will of certane noblemen of his faction, enjoyaed the realme, contrary to the law of God and man; who, not long after, having es-
tablyshyd all thinges at London according to his owne fantasy,
tooke his journey to York, and first he went streight to Glocester,
where the whyle he taryed the haynous guylt of wicked conscyence
dyd so freat him every moment as that he lyvyd in contynuall
feare, for thexpelling wherof by any kind of meane he determynyd
by death to dispatche his nephewys, because so long as they lyvyd

Order
g e
the leefte
nant of the

murthere
the yonge
p........

Edward E.
a
wick, son
to George

Clarence,
sent pri-
soner to
Seryhoo-

Braken-
1
fused to
e the

of the
:es.

a
T rrell was
made leef-
na
tne towere
who per-
formed the
exployt.

he could never be out of hazard; wherefore he sent warrant to Robert Brakenbury, lyvetenant of the towr of London, to procure ther death with all diligence, by some meane convenyent. From thence he departyd to York, wher he was joyfully receavyd of the cytecyns, who for his comyng mayd certane days publyk and open tryumph; but king Richard, that he might advance himself openly to all men, yea to the country people (so desyrus was he to prowle after vane plause and congratulation), denouncyd a day wherin the archbisshop of York, at his request, apoyntyd general procession, in the solemnytie wherof himself and the quene went crownyd. King Richard caryed with him Edward earle of Warweke, the soone of his brother George duke of Clarence, by reason of whom least any danger might to himself be deryvyd, he sent him to be kept in ward at a castle caulyd Shyriff Huton. But the lyvetenant of the towr at London after he had receavyd the kinges horryble commyssion was astonyed with the creweltie of the fact, and fearing least yf he showld obey the same might at one time or other turne to his owne harme, dyd therfor dyffer the dooing therof in hope that the kinge wold spare his owne bloode, or ther tender age, or alter that heavy determynation. But anv one of those poynts was so fur from taking place, seing that the mynd therin remanyd immovable, as that when king Richard understoode the lyvetenant to make delay of that which he had commandyd, hee anon commyttyd the charge of hastening that slawghter unto another, that is to say James Tyrrell, who, being forcyd to do the kings commandment, rode sorowfully to London, and, to the woorst example that hath been almost ever hard of, murderyd those babes of thyssew royall. Thys end had Prince Edward and Richarde his brother; but with what kinde of death these sely chyldren wer executyd yt is not certanely known. But king Richard, delyveryd by this fact from his care and feare, kept the slaughter not long secret, who, within few days after,

permyttyd the rumor of ther death to go abrode, to thintent (as
we may well beleve) that after the people understoode no yssue
male of king Edward to be now left alyve, they might with better
mynde and good will beare and sustayne his governement. But
whan the fame of this notable fowle fact was dispersyd throwgh
the realme, so great griefe stroke generally to the hartes of all
men, that the same, subdewing all feare, they wept every wher,
and whan they could wepe no more, they cryed owt, 'Ys ther trewly
any man lyving so farre at enemytie with God, with all that holy
ys and relygyouse, so utter enemy to man, who wold not have ab-
horryd the myschief of so fowle a murder?' But specyally the
quenes frinds and the chyldrens exclamyd against him, 'What
will this man do to others who thus cruelly, without any ther
desert, hath killyd hys owne kynsfolk?' assuring themselves that
a marvalous tyrany had now invadyd the commanwelth. Emongest
all others the news herof was unto thynfortunate mother, who
yeat remanyd in sayntuary, as yt wer the very stroke of death :
for as soone as she had intelligence how her soons wer bereft thys
lyfe, at the very fyrst motion therof, the owtrageousnes of the
thinge drove her into suche passion as for feare furthwith she
fell in a swowne, and lay lyveles a good whyle ; after cooming to
hir self, she wepeth, she cryeth owt alowd, and with lamentable
shrykes made all the house ring, she stryk hir brest, teare and
cut hir heire, and, overcommyd in fyne with dolor, prayeth also
hir owne death, cawlyng by name now and than emong hir most
deare chyldren, and condemning hirself for a mad woman, for that
(being deceavyd by false promyses) she had delyveryd hir yownger
soon owt of sayntuary, to be murderyd of his enemy, who, next
unto God and hir soons, thought hir self most injuryd ; but after
long lamentation, whan otherwise she cowld not be revengyd, she
besowght help of God (the revenger of falshed and treason)
as assuryd that he wold once revenge the same. What man ys

ther in this world, who, yf he have regard unto suche noble children thus shamefully murderid, wyll not tremble and quake, seing
that suche matters often happen for thoffences of our ancestors,
whose faults doo redownd to the posterytie? That fortunyd peradventure to these two innocent impes because Edward ther
fathyr commytted thoffence of perjury, by reason of that most
solemne othe which (as we have in the former booke mentionyd)
he tooke at the gates of the cytie of York, meaning one thing inwardly and promysyng an other in expresse woordes outwardly, as
furthwith appearyd : and for that afterwardes, by reason of his brother the duke of Clarence death, he had chargyd himself and his
posterytie before God with dew desert of grevous punysshement.

　　Whyle this stere was abrode otherwher, the day of generall
procession was at hand, wherin ther was great eonfluence of people,
for desire of beholding the new king. In which procession very
solemly set furth and celebratyd by the clergy, the king was present in parson, adornyd with a notable riche dyademe, and accompanyed with a great number of noble men : the quene folowyd
also with a crowne uppon hir head, who led by the hand hir soon
Edward crownyd also with so great honor, joy, and congratulation
of thinhabytants, as in shew of rejoysing they extollyd king
Richard above the skyes. Whan this solemne pomp of prayer

R. 3
somoned a
parliament
at York.
was fynysshyd, the king not long after cawlyd a parlyament, in the
which, after many matters wer establishid towching the state of
that province, his only soon Edward, abowt ix^{ne} yeres owld, was

John Ho-
ade
duke of
Norfolk
made prince of Wales, and John Haward, a man very pollytyke
and skilfull in warres, was made duke of Norfolk, and his soon
Thomas, a lusty and noble young gentleman, earle of Surrey. Also

soone E.
of Surrey.
tne number of the kinges cownsayll was augmentyd with soom
noble men of that countre, because king Richerd had in ther
fidelytie most confydence as we have before declaryd. Fynally,
because ther was no myschyef, none adversytie, which the kinges

head, guiltie of so many crymes, dyd not mystrust, provysyon was
made that the kings enemyes, desyrus to disturb all things,
might not be hable to caule home againe into England Henry
earle of Richemond. And so Thomas Hutton, a man of pregnant
wyt, was appoyntyd ambassador to deale with the duke of Bryt-
tayn by all force of fayre woords and money that he wold detane
the erle in perpetuall pryson at the least, according as he had
doone hytherto at the request of his brother Edward, who transportyd furthwith into Brytayny. Whan these thinges wer doone
the king returnyd to London, whom all the cyty for dewties sake
cam furth to mete. Thus had kinge Richerd by a strange kinde
of owtrageous creweltie attayned the type of glory and promotion,
and in the eye of the people was accountyd a happy man, whan as
soon after he perceavyd himself to declyne from his state by
lyttle and lyttle, that he could not kepe fast therein by any
pollycy. Surely after the murder of king Edwardes soons as oft
as any evell storme was presently immynent or lyke to ensew, the
people, remembring suddaynly the kings late abhomynable fact,
layd the blame thereof only uppon him, exclaming that God did
revenge the kinges wickednes uppon the powr Englishe people;
whom therfor they accusyd, detestyd, and fynally besowght God to
take extreame vengeance uppon. Thus when king Richard was
spoken of at all hands, and though hee [was] not ignorant from
whom these speaches dyd procede, yeat for all that durst not by
violence revenge the same, supposing yt an unwyse part not to
beare soom time with suche as towld him of his fault, he fell agane
from so great felycytie into a feare and heavynes of hart, and, because he could not reforme the thing that was past, he determynyd to abholishe by all dewtyfulnes the note of infamy wherwith his honor was staynyd, and to geave suche hope of his good
governement that from thencefurth no man showld be hable to
lay any calamytie that might happen to the commonwelth unto

(margin notes) Thomas Hutton sent ambassador to of Brittany to detayne Richmond in prison.

his charge. But hard yt ys to alter the naturall disposition of ones mynde, and suddaynly to exterp the thing therin settlyd by dayly conversation. And so, whether yt wer for that cause, or (as the brute commonly goeth) because he now repented of his evell dedes, he began afterward to take on hand a certane new forme of lyfe, and to geave the shew and cowntenance of a good man, wherby he might be accowntyd more righteous, more mylde, better affectyd to the commonaltie, and more lyberall especially toward the powr; and so first might meryte pardon for his offences at Gods hand; than after appease partly thenvy of man, and procure himself good will, he began many woorks as well publick as pryvate, which (being prevented by death before his tyme) he perfyted not. He fowndyd a colledge at York of an hundreth priests. Also he began now to geave eare to the good admonition of his frindes. But anon after yt appearyd evydent that feare, which seldom causeth continewance of dewtyfull dealing, made king Richard so suddainly good, for as much as the bowntyfulnesse of the man beinge but counterfayt waxed cold agane quickly; by reason wherof all his proposyd practyses began straightway to coom to naught. For fyrst he lost Edward his only soon the third month after he had bene made prince of Wales; after that, a conspyracy was contryvyd agaynst him by meane of Henry duke of Buckingham, which, though yt wer by one of the conspyrators discoveryd before yt grew great, yeat was he trublyd in suppressing therof. And for as muche as we be now coommyd to this place, yt is nedefull to make convenyent rehersall of certane thinges premvsyd wherby we may explane the first cause of the discord begun betwixt the king and the duke: for Humfrey soomtyme erle of Hereforde, of whose death we have made mention before in the xviii^{th}. booke, left of his body begotten two dawghters, and them he made his heyres; that ys to say, Mary who maryed to Henry erle of Darby, theldest soon to John duke of Lancaster,

R 3 founded a colledge at York.

His son Edwarde

The discencion be R. 3 and the duke of Buckingham.

who aftirward having gotten the crowne was caulyd Henry the
Fourth, and Alyenore whom Thomas of Woodstok duke of
Glocester and erle of Buckingham tooke in maryage. Of this
Thomas and Alyenore yssewyd and remanyd onely alive one
dowghter caulyd Anne, to whom by right discendyd after the con-
fiscation of hir fathers possessions in the time of Richard the
Second, who put the duke to death, hir mother Alyenors inherytance. This lady was first handfast to Thomas Stafford, but he
dying before marriage, she also beinge but very young, was after-
ward maryed to Edmund brother of the sayd Thomas erle of
Stafforth. He begot Humfrey duke of Buckingham, and Humfrey
Henry. And so by the maryage of Anne and Mary was therle of
Herefoords inherytance devydyd, thone moytie to thowse of Lancaster, thother to the bloode of Staffoords, from whom the dukes
of Buckingham deryve ther pedygre. And after a few yeres all
the rase of king Henry the Fourth faylyd in prince Edward,
Henry the Syxtes soon : which howse extynguyshyd, Henry of
Buckingham thowght that he might by good right demand that
part of therle of Herefords patrimony which in the right of Mary
had coommyd to the howse of Lancaster, which than king Richard
held in right of the crown, with thother possessions of the howse
of Lancaster. Therfor the duke within few days after, having gotten
fytt occasion to talke of the matter, demandyd of king Richerd
that part of therle of Herefoordes patrymony that to him by right
of inherytance was dew. To this king Richerd, who supposyd
that matter to have bene now forgotten, ys reportyd to have awn-
swered furthwith in great rage : ' What now, duke Henry, will yow
chalenge unto you that right of Henry the Fourth wherby he
wyckedly usurpid the crowne, and so make open for yourself the
way therunto ?' Which king Richerds awnswer settlyd depe into
the dukes breste, who from that time furth, movyd muche with ire
and indignation, began to devyse by what meane he might thrust

The duke of Buck- demanded of the g(part of the E. of H ords lands.

owt that ungratefull man from the royall seat for whose cause he
had right often doone many thinges agaynste his owne conscyence
otherwise than before God he lawfully might. The duke thus
affectyd accompanyed king Richerd not long after as he journeyed towardes Yorke unto Glocester, from thence with his consent he repayred into Wales, wher a great part of his lyvings
lay. Heare the while of his tary, provokyd partly by freshe
memory of the late receavyd injury, partly repenting that hitherto
of himself hee had not resystyd king Richardes evell enterpryse,
but much had furtheryd the same, he resolvyd to seperate himself
from him (though in dede he showld so have doon in the begyn-
nyng), and to bring to passe the thing which he had long revolvyd

A consul-
tation
between
the duke of
ham and
the bishope
]
towching
the earl of
Richmonds
title.

in mynde : and so he began to discover his intent to John bishop
of Ely whom (as we have before remembryd) he had in Brechnoch
castle. The bisshop suspecting treason, demandeth why he
goetn abowt that matter, and prayeth to do him no harm ; afterward whan he understood his just cause of hatred, which king
Richerd had well deservyd long ago, he refusyd not to conferre of
the conspiracy. Than the duke unfoldyd all thynges to the
bisshop of Ely, and dyscoveryd himself wholy, shewing how he
had devysyd the meane wherby both the bloode of king Edward
and of Henry the Sixth that yeat was remaining, being conjoignyd
by affinytie, might be restoryd to the domynion dew unto both ther
progenyes. The meane was this, that Henry erle of Richemond,
who (as the report went) was, after knowledge of king Edwardes
death, delyveryd by Francys duke of Brytayne owt of prison,
might be sent for in all hast possyble, and assystyd with all that
they might do, so that he wold promyse before by solemne othe,
that after he had once obtaynyd the kingdom he wold take to
wyfe Elyzabeth, king Edwards eldest dawghter.

    The bishop of Ely alowyd as well the dukes devyse as the
maner of performing the same, and procuryd one Renold Bray,

servant to Margaret erle Henry his mother, who had maryed Renold
Thomas lord Standley, to coome unto the duke into Wales, and countys of
his pleasure knowen to returne spedely unto the said Margaret, Richmonds
servant.
and certify hir of all thinges which had bene delyberatyd betwixt sent for to
him and the duke concernyng common saftie. This trewly was of Buck-
the matter for the which dissention sprang betwyxt the king and ingham.
the duke, and wheruppon the conspyracy was made agaynst him.
But the comon report was otherwyse; for the multytude sayd that
the duke dyd the lesse disswade kinge Richerd from usurping the
kingdome, by meane of so many mischievous dedes, uppon that
intent that he afterward, being hatyd both of God and man, might
be expellyd from the same, and so himself be caulyd by the commons to that dignytie, wherunto he asspyryd by all meanes possible, and that yerfor he had at the last stirryd upp warr agaynst
kinge Rycherd: but let us returne to owr purpose.

Now before the duke all in a rage had begun to be alyenate in Lewis a
mynde from king Richerd, the same very time a plot of new con- physetyon
used be-
spiracy was layd at London betwixt Elyzabeth the quene, wyfe to tweene Q.
king Edward, and Margaret mother to erle Henry, in this sort: and the
This Margaret for want of health usid thadvyse of a physition countys of
R   d
namyd Lewys, a Welsheman born, who, because he was a grave for a match
man and of no smaule experience, she was wont oftentimes to to be had
betweene
conferre frely with all, and with him famylyarly to lament her their
adversitie. And she, being a wyse woman, after the slaughter of children.
king Edwardes children was knowen, began to hope well of hir
soones fortune, supposing that that dede wold withowt dowt
proove for the profyt of the commonwelth, yf yt might chaunce
the bloode of king Henry the Sixth and of king Edward to be
intermenglyd by affynytie, and so two most pernicious factions
should be at once, by conjoynyng of both the howses, utterly
taken away. Wherfor furthwith not neglecting so great oportunytie, as they wer consulting togythers, she utteryd to Lewys that

the time was now coom when as king Edwardes eldest dowghter
might be geaven in maryage to hir soon Henry, and that king
Rycherd, accountyd of all men enemy to his countree, might easyly
be dejectyd from all honor and bereft the realme, and therfor prayd
him to deale secretly with the quene of suche affayre; for the
quene also usyd his head, because he was a very learnyd physytion.   Lewys nothing lyngeryng spak with the quene, as yeat remaning in sayntuarie, and declaryd the matter not as delyveryd to
him in charge but as devysyd of his owne heade.   The quene was
so well pleasyd with this devyse, that she commandyd Lewys to
repare to the cowntes Margaret, who remaynyd in hir husbands
howse at London, and to promyse in hir name that she wold do
hir indevor to procure all hir husband king Edwards frynds to
take part with Henry hyr soon, so that he might bee sworne to
take in maryage Elyzabeth hyr dowghter, after he shalle have
gotten the realme, or els Cycyly, the yownger, yf thother showld
dye before he enjoyed the same.   Lewys, by and by, doing as he
was commandyd, made up the matter easyly betwyxt the two
women, who because of his scyence becam a messenger betwene
them, and was assocyat unto them in this new conspyracy against
king Richerd withowt any suspytion. Thus Margaret being browght

Rainold
in good hope apoyntyd Raynold Bray her servyteur, a man most
confedera-
cion of the
contesse of faythfull and trustie, to be the chief dealer in this conspyracy, and
commanded him to draw unto her partie, as secretly as might be,
Rich-
monds soom such noble or woorshipfull men as wer wyse, faythfull, and
party. actyve, who wer hable to make help in the cause. Raynold within
few days gathered into the socyetie of that conspyracy Gyles
Dawbney knight, Richerd Gylfoord, Thomas Ramney, John
Cheney, and many mo, having taken an oathe beforehand of every
man perticulerly. The quene also maketh hir frindes partakers of
this devyse and busynes to be set forward with all spede convenyent. But Margaret the meane whyle tooke into hir famyly

Christopher Urswyche, an honest, approovyd, and serviceable priest, Christofor
and after he was sworn unto hir, she discoveryd to him all hir ~~Urswyck~~ sent into
intent, trustyng that she might so do safely because Chrystopher Brittany to
was alway a favorer of king Henry the vj^(th), and commendyd to Riche-
hir by Lewys the physytion.   Thus the mother, carefull for the mond.
well doing and glory of hir soon, gave Christopher in charge to go
unto erle Henry into Bryttany, and to signyfy unto him all that
was doone with the quene.   But before he began to take his journey behold she was suddanely advertysid of the same practyse
purposyd by the duke of Buckingham, as we have before remembryd; which whan she knew she alteryd hir intent, staying Chris- Christofer
topher at home, and sent Hugh Conwey into Bryttane unto hir Jrswic
soon Henry with a good great sum of money, commanding him to stayed,
utter all thinges, and exhort hys returne, and especyally to advyse Conwaye
him to arryve in Wales, wher he should fynde ayd in readines. sente to the
Also, Richerd Gilfoord sent after him owt of Kent Thomas Riche-
Romney with the same message.   They having spedy passage mond.
cam unto erle Henry almost at one time, whom we have before Rumney
sayd to have bene with the duke of Bryttany, now after the death sent by
of king Edward at his owne lybertie.   Henry having receavyd the Gylford to
message gave thanks to God, supposing his whole harts desyre earle Richmond.
cowld not have happenyd without Gods speciall provydence; and
therfor, rejoysing woonderusly, he conferryd all thinges with the
duk, shewing that he had conceavyd an assuryd hope of obtanyng
the realme of England, and prayd therfor that the same might be
browght abowt both by his good help and assent, whiche whan so
ever habylytie showld serve he wold not fale to requyte.   The duke,
althowgh he had bene laboryd from king Richerd both with money
and muche sute by Thomas Hutton his ambassador, whom we
have before declaryd to have bene sent thyther, that he wold
thrust erle Henry agane into ward, yeat he promysyd ayd and
willingly gave yt.   Than Henry premysyd into England Hewgh

Conway and Thomas Ramney to geve notice of his coomming, that
his frinds might take order hedefully for all other thinges which
by pollycy might be provydyd for; hys owne pleasure was to stay
ther untill that all thinges nedefull for saling wer preparyd. In the
meane time in England the heades of the conspyracy went abowt
many matters; soome held furnyshyd fyt places with force of men;
soome secretly solycytyd the commonaltie to sedytion; others
earnestly mynded, and wer redy, so soone as they should know of
Henryes arryvall, to begin the warre; others fynally, of which
number John Morton bisshop of Ely was chief, provokyd, by
secrete messengers, all men to this new conspyracy whom they
knew assurydly to hate king Richerd no lesse than themselfes did.

While these thinges wer a doing king Richerd was informyd of
the conspyracy of these noble men, who being dryven into per-
plexitie by dubble mischief, for because he nether had army in
readynes, nether yeat, yf he showld make warre uppon the suddayn,
knew suffycyently wher to encownter thenemy, wher to tary nor
whyther to go, determynyd to dyssemble the matter a while till he
might gather an army, and that by speache of the people, and
dylygence of espyall, the devyses of his adversaryes wer searchyd
owt, conceavyd, manyfestyd, and discoveryd, or that by thys kinde
of sleyght he might apprehend soome of the conspirators; for that
ther is no deceyt more depe and secrete than that which lurketh in
the dissembly of understanding, or under soome colour of curtesy.
The kynge And because he knew the duke of Buckingham to be the head of
duke of ^{t e} the conspyrators, therfor first of all he thowght best, ether by
Bucking- fraude or force, to cut of the same; and therfor he sent exceding
he reffused. curteous letters unto the duke that he wold coome unto him, and
gave the messenger who caryed the letters in charge to make in
his name many fayre promyses, and by soome good meane perswade him to coome unto the court. The duke, alledging infyr-
mytie of stomake, awnsweryd the messenger that presently coome

he cowld not. King Rycherd wold admyt none excuse, but sent for him agane with threatening woords. Than the duke openly denyed that he wold coom to his enemy, and withall made ready for warre, and perswadid his confederates furthwith, soom one wher soom other, to rase the people. So almost at one moment and time Thomas marquyse Dorset, who was gone owt of sayntuary and preservyd from all danger by meane of Thomas Rowell, in Yorkshire, Edward Courtney, with Peter his broother, bisshop of Excester, in Devonshire, Richerd Gylfoord, with certane of great reputation, in Kent, rasyd upp the commons every wher to armor, and made a begynning of warres. But king Richerd the meane season having gatherid an huge host of armyd men, because he wold not dissypate his forces, the while he was willing to pursew every of the conspyrators, resolvyd to omyt the resydew, and turne his whole army agaynst the head, that was the duke, who removing from London tooke his journey towardes Salsbury, to thintent he might dyvert owt of that way agaynst the duke whersoever he could learne that he wer encampyd. And now was he coommyd within two days journey of the towne, whan the duke with great force of Walse soldiers, whom he, as a sore and hard dealing man, had brought to the feild agaynst ther wills, and withowt any lust to fight for him, rather by rigorus commandment than for money, which was the cause of the revolt, went earnestly abowt to encownter the king, but he was forsaken suddaynly of the more part of his soldiers, and compellyd thereby to fly, during which flight, being in great terror by reason of this suddane chaunge of fortune, whan he knew not well what way to take, he got himself into the howse of a certane servant of his namyd Humfrey Banyster, whom because he had found an honest man eaven from his chyldehoode, therfor he trustyd to fynde him most faythfull, and commyttyd himself to hys fydelytie, meaning to remane secret with him untill the tyme that he might advyse

The duke of Buckinghames confederates.

R. 3 gone with an army against the Buckingham.

The duke of Buckingham forsaken of diers.

ether how to repare for his owne defence a new army, either els to
go unto therle Henry into Brytayn. But whan his confederates,
who had now begoon warre, knew that the duke was forsaken of
his people, and fled no man wyst whyther, they wer suddainly
dismayd, every man fled without hope of saftie, and other got into
sayntuaryes or wyldernes, or assayed to sayle over the seas, wherof
a great part came safe soone after into Brytayne. Emongest that
company was Peter Cortney bisshop of Excester, with Edward his
broother, erle of Devonshire, Thomas marquise Dorcest, with
Thomas his soon, a very chylde, John Bursher, John Welles,
Edward Woodvill, a valyant man of warre, brother to quene Elizabeth, Robert Wylloughbie, Gyles Dabeney, Thomas Arundell,
John Cheyney, with hys two brothers, William Barchley, William
Brandon, with Thomas his broother, Rycherd Edgecombe, and all
these almost of thorder of knighthoode: also John Halvell,
Edward Peningham, chiefe captane of tharmy, Christopher Urswyche, and John Morton bysshop of Ely, with many other noble
men, transportyd over abowt the same very time into Flanders.

But king Richerd, a man muche to be feared for circumspection
and celerytie, who now was coomyd to Salsbury, after that he
knew the duke and others of the conspyracy to be fled, determynyd to pursew them, and first sent soldyers anon to all the
portes nighe therabowts, to take, kepe, and hold all passinge owt
by sea, and to let tnem tnat fled from transporting; than after,
to any man that showld tell of the duke he proclamyd large
reward; to the bond, libertie; to the fre pardon from punishment and a M^{li}. And because he had receavyd of late intellygence by Thomas Hutton, being returnyd owt of Brytayne, that
the duke thereof was so farre from condiscending to kepe erle
Henry in pryson for his sake, yea as that he was busyly abowt-
ward to ayd therle with succor and supply against him, he disposed
withall certane shipps well furnysshyd alongest the sea coste that

The duke
uck-
'n h
confede-
s e e
into Brit-
tany.

A procla-
e
against the
duke of
ing-
ham.

tendeth toward Brytayne, to thintent that, yf erle Henry showld by chaunce coom, he might ether be interceptyd or kept from the shore. Moreover, to make marvalus strayt watche every wher, he disposyd some soldiers in places convenyent to beset ways, paths, and all kynd of passages: he sent owt others every way, to seke yf yt were possyble to fynde and apprehend any wher the duke or any his confederats. To these men seking owt all thinges narrowly, Humfrey Bannister, whether for feare or money yt is soom dowt, betrayed his guest Henry the duke, who brought him furthwith to Salsbury unto king Richerd. The duke was dily- gently examynyd, and what he knew uppon demand he tould without torture, hopynge because he frely confessyd, that therfor he showld have lybertie to speake with king Richerd, which he most sore desyryd; but after he had confessyd thoffence he was beheadyd. This death dyd the duke suffer of king Richerd, whom he had aydyd agaynst his own conscience (as the saing is), with whom he had by this meane conjoignyd socyetie of perill more trewly than of empire. Hereof surely may we marke, that he loseth his labor, and chargeth his owne lyfe with haynous offence, who helpeth an evell and wicked man, seing that he both re-ceaveth of him for the most part an evell dede for a good, and of God alway in the ende condigne punishment.

Whyle these thinges were doone in England, Henry erle of Richemoond had preparyd an army of v.M. Bryttaynes, and fur-nyshyd a navy of xv^tn. shipps, and now was approchyd the day of his departure, who began to sayle with prosperous wynd the vj^th. ides of October in the yere of helth M.CCCC.lxxxiiij., and the second king Richerd began his raigne. But a little before even suddayn tempest arose, wherwithall he was so afflyctyd that his shipps wer constraygnyd by force of a crewell gale of wynde to turne ther course from one way from another; divers of them wer blowen bak into Normandie, others into Bryttany. The ship wherin

Marginal notes: The duke ingham betrayed Banystere his set ranger.

ultra aras.

The earle mond c.- taketh his towards England.

Henry was, with one other, tossyd all the night long with the waves, cam at the last very early in the morning, whan the winde grew calme, uppon the south coast of the iland, agaynst the haven caulyd

Polam. Pole. From hence erle Henry, viewing afur of all the shore beset with soldiers, whiche king Richerd, as we have before shewyd, had every wher disposyd, gave open commandment that not one man of them all showld take landing before the resydew of the ships showld come togythers ; which, while he taryeth for, he sent owt a bote to try whether they wer his frindes which hoovyd so in the same place. Than those who wer sent wer earnestly desyryd by the soldiers from the shore to come a land, crying that they wer

The earle sent from the duke of Buchingham to be ready for the accom-
ᴏꜰ ʀɪᴄʜ-
monds panying of erle Henry safe unto the camp, which the duke himself
shipes nad at nand with a notable excellent army, so that joigning ther
being
scatered forces they both might pursew king Richard who was fled. But
durst not erle Henry suspecting yt to be a trayn, as yt was in dede, after
länd.
that he dyd see none of his owne ships within view, hoysyd upp sale, and with prosperus wynde came into Normandy, so that a man may think the very blast of the wynde drove him bak from danger. Here he, tarying uppon the shore the space of thre days for the refreshing of his soldiers after ther toyle and travaille, de-termynyd to returne with part of his retynew a foote into Bry-tayne, and in the meane time sent ambassadors to demand of Charles theight, king of Fraunce, who had succeeded Lewis his father lately dead, leave to passe throwghe Normandy. The king pytying therles fortune, dyd not onely grant him passage with good will, but also money to beare his charges. Howbeyt himself, trusting uppon the kinges courtesy, had sent his ships home before and was enteryd on his journey; yeat he had not gone fur whan thambassadors returnyd, so that greatly comfortyd by that benyfyt and replenished with good hope he returnyd into Brytayne, supposing that from thencefurth he must take an other

course. But being in Brytayne he had intelligence by his frindes The mar-
that the duke of Buchingham was beheadyd in England; that the que Dorset
marquyse Dorset, with a well great number of thinglishe noby- aryved in
lytie, was commyd thither a little before to seke him, and remanyd Brytany.
at Vanes; which newys whan he understoode to be trew, he muche
lamentid that the first attempt of those noble personages had
fallen so evell owt, yet on thother syd rejoysing that he had so
many notable captanes partakers of that warre, and withall conceaving eaven than almost an assuryd opynion that all his affayres
wer firmly strengthenyd, and that his cause wold coome well to
passe, he adjudgyd yt mete for him to use celerytie. Wherfor, going
unto Reynes, he sent furthwith certane of his retynew to bring Rhedones.
the marquyse and thother noble and woorshipfull unto him. They
having knowledge that erle Henry was, after long wandering, returnyd safe into Brytayne, rejoysed woonderusly (for, being ignorant
in what part of the world he was become, they fearyd least he had
faullen into the handes of king Richerd) and so reparyd to him in
all hast thick and threfold. Heare, after muche mutuall congratulation made, and that they had delyberatyd of dealyng in their
causis certane days, the day of Chrystes natyvytee was coomyd
uppon, which, meting all in the churche, they ratyfied all other
thinges by plyghting of their trouths and solemne covenantes; and
first of all erle Henry uppon his othe promysyd, that so soone as
he showld be king he wold mary Elyzabeth, king Edwards
dowghter; than aftir they swore unto him homage as thowghe he
had bene already created king, protesting that they wold losse not
onely ther landes and possessions, but ther lyves, before ever they
wold suffer, beare, or permyt, that Richerd showld rewle over
them and theirs. Whan this was done erle Henry reportyd all to
the duke, and prayd him hartely to ayde him with more ample
supply, that he might returne furthwith into his cowntry, much
desyringe his presence, and especially to lend him money, for so

much as that which he had already receavyd of his frindes was
spent in furnishing of the former warre, and promysyd that he
wold faythfully repay what soo ever he showld receave, and in
time to coome plentyfully requyte the dukes singular lyberalytie

with all indevor, care, and diligence. The duke promysyd him
ayde, whereuppon trusting he took uppon him agane the care of
preparing a navy, and made himself ready to the sea, that he
showld not be hinderyd from any attempt by laches of time.   '

In the meane whyle king Richerd, being returnyd to London,
commandyd certane that wer guyltie of the conspyracy who wer
taken in sundrye places all at once, and emong them George

Broune, Roger Clyffoord, Thomas Selenger, knightes, also Thomas
Ramney, Robert Clyffoorth, and dyvers others, yea of his owne
howsehold, to be put to death. Afterward he assemblyd a parlyament, wherin he procuryd all thexyles to be denoncyd traytors to
ther countree by act of parlyament; then all ther goodes to be con-
fiyscate, and not content with that pray, though very riche, he
fynally causyd a great tax of money to be imposyd uppon the
people, for he had bene of late so lavashing in rewards, seking by
suche meane to purge himself, and win favor of the commonaltie,
that he began now to be nedy. But yt went very hard that
Thomas Stanley also was not accowntyd emongest the number of
the kinges enemyes, by reason of the practyses of Margaret his
wyfe, mother unto erle Henry, who was commonly caulyd the
head of that conspyracy; but, for as muche as the woorking of a
womans wit was thowght of smaule accounte, the cownsell therfor

set downe and commandyd that Thomas, who proovid himself
guiltles of the offence, showld remove from his wyfe all hir servantes, and kepe hir so strayt with himself that she showld not
be hable from thencefurth to send any messenger nether to hir
soone, nor frinds, nor practise any thing at all agaynst the king;
which was doone accordingly. Also by authorytie of the same

parlyament a peace was made with the Scottes, who a lyttle A peace
before had run forrows about the borders. Whan these thinges land.
wer thus concludyd, all the conspyracy semyd in a maner extin-
guyshyd; the duke beinge taken away and other his confederates
partly executyd, partly exylyd into foreyn countreys. But king
Richerd, as yeat more dowtynge than trusting in his owne cause,
was vexyd, wrestyd, and tormentyd in mynd with feare almost
perpetually of therle Henry and his confederates returne ; wherfor
he had a myserable lyfe, who to ryd himself of this inward gryefe,
determynyd fynally to pull up by the rootes all matter of feare
and tumult, and other by guyle or force to bring the same abowt.
And so after suche resolution taken he thought no way more fytt
or commendable than to solycit agane the duke of Brytayne, for
money, prayer, and reward, because yt lay in his hand to dispatche
him quyte of all perill, and therfore he sent furthwith specyall messengers to the duke, who, besydes great gyftes which they caryed R. 3 sent a
with them, showld promise to geave him yerely the whole revenues ew mes-
sen-ere to
of all the lands appertaining to earle Henry, and the resydew of the duke
thinglishe nobylyte that wer with him, yf he wold from thence- o or any
romy-
furth kepe them with him in ward. The messengers being gone synge
with this maner message could not deale this matter with the duke, rewardes.
for that he was becoome feble by reason of sore and dayly siknes and
began to maddle; wherfor Peter Landofe his treasurer, a man both
of sharpe wit and great authorytie, rewlyd all matters as himself lyst,
who for that cause had stirryd upp grevously agaynst himself thenvy
of the Bryttishe nobylytie. This man dyd thiglyshe ambassadors
deale withall, and explaning ther commyssion besowght him earnestly that he, who might do all thinges as hym lyst, wold fulfill
king Richerds dayly desire. Peter, who was in great hatryd of his
owne countrymen, supposing that yf he showld satisfy king Richerd
he showld be more mightie againe his adversaryes, awnsweryd
that he wold do the thing which king Richerd requyryd, so that he

wold kepe promyse. And all this dyd he by reason of cyvyll enemytie; for he hated not earle Henry, whom, as we have shewyd
in the former booke, he had before delyveryd from danger, at
saint Maloes. Thus ever with cause we offend. But the fortune
of thinglishe commonwelth was the let why this mortall covenant
was not performyd : for whyle that many messengers and often
letters dyd fly to and fro betwixt Peter and the king, for dispatche

R. 3 prac-
tyce with
n
of the duke
ta   dis-
covered to
the L. of
Rich-
monde.
of the busynes, John bysshop of Ely, who lyvyd in Flanders,
being certyfyed of that practyse from his fryndes owt of England,
gave intelligence to Henry furthwith of the plot that was layd, by
Christopher Urswyke, who was coomyd to hym owt of England
abowt the same time, and advysyd therle that he showld get himself and thother noble men as soone as might be owt of Brytayne
into France. Henry was than at Vanes whan he had intelligence
of the fraude, who, without any stay, sent Christopher as ambassador to king Charles, to pray that he myght lawfully passe
into France; which thing easyly obtanyd, thambassador returnyd
spedyly unto his prince.

Than earle Henry, thinking yt mete to provyde for his affaires
with all dylygence, imparteth his purpose to few of his company,
and, having learnyd the way, he sent before all thinglyshe nobilytie,
faygnyng that he wold send them for supply of his pryvate causes
unto the duke, who as than lay for his pleasure not farre from the
boundes of Fraunce, and secretly warnyd therle of Pembruch,

The earle
of Riche-
his frendes
flye into
Fraunce.
cnief of thambassage, that whan they showld be at the borders of
Brytayne, leaving suddaynly the right way, they showld get themselves into Fraunce ; who, doing as they wer directyd, procedyd
in ther journey contynewally withowt intermytting any one moment of time, and went unto the country of Angeow. Hymself
two days after departing from Vanes, and accompanied with fyve
onely servantes, feignyd to go unto a frind, who had a maner not
farre of, and, because an huge multitude of Englishe people was

left in the towne, nobody suspectyd his voyage; but whan he had
journayed almost five myles he withdrew hastely out of the highe
way into the next wood, and doing on a serving mans apparell, he
as a servant folowyd one of his owne servants (who was his
guyde in that journay) as thowghe he had bene his maister, and
rode on with so great celerytie, keping yeat no certane way, that
he made no stay any where, except yt were to bate his horses,
before he had gotten himself to his company within the bounds of
Angeow. Moreover, fowre days after that erle Henry had escaped
by flight, Peters intent was to have set owt certane force of men,
musteryd with ther captanes (which he had chosen owt to perform
his wicked determynation), under pretence that he wold delyver
them to erle Henry, as yt wer to accompany hym in his returne
to his country, but in very dede meaning to have browght therle
unwares, and suspectyng no guyle, with the resydew of the nobylyte, suddanly into pryson; that by suche haynous fact he might
satisfy kinge Rycherd for the trybute which he had promysyd.
But this Peter the treasurer, who wantyd no subtiltie, whan he
understood that Henry was departyd, wherof his mynde gave him,
sent owt horsemen incontinent every way to pursew, and if they
cowld overtake him, to apprehend and bring the earle to him.
The horsemen made such haste as that ther was never thing more
nighe thachieving than thovertakinge of the earle; hee was scarse
ne h owre entryd the boundes of France whan they cam thyther.
But thinglishe men (abowt three hundreth in number), who
remained at Vanes, whan they knew that erle Henry was fled,
because they were not pryvy therunto, became so afeard that they
wer now in utter despeare of safety; howbeyt the matter fell owt
otherwyse than they demyd fyt for them to feare; for the duke,
takinge yt in evell part that Henry was so uncurteously entertaynyd as that he was forcyd to fly owt of his domynyon, and for
the same cause being very angry with Peter, uppon whom, thowghe

himself was ignorant of all the practyse, he layd the blame of
that offence, cawlyd unto him Edward Ponings, and thother
Edward Woodvyll, and geaving them money to beare the charges
of ther journey, commanded them to conduct all thinglishe men to
therle. And so earl Henry, having receavyd all his retynew, was
woonderus glad, who, because he wold not be accowntyd unthankfull, sent back dyvars unto the duke tadvertyse on his behalf,
that presentlv hee thankyd him for the saftie of himself and all his
company, which thereafter in time he wold not fale to requyte.
But hee within few days after reparyd unto king Charles, who was
at a towne sytuate uppon the ryver of Loire caulyd Angiers ; unto
whom, after thankes geaven for the benefytes receavyd, he first
explanyd the cause of his cooming, than he besowght ayd wherby,
throwgh his immortal benyfyt, he might returne safely unto his
owne nobylytie, of whom he was generally caulyd unto the kingdom, so muche dyd they abhorre the tyranny of king Richerd.
King Charles promysyd him ayd, and bad him be of good chere,
for he wold willingly shew his goodwill, who furthwith after
departyd to Montarge, taking Henry with him and all the trane of
his nobylytie. During the time of Henry his abode heare John
earle of Oxfoord, whom we have above mentionyd to have bene
holden in ward of king Edward in the castle of Hammes, togyther
with James Blunt the captane therof, and John Fortescew knight,
the gentleman porter of Calys, subornyd by the erle, cam unto him ;
but captane James, because hee left his wyfe in the castle, had fur-
nissyd the same with new garryson before his departure thence.
Whan Henry saw therle he was ravisshyd with joy incredible
that a man of so great nobilytie and knowledge in the warres, and
of most perfyte and sownd fydelytie, most earnestly bent to his
syde, was at the last by Gods assistance delyveryd owt of ward,
and in so fyt tyme coommyd to help him, in whome he might
repose his hope, and settle himself more safely than in any other ;

The duke
send the r ny
residue of
earl
Henryes
trayne after
France
char e ɩ is

Angeu.

King
France s o
yelds ayd
Henry.

The earle
of Oxford
came over
into
Trance to
the earle
or Riche-
mond.

for he was not ignorant that others who had holden on king
Edward syde yealdid unto him by reason of the evell state of
time, but this man who had so oft foughte for king Henry was he
thowght delyveryd from that ward by the hevenly help, that he
might have one of his owne faction to whom he might safely
commyt all thinges; and therfor rejoysing above all measure for
therle of Oxfoorthis cooming, he began to hope better of his
affaires.

Not long after king Charles removyd to Paris, whom erle Henry
folowyd, and sowght there to bring to passe his sute, requesting
king Charles agane to take him wholy to his tuytion, so that yf he
and his confederates showld be in safetie they might all lykewyse
also acknowledge the same receavyd at his hand. In the meane
time very many Englishe men, who ether dyd flok contynewally
owt of England, or were ther studyouse of learning, gave and
vowyd upp themselves wholy to take his part. Emongest these
was Richard Fox, priest, a man of an excellent wyt, a man learnyd,
whom Henry receavyd immediatly to be of his privy counsaile,
and browght within short whyle to great honor, who is now bisshop
†of Wynchester.

Richard
afterbishop
of Win-
came to
earl Henry
to France.

Richerd in the meane time having intelligence what covenants
the confederats in Brytayn had made emongest themselves, and
how they had all escapyd into France by the conduct of earle
Henry, thowgh he wer greatly disapoyntyd because his craftie
practyse had not procedyd, yeat he determynyd to prevent by an
other way that thearle Henry showld not coom unto the kingdom
by maryage of hys nece Elyzabeth. And because, in comparyson
of thorrible factes which, blyndyd with desyre of soveraigntie, he
had before enterprysyd, all other thinges that he showld do aftirward semyd in his estimation but smaule matters (according as
the proverb putteth us in remembrance, He will lyft up an oxe
that hath caryed a calfe), ther cam therfor into his mynde matter

the most wickyd to be spoken, and the fowlest to be commyttyd, that ever was herd of. For whyle he revolvyd with himself how great heap of myschiefe wer immynent yf Henry should be avaunced by maryage of his nece, uppon thonly rumor wherof he herd of dyvers who semyd already carefull for therles affayres ;

he therfor determynyd, by all meanes possyble, to reconcyle unto him Elyzabeth the quene, that she myght yeald hir self and hir dowghters into his handes, and Henry by that meane defraudyd from thaffynitie of his nece ; and yf yt wer not possible to salve the sores immynent otherwyse, and that by hap it myght fortune his wyfe too dye, than he wold rather mary his nece himself than by thaffynytie aforesayd to danger the state, as thowgh by his faule the ruyne of the realme must nede folow. And so he sent into the saintwary often messengers unto the quene to make unto hir purgation of his fact, and by promysing mountaynes both unto hir and hir soon Thomas the marquise to put the woman in passing great hope. The messengers being grave men, though at the first by reducyng to memory the slawghter of hir soonnes they soomwhat wowndyd the quenes mynde, and that hir gryefe semyd scarse hable to be comfortid, yeat they assayed hir by so many meanes, and so many fayre promisses, that withowt muche adoe they began to mollyfy hir (for so mutable is that sex), in so muche that the woman herd them willingly, and fynally sayd she wold yeald hir selfe unto the king ; and so not very long after, forgetting

injuryes, forgetting hir faith and promyse geaven to Margaret, Henryes mother, she first delyvered hir dowghters into the handes of king Richerd ; than aftir by secret messengers advysyd the marquyse her soon, who was at Parys, to forsake erle Henry, and with all speede convenyent to returne into England, wher he showld be sure to be caulyd of the king unto highe promotion. Whan the quene was thus qualyfyed, king Richerd receavyd all his brothers dawghters owt of saintuary into the court. Thonely

matter now remaning was to acquyte himself of marriage, which he
adjudgyd best for him to do by all meane possible; but this savage
and crewell mynde of his was no lytle fearyd from so great and
owtrageous fact, for that (as we have before mentyonyd) he had
of late counterfaytyd to be a good man, and therfor was afeard
least by the untymely death of his wyfe he showld hinder the good
opynyon which he belevyd the people had conceavyd uppon him.
But the wickyd intent wan the mastery in the wyt wayward from
all righteousnes; for first he forbare to lye with her, and withall
began to complane muche unto many noble men of his wyfes un-
fruytfulnes, for that she browght him furth no children, and that
chiefly dyd he lament with Thomas Rotheram archebysshop of
York, because he was a grave and good man, whom he had a lyttle
before let owt of prison (who thereuppon gatheryd and supposyd
yt wold come to passe that the quene should not long lyve, and
-foreshewyd the same to dyvers his frinds). Than after he procuryd a rumor (uncertane from whom) to be spred abrode of the
quene his wyfes death, that ether the woman being browght in
great dolor, by report and fame of the matter, might faule into
siknes, ether els that he might therby take a proofe yf the same
showld happen afterward whether the people wold lay the blame
therof unto his charge. But whan the quene herd of suche terrible
rumors dispersyd already of hir owne death, supposing that hir
days wer at an end, she went unto her husband very pensyffe and
sadde, and with many teares demandyd of him what cause ther
was why he should determyne hyr death. Hereunto the king,
least that he might seme hard hartyd yf he showld shew unto his
wyfe no signe of loove, kissing hir, made awnswer loovingly, and
comfortyng hir, bad hir be of good chere. But the quene, whether R. 3 his
-she wer dispatchyd with sorowfulnes, or poyson, dyed within few queen ule sodenly.
days after, and was buryed at Westmynster. This ys Anne that
thone of the daughters of Richerd erle of Warweke who was soom

tyme covenantyd to prince Edward, soon to king Henry the Sixt. The king, thus lowsyd from the bond of matrimony, began to cast an eye uppon Elyzabeth his nece, and to desyre hir in maryage ; but because both the yowng lady hirself, and all others, did abhorre the wickednes so detestable, he determynyd therfor to do every thing by leysure, for so muche especially as he was overwhelmyd with pinching cares on every hand ; for that soom man of name passyd over dayly unto Henry, others favoryd secretly the parte-

The lo. Stanley and others of the con- the E. of Richmond.
ners of the conspyracy. Emongest these principally was Thomas Stanley, William his brother, Gylbert Talbot, and others innu- merable, whose inward mynde thowgh Richerd was ignorant of, yeat he trustyd never one of them all, and Thomas Stanley least of all others, because he had in maryage Henryes mother, as the matter yt self made manyfest shew ; for whan he at that time wold have gone into his countrie, for his pleasure as he sayd, but indede that he might be ready to receave erle Henry as a frind at his cooming, the king forbad him, and wold not suffer him to depart before he had left George lord Strange his soone as a pledge in the court.

R. 3 had oti ıa the castell of Hames the E. of Richmond.
Whyle king Richerd was thus occupied in so great trouble of mynde and alteration of devyses for feare of stirre to coome, beholde he heard that the same was broken owt, for hee had intelligence that the castle of Hammes held with Henry by meane of tnerle of Oxfoorth, and that he, with James Blunt, captane therof, were fled to Henry himself ; wherefore thinkinge yt best to withstand the begynning, he sent furthwith to recover the hold, a good part of the garryson which was at Calys. Those who wer within the castle, whan they saw thadversary approche, armyd themselves quikly to the defense, and anon sent messengers to erle Henry to demand ayd. Henry withowt delay commandyd therle of Oxfoorth with choyse soldiers to go and help his frinds, who in ther first arryvall encampyd themselves not farre from the

castle; the whyle they held ther enemys intentyve uppon that part, Thomas Brandon, with thirtie valyant man, entryd the castle by the marishe, which joingneth unto the place. Than they who wer within, having receavyd new supply, skrymysshyd with thennemy from the waule more sharply than before. Therle of Oxfoorth also at ther bakes was no lesse earnest; wherby yt fell owt that thenemyes of ther owne free will gave unto the besegyd fre lybertie to depart with bagg and baggage, which condytion therle of Oxfoorth, who came for that ende to delyver his frindes from danger, and especyally the wyfe of James, the captane therof, - dyd not refuse, but leaving the castle returnyd safe with his company to Parys. King Richerd after this understoode by his spyalls that Henry, hinderyd emongest the Frenche by reason of the time, grew weary with contynuall demaunding of ayd, that he profytyd nothing, nor that any thing went forward with him, but that all thinges which he dilygently had devysyd fell owt not well; which whan he belevyd to be so, as thowgh he had vanquisshed the whole warres, and had bene delyveryd from all feare, supposyd that ther was no cause why he showld take such care in a matter of no danger, caulyd his shipps from ther stations, and all the soldiers which he had before placyd heare and there to kepe of thenemy; but least he might be found altogether unready, he commandyd noble men and gentlemen dwellynge about the sea coste, and chiefly the Walshe men, to kepe watche by course after ther country maner, to thintent that his adversaryes showld not have ready recovery of the shore and coome a land; for thinhabytantes about the sea costes place, in the time of warre especyally, on the hylls adjoyning lampes fastenyd upon frames of timber, and whan any great or notable matter happeneth, by reason of thapproche of enemyes, they suddenely lyght the lampes, and with showtes through towne and fielde geave notice therof; from thence others aftirward receave and utter unto ther neighbors

(marginalia:) Hames delyvered by the earle of Oxford monds people.

(marginalia:) Beakones pre in Wales and all places.

notice after the same sort. Thus ys the fame therof caryed spedyly to all villages and townes, and both country and towne arme themselves agaynst thenemy. And thus king Richerd, soomwhat easyd of his griefe, began to be more careles, least otherwise he might by dylygence have avoydyd the desteny that hang over his head; for suche is the force of the divine justice, that a man lesse seath, lesse provydeth, and lesse hede taketh when he ys nighe the yealding of punishement for his haynous offences.

At that time that Henry stayd in France for thobtaning of ayde very many noble men were, by reason of king Charles his age, rewlers of the realme, not muche agreing emong themselves, of which pryvy hatryd Lewys duke of Orleance was head, who, seing he had in maryage Joan syster to king Charles, strove to beare chief sway in the government of the commonwelth ; by which occasyon yt cam to passe that the charge of thempire was commyttyd to no one man ; and erle Henry, who day and night omyttyd no oportunytie of hastening his voyage into his country, was compellyd to go and make earnest sute unto every man particularly. So was the matter driven of, when Thomas marquise Dorcest, whom we have before sayd to have bene cauled home of his mother, partely despearing for that cause of erle Henryes successe, partly subornyd by king Richerds fayre promyses, departyd pryvyly in the night time from Parys, and with great journeys travalyd into Flanders ; which thing as soone as therle and thother Englishe nobylytie understoode they were muche moovyd, and desyryd of king Charles that they might by his commandment -stay the man who was pryvy to all ther purposes whersoever he should be fownd, and ther sute obteynyd began to ryde owt every way. But Humfrey Cheyney, savoring most subtilly the trace of him that went before, followyd the right way, and overtooke the marquise at the towne of Compiegne, and so perswadyd him that a little after he returnyd to his felowes. Erle Henry, easyd of that

marques Dorset

towards England from the E. of Rich-

T e ues Dorset came back the per- swasyon of Cheyney.

griefe, determynyd that yt was not for him to linger, but to use all
the celerytie that might be, least by dowting and differring of time
he should losse great oportunitie, or least longer looking for might
trooble more the myndes of his frinds who awaytyd for his
coomming. And so, obtaynyng of king Charles a sclender supply, Pledges left
h
and borowyng as well of him as of other pryvate frinds certane king of
money, for the which he left sureties, or rather pledges, the mar- Fr   for
moneye
quyse and John Burschere, he departyd to Roan. While he lente E.
taryed here, and riggyd his navy at the mouth of Seyne, a rumor Henry.
came unto his eare that king Richerd, his wife being dead, was
amyndyd to mary Elizabeth, his brother Edwardes dowghter, and
that he had maryed Cecyly, Edwards other doughter, unto an
obscure man of no reputation. This matter being of no smaule
weyght, as the which cut away from the confederates all hope of
executyng ther delyberat resolution, pinchid Henry by the veray
stomak, because therby he saw that he cowld not now expect the
marriage of any of king Edwardes dowghters, wherfor he thowght
yt was to be fearyd least his frindes showld forsake him. The
matter therfor being browght to consultation of a few, yt lyked
them to prefer the same, before the profection, that they might The E. of
assay if any other cowld be adjoignyd, and yt was thowght to uci mo   e
sent   s-
stand with ther profyt yf by affynytie they cowld draw into sengers to
suryetie of that warre Gwalter Harbert, a man of ancyent autho- Harberte
rytie emong the Welshe men, who had with him a sister marrage- to have his
de. nd
able; and to procure the same messengers were sent to Henry promysed
earl of Northumberland, who had in marriage Gualters other sister, o i a
his sister.
that he wold deale in that cause; but the ways were so beset that A messen-
none of them could coome unto him. But a better messenger ger frō
Mor
came from John Morgan, a lawyer, who signyfyed the same tyme monisne ͞r.
that Richerd, by surname Thomas, a man of great service and of Rich-
valyant, and John Savage, wer wholy geauen to erle Henryes mond to
haste into
affayres, and that Reynold Bray had made up no smaule summ of England.

money to pay soldyers wages withall, and therfor advysyd him
that as soone as oportunytie showld serve he wold take the streight
way into Wales.

Than Henry, thinkinge yt nedefull to make haste, that his
frinds showld not be any longer kept in perplexytie betwene
hope and drede, uncertane what to do, after he had made his
prayers to God that he might have an happy and prosperous
journey, he lowsyd from the mowth of Seyne with two thousand
onely of armyd men and a few shippes, the calends of August, and
with a soft suthren wynde.   The weather being very fayre he
came unto Wales the 7th day after, a lyttle before soone set, wher,
entring thaven caulyd Milford, and furthwith going a land, he took
first a place the name wherof ys Dalley, wher he herd that certane
companyes of his adversaryes had had ther stations the wynter by
past to have kept him from landing.   From thence departing in
the breake of day he went to Haverforde, which ys a towne not
xne. myles from Dalley, wher he was receavyd with great goodwill
of all men, and the same he dyd with suche celerytie as that he
was present and spoken of all at once.   Heare he understandeth
that Rycherd Thomas and John Savage, with all ther force and
frindes, dyd help king Richerd to thuttermost of ther power, clene
contrary to tnat ne was certyfyed of in Normandy.   But thinhabytants of Pembrough at the same very time comfortyd all ther
dysmayed myndes, for they gave intelligence, by Arnold Butler, a
valyant man, demanding forgeavenes of ther former offences, that
they wer ready to serve Jaspar ther erle.   Henry, his army thus
augmentyd, departyd from Hareford, and goeth forward v. myles
toward Cardygan.   The whyle the soldyers refreshyd themselves
hear a rumor was suddaynly spred throwgh the whole camp,
thautor wherof was uncertane, that Gwalter Herbert and those
who wer in camp at the towne of Carmardyne wer at hand with
an huge army.   Wheruppon a stirre rose streightway, every man

mayd ready his armor, assayd his weapon, and began to advance
the same, and all men wer in feare therwith a lyttle whyle, whan
as thorsemen sent owt before hand to scurrey by erle Henry .
brought home woord that all thynges (as they wer in dede) wer
quiet, and that ther was no hinderance to ther voyage immynent;
but one Gryfyne, a man of highe parentage, did above the rest One Grif-
make them all mery, who, thowgh before he had joingnyd with broughte
Gualter Harbert and Rycherd, yeat almost at the very same instant his forces
revoltyd with his company of soldiers, few though they wer, to erle Richmond.
Henry. The same very day also John Morgan came to the sayd Jo. Mor-
Henry. Thus Henry went forward without stay almost in any place, gane
and that he might have more ready passage he set uppon dyvers for- his foarces
tresses furnyshyd with garryson of his adversaryes, and the same wan Henry.
without any difficultie; and whan as after these thinges he understoode by the scowtts that Harbert and Rycherd wer before him
in armes, he resolvyd to go agaynst them, and whan he had ether
put them to flight or receavyd them into his obedience to make
haste against king Richerd. But that he might advertise his The E. of
frinds of his proceedinges, he sent unto Margaret his mother, to mond sent
the Stanleys, to the lord Talbot, and others, certane of his most o the
faythfull servants with secrete messages, theffect wherof was that and his
he, trusting to the ayde of his frynds, had determynyd to passe advertis
over Severn, and throwgh Shropshire to go to London, and therfor them of his
desyryd them to mete him, with whom in place and time convenyent he wold impart more of his intent. Thus having dispatchyd Ric.
the messengers with this message, himself procedyd forward toward Thomas
Shrewsbury, whom Richerd Thomas met by the way with a great poure with
bande of soldiers, and with assuryd promysse of loyaltie yealdyd Riche-
himself to his protection. Two days before Henry had promysyd mond.
to Richerd Thomas the perpetuall lyvetenantship of Wales, so that Thomas
he wold coome under his obedience, which afterward when he had promysed
obtanyd the kingdom he gave lyberally. In the meane time the nancye of
Wales.

messengers having executyd ther charge with dylygence, and loden
with money which they had receavyd of every man to whom they
wer sent, returnyd unto Henry the same very day that he came to
Shrewsbury, and signyfyed that his frinds wold be ready to do
ther dewties in time convenyent. Herewithall Henry beinge
browght in good hope, contynewyd furth the journey he had
begun and cam to a village which thinhabytants caule Newport,
and, pightching his tentes uppon the next hill, taryed ther all the
night. Ther came unto him in the evening Gilbert Talbot, with
v.ᶜ· and moe armyd men. After that he marchyd on to Staffoord,
unto whom, the while of his abode ther, came William Stanley,
with a smaule retynew, who, having short talk with him, returnyd
to his soldiers, whom he gathered togythers. From thence departing ne went to Lychefelde, and that night taryed withowt the
waule. The next day after, very early in the morning, he enteryd
the towne, and was honorably receavyd. The third day before,
Thomas Stanley had bene at the same place, gardyd with few lesse
than fyve thowsand men well armyd, who, understandinge of
Henryes approche, went before, without delay, to a village caulyd
Aderstone, meaning ther to tary till Henry showld draw nere.
This he dyd to avoyd suspition, fearing yf before they showld
coome to hand strokes he showld overtly shew himself to stand
and hold with erle Henry, least that king Richerd, who as yeat
did not utterly mistrust his loyaltie, might kill his soone George,‒
whom, as we have before sayd, he held in custody as a pledge.

    But Richerd in the meane time, being then at Notingham, was
certyfyed that Henry and thother exiles who tooke his part wer
coommyd into Wales, and that he was utterly unfurnyshyd and
feble in all thinges, contrary wyse that his men whom he had disposyd for defense of that province wer ready in all respectes.
That rumor so puffyd him upp in mynde that first he estemyd
the matter not muche to be regardyd, supposing that Henry,

Gylbert
Talbot
comes to
yᵉ E. of
Richе-
mond.
Wᵐ Stan-
ley a ᵉ to
  ᵉ E of
Riche-

ᴵ
lord Stan
ley came to
      ᴼ
Riche-
mond.

having procedyd rashly, consydering his smaule company, should surely have an evell ende whan he showld coome to that place, wher ether he should be forcyd to fyght against his will, or taken alyve by Gualter Harbert and Richard Thomas, who rewlyd in Wales with equal authoritie. But afterward, waynge with him self that a smaule matter in the warres made soome time great stirre, and that yt was a poynt of wysdom not to contemne the forces of hys enemye, thoughe they wer but smaule, he thowght best to provyde in time for the event to coom ; and therfor he commandyd Henry erle of Northumberland, and other noble men that wer his _frinds, who he hoped wold prefer his safety before all that ever they had, to make furthwyth muster of soldiers, and with ther forces furnysshyd to repare spedely to him. Also by often mes- R. 3 sent sengers and letters he commandyd Robert Brakenbury, lyveten- o Robert Brak nant of the towr of London, to coome to him in all haste, and bury the to bring with him, as felows in warr, Thomas Burshere, Gwalter of the ᴵᵃⁿᵗ Hungerfurd, and many other gentlemen of thorder of knighthoode, towere, whom he had in suspicion. While these thinges wer a doing, yt ing him to was reportyd that Henry, withowt any annoyance receavyd, was brin₂ with him some coomyd unto Shrewsbury ; with which message the king, much of his pri- movyd, began with grief to be in a fervent rage, and cry vehe- sꞇners. mently out uppon the falshood of them who had broken promyse, and withall to have less confydence in others, in so muche that the very first day that oportunitie wold permyt he determynyd to go agaynst his enemyes, and suddanely sent furth scurryers to view what way they held. The scurryers, doing ther devoyr dilygently, returned not long after and advertysyd that Henry was encampyd at Lichefelde : which whan he knew, because an huge number of men in armes wer now assemblyd, his soldyers beinge brought furth into good aray, he commandyd the armye to marche forward in square battayll that way by the which they understoode ther enemies wold coome, and, all impedimentes being

gatheryd into the middest of tharmy, himself, with his gard, dyd
folow the wings of horsemen ranging on both sydes; so, keping
ther aray, they came unto Leycester a little before the soone sett,
whan as the meane while Henry, removing from Lichefelde, travalyd to go unto the next village, which is caulid Tamworth, whom
Gualter Hungerford, Thomas Burscher, and many other met by
the way, who yealdyd themselves to his obeyssance; for they,
perceavynge that king Richerd had them in jelosy, because they
wold not be brought to ther enemy agaynst ther willes, forsaking
Robert Brakenbury a lyttle beyond Stony Stratford, went away to
therle Henry in the night season. Ther flockyd to him also
many other noble men of warre, who from day to day hatyd king
Richerd woorse than all men lyving.

Waltere
Hu gei
fo d   d
Tho. Bour-
c me
to the E
of Rich-
mond.

Ther happenyd in this voyage unto erle Henry a chance worthy
memory; for thoughe he wer of noble corage, and that his forces
augmentyd every wher, yeat was he in great feare, because he
thought that he cowld not assure himself of Thomas Stanley, who, as
I have shewyd, for that he fearyd the danger that king Richerd
might doo his soon, dyd enclyne as yeat to nether partie; and as
touching king Richardes causes, yt was told him muche otherwyse
than his frinds had signyfyed, which was, that nothing was more
firme, nothing better furnysshyd : wherfor, consydering his feare
was not for nothing, himself, accompanyed with xxtie armed men
onely, stayed by the way, uncertane what was best as to delyberat
what he might do.   Moreover he herd that king Richerd, with an
host innumerable, was at hand.   While he thus, soomwhat sadd,
folowyd alofe, all tharmy cam to Tamworth, and whan as by reason of the night which came uppon him he could not discerne the
trace of them that wer gone before, and so after long wandering
could not finde his company, he cam unto a certane towne more
than thre myles from his camp, full of feare ; who, least he might
be betrayed, durst not aske questyons of any man, but taryed ther

all that night, no more afrayed for the present than for the perill
to coom; for he was afeard that the same might be a signe of
soom maner plague to ensew. Nether was the army lesse heavy
for the suddane absence of ther captane, whan as Henry the next
day after, in the gray of the morning, returnyd to the hoste, ex-
cusing himselfe that he was not deceavyd in the way, but had
withdrawen from the camp of set purpose to receave soome goode
newys of certane his secret frindes. After that he went pryvyly
to Adderstone, wher Thomas Stanley and William lay encampyd.
Here Henry dyd mete with Thomas and William, wher taking one
an other by thand, and yealding mutuall salutation, eche man was
glad for the good state of thothers, and all ther myndes wer movyd
to great joy. After that, they enteryd in cownsaylle in what sort
to darraigne battayll with king Rycherd, yf the matter showld
coome to strokes, whom they herd to be not farre of. A lyttle
before thevening of the same day, John Savage, Bryan Sanfoord,
Symon Digby, and many others, revolting from king Richard,
came to Henry with a choyse bande of armyd men, which matter
both augmentyd the forces of erle Henry, and greatly replenyshyd
him with good hope.

The earle of Rich-e, Tho. lord Stanley mette

John Sa-others come to e Richmond.

In the meane time king Richard, hearing that thennemy drew
neare, came first to the place of fight, a little beyond Leycester
(the name of that village ys Boswoorth), and ther, pightching his
tentes, refresshyd his soldiers that night from ther travale, and
with many woords exhortyd them to the fyght to coome. Yt
ys reportyd that king Rycherd had that night a terryble dreame;
for he thowght in his slepe that he saw horryble ymages as yt wer
of evell spyrytes haunting evydently abowt him, as yt wer before
his eyes, and that they wold not let him rest; which visyon
trewly dyd not so muche stryke into his brest a suddane feare, as
replenyshe the same with heavy cares: for furthwith after, being
troublyd in mynde, his hart gave him theruppon that thevent of

The batle worthe. R. 3 his fatall dreame.

the battale folowing wold be grevous, and he dyd not buckle himself to the conflict with such lyvelyness of corage and countenance as before, which hevynes that yt showld not be sayd he
shewyd as appallyd with feare of his enemyes, he reportyd his
dreame to many in the morning. But (I beleve) yt was no dreame,
but a conscyence guiltie of haynous offences, a conscyence (I say)
so muche the more grevous as thoffences wer more great, which,
thowght at none other time, yeat in the last day of owr lyfe ys
woont to represent to us the memory of our sinnes commyttyd,
and withall to shew unto us the paynes immynent for the same,
that, being uppon good cause penytent at that instant for our evell
led lyfe, we may be compellyd to go hence in heavynes of hart.
Now I return to my purpose. The next day after king Richerd,
furnysshyd throwghly with all maner of thinges, drew his whole
hoste owt of ther tentes, and arraieth his vanward, stretching yt
furth of a woonderfull lenght, so full replenyshyd both with foote
men and horsemen that to the beholders afar of yt gave a terror
for the multitude, and in the front wer placyd his archers, lyke a
most strong trenche and bulwark ; of these archers he made leder
John duke of Norfolk. After this long vanward folowyd the king
himself, with a choyce force of soldiers. In this meane time
Henry, being departyd bak from the conference with his frinds,
began to take better hart, and without any tary encampyd himself
nighe his enemyes, wher he restyd all night, and well early in the
morning commandyd the soldiers to arm themselves, sending
withall to Thomas Stanley, who was now approchyd the place of
fight, as in the mydde way betwixt the two battaylles, that he
wold coom to with his forces, to sett the soldiers in aray. He
awnsweryd that the earle showld set his owne folkes in order,
whyle that he should coome to him with his army well apoyntyd.
With which answer, geaven contrary to that was looked for, and to
that which thoportunytie of time and weight of cause requyryd,

thowghe Henry wer no lyttle vexyd, and began to be soomwhat appallyd, yeat withowt lingering he of necessytie orderyd his men in this sort. He made a sclender vanward for the smaule number of his people ; before the same he placyd archers, of whom he made captane John erle of Oxfoord ; in the right wing of the vanward he placyd Gilbert Talbot to defend the same ; in the left veryly he sat John Savage ; and himself, trusting to thayd of Thomas Stanley, with one troup of horsemen, and a fewe footemen dyd folow ; for the number of all his soldiers, all maner of ways, was scarce v.^M. besydes the Stanleyans, wherof about 3.^M. wer at the battaill, under the conduct of William. The kings forces ‑were twyse so many and more. Thus both the vanwardes being arrayed, as soone as the soldiers might one se an other afur of, they put on ther head peces and preparyd to the fyght, expectyng thalarme with intentyve eare. Ther was a marishe betwixt both hostes, which Henry of purpose left on the right hand, that yt might serve his men instede of a fortresse, by the doing therof also he left the soon upon his bak ; but whan the king saw thenemyes passyd the marishe, he commandyd his soldiers to geave charge uppon them. They making suddanely great showtes assaultyd thennemy first with arrowes, who wer nothing faynt unto the fyght but began also to shoote fearcely ; but whan they cam to hand strokes the matter than was delt with blades. In the meane tyme therle of Oxfoord, fearing lest hys men in fyghting might be envyronyd of the multitude, commandyd in every rang that no soldiers should go above tenfoote from the standerds ; which charge being knowen, whan all men had throng thik togethers, and stayd a whyle from fighting, thadversaryes wer therwith aferd, supposing soom fraude, and so they all forbore the fight a certane space, and that veryly dyd many with right goodwill, who rather covetyd the king dead than alyve, and therfor fowght fayntly. Than therle of Oxforth in one part, and others in an other part,

with the bandes of men closse one to an other, gave freshe charge
uppon thenemy, and in array tryangle vehemently renewyd the
conflict.   Whyle the battayll contynewyd thus hote on both sydes
betwixt the vanwardes, king Richard understood, first by espyalls
wher erle Henry was a farre of with smaule force of soldiers
abowt him ; than after drawing nerer he knew yt perfytely by
evydent signes and tokens that yt was Henry ; wherfor, all in-
flamyd with ire, he strick his horse with the spurres, and runneth
owt of thone syde withowt the vanwardes agaynst him.   Henry
perceavyd king Richerd coome uppon him, and because all his
hope was than in valyancy of armes, he receavyd him with great
corage.   King Richerd at the first brunt killyd certane, overthrew

in-done the standerd ;a E of Rich mond over-throwne. Henryes standerd, toygther with William Brandon the standerd
bearer, and matchyd also with John Cheney a man of muche
fortytude, far exceeding the common sort, who encountered with
him as he cam, but the king with great force drove him to the
ground, making way with weapon on every syde.   But yeat
Henry abode the brunt longer than ever his owne soldiers wold
have wenyd, who wer now almost owt of hope of victory, whan as
loe William Stanley with thre thowsand men came to the reskew :
than trewly in a very moment the resydew all fled, and king
R. 3. slayne. Richerd alone was killyd fyghting manfully in the thickkest presse
of his enemyes.   In the mean time also the erle of Oxfoord after
a lyttle bickering put to flight them that fowght in the forward,
wherof a great company wer killed in the chase.   But many mo
forbare to fyght, who came to the fielde with king Richerd for
aw, and for no goodwill, and departyd withowt any daunger, as
men who desyryd not the safety but destruction of that prince
Noblemen whom they hatyd.   Ther wer killyd about a m. men, and
emongest tnem of noblemen of warre John duke of Norfolk,
Gwalter L. Ferryse, Robert Brakkenbury, Rycherd Ratclyff and
many moe.   Two days after at Leycester,William Catesby, lawyer,

with a few that wer his felowys, were executyd. And of those Wm.
~~Catesby~~
with others
executed at
———————
that tooke them to ther fete Frauncis L. Loovell, Humfrey
Staffoord, with Thomas his brother and muche more company, fled
into the sayntuary of Saint John which is at Colchester, a toune
by the sea syde in Essex. As for the number of captyves yt was
very great; for whan king Richerd was killyd, all men furthwith
threw away weapon, and frely submyttyd them selfes to Henryes
obeyssance, wherof the most part wold have doone the same at
the beginning, yf for king Rycherds scurryers, scowring to and
fro, they myght so have doone. Emongest them the chiefe wer
Henry erle of Northumberland, and Thomas erle of Surrey. This
man was commyttyd to ward, wher he remaynyd long ; he as frind
in hart was receavyd into favor. Henry lost in that battayll
scarce an hundreth soldiers, emongst whom there was one princy-
pall man, William Brandon, who bare erle Henryes standerd. Wm.
Brandone
slayne.
The feilde was fowghten the xj[th]. calends of September, in the
yere of mans salvation M.CCCC.lxxxvj, and the fight lasted more
than two houres.

The report is that king Richerd might have sowght to save
himself by flight; for they who wer abowt him, seing the soldiers
even from the first stroke to lyft up ther weapons febly and faynt-
lye, and soome of them to depart the feild pryvyly, suspectyd
treason, and exhortyd him to flye, yea and whan the matter began
manyfestly to qwaile, they browght him swyft horses ; but he, who
was not ignorant that the people hatyd him, owt of hope to have
any better hap afterward, ys sayd to have awnsweryd, that that
very day he wold make end ether of warre or lyfe, suche great
fearcenesse and suche huge force of mynd he had : wherfor, knowinge certanely that that day wold ether yeald him a peaceable
and quyet realme from thencefurth or els perpetually bereve him
the same, he came to the fielde with the crowne uppon his head,
that therby he might ether make a beginning or ende of his

raigne. And so the myserable man had suddaynly suche end as
wont ys to happen to them that have right and law both of God
and man in lyke estimation, as will, impyetie, and wickednes.
Surely these are more vehement examples by muche than ys hable
to be utteryd with toong to tereyfy those men which suffer no
time to passe free from soome haynous offence, creweltie, or
mischief.

Henry, after the victory obtaynyd, gave furthwith thanks unto
Almightie God for the same ; than after, replenysshyd with joy
incredible, he got himself unto the next hill, wher, after he had commendyd his solders, and commandyd to cure the woundyd, and to
bury them that wer slane, he gave unto the nobylytie and gentlemen immortal thankes, promysing that he wold be myndfull of
ther benyfyttes, all which meane whyle the soldiers cryed, God
save king Henry, God save king Henry ! and with hart and hand
utteryd all the shew of joy that might be ; which whan Thomas
Stanley dyd see, he set anon king Richerds crowne, which was
fownd among the spoyle in the feilde, uppon his head, as thoughe he
had bene already by commandment of the people proclamyd king-
after the maner of his auncestors, and that was the first signe of
prosperytie. After that, commanding to pak upp all bag and baggage, Henry with his victorious army procedyd in the evening to
Leycester, wher, for refresshing of his soldiers from ther travaile
and panes, and to prepare for going to London, he taryed two
days. In the meane time the body of king Rycherd nakyd of all
clothing, and layd uppon an horse bake with the armes and
legges hanginge downe on both sydes, was browght to thabbay of
monks Franciscanes at Leycester, a myserable spectacle in good
sooth, but not unwoorthy for the mans lyfe, and ther was buryed
two days after without any pompe or solemne funerall. He
raigned two yeres and so many monethes, and one day over. He
was lyttle of stature, deformyd of body, thone showlder being

_higher than thother, a short and sowre cowntenance, which semyd to savor of mischief, and utter evydently craft and deceyt. The whyle he was thinking of any matter, he dyd contynually byte his nether lyppe, as thowgh that crewell nature of his did so rage agaynst yt self in that lyttle carkase. Also he was woont to be ever with his right hand pulling out of the sheath to the myddest, and putting in agane, the dagger which he did alway were. Trewly he had a sharp witt, provydent and subtyle, apt both to counter-fayt and dissemble ; his corage also hault and fearce, which faylyd him not in the very death, which, whan his men forsooke him, he rather yealded to take with the swoord, than by fowle flyght to prolong his lyfe, uncertane what death perchance soon after by sicknes or other vyolence to suffer.

THEND OF THISTORY OF KING RICHERD THE THIRD.

ERRATA.

Page 181, line penult. for *hart,* read *hurt.*

„ 187, line 25, for *enjoyned,* read *enjoyed.*

„ 205, line 26, for *thiglyshe,* read *thinglyshe.*

„ 213, line 2, for *man,* read **men.**

INDEX.

C

LONDON:

J. B. NICHOLS AND SON, 25, PARLIAMENT STREET.

Printed in Great Britain
by Amazon